THE
FINELY FITTED
YACHT

THE FINELY FITTED YACHT

Volumes I and II

by

Ferenc Maté

Illustrations by Candace Maté

Photographs by the author

ALBATROSS PUBLISHING HOUSE

Édesapámnak

VOLUME II
EXTERIOR

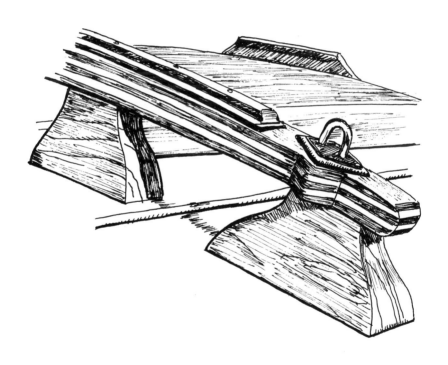

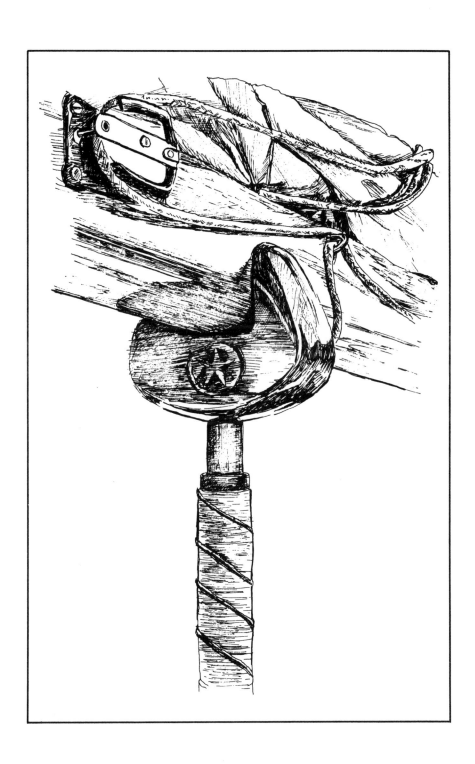

TABLE OF CONTENTS

SECTION I: COCKPIT

SECTION II: ON DECK

SECTION III: MAST AND RIGGING

SECTION IV: SAFETY

SECTION V: GROUND TACKLE

SECTION VI: BIBELOTS

SECTION VII: CANVAS AND SAILS

SECTION VIII: TOOLS

cockpit

COCKPIT BILGE PUMP

You will probably have noticed by now that if you install half of the items suggested in this chapter into the average cockpit, the crew will have to dangle over the sides for lack of room. But, if you have room for only one item in your thimble-sized foot soaker, *this* is the one it should be.

Every yacht should have two bilge pumps, just in case one gets jammed with whatever grotesque things bilge pumps get jammed with, and of the two, one should certainly be in the cockpit. One never knows when one will have to single-hand the boat because of illness or injury or volition, so early preparation would be a nice idea.

One of the best pumps for this type of work is a medium size diaphragm pump like the Whale Ten. Diaphragm pumps are very reliable machines and easily maintained and serviced, and this particular model has the spectacular quality of movable brackets which can be turned 90° so they can be installed very serviceably regardless how your structural supports are positioned. The Whale Ten is designed specifically for flush mounting and has a tidy cover plate that protrudes no more than 1/4" from the cockpit wall.

Location should be carefully thought out. It should be placed close enough to the helmsman that he can work it without releasing the helm, yet far enough away so that someone else can work the pump without getting in the helmsman's way. When finding a location, don't forget to allow for unobstructed movement of the handle. An up and down movement is preferable. Pumping is made much easier if the one stroke (down) can be accomplished by simply applying weight. The body of the pump will, of course, be belowdecks. Total and quick access to all its parts are mandatory. Remember to allow space for hands and tools. Some sort of light, either natural or artificial, should be provided since pump removal and cleaning will require two hands. The entire servicing can be accomplished in minutes assuming that the above hints have been followed. If not, your boat might just sink like a rock.

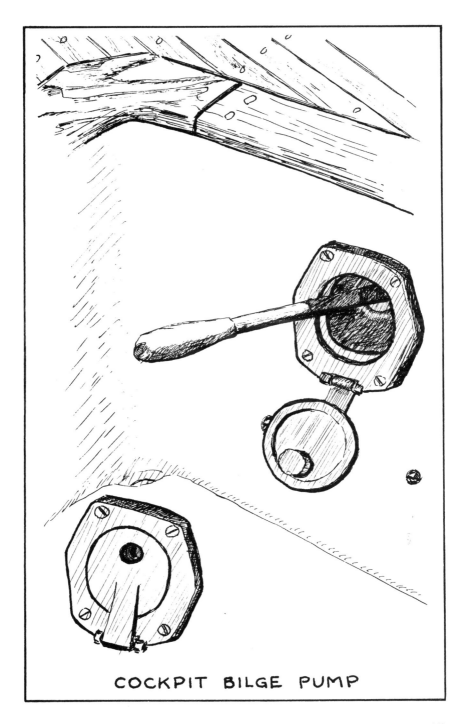

COCKPIT BILGE PUMP

THRONES FOR THE HELMSMAN

I have always advocated the use of tillers on small yachts, arguing that wheel systems are too involved and vulnerable to perform such a basically artless task, and now, my case has been buttressed unshakably, for as it turns out, not only do you need gears and levers and chains and cables to sustain a wheel, but you also need abstruse butt-supports to humour the helmsman (see photo).

The one advantage that these thrones have is that they can be nicely incorporated into small storage areas which are most valuable in any cockpit. The angular one is from *Nightingale*, a lovely little ketch from Newport Beach, while the curved one can be found on the Cheoy Lee 41's. (By the way, notice the nice compromise on its steering wheel that incorporates the beauty of a traditional wood wheel with the smooth and safer function of the modern destroyer type.)

The Angular Seat

This is made of solid 13/16″ teak with let-in corners. It's secured to the deck by an interior run of cleat stock. Alternately, you could screw into the teak base itself from below by putting the box into place, scribing its outline onto the deck, then drilling the pilot holes from above. The ideal height for the seat would be such that allows the helmsman unobstructed vision over the cabin top. The lid is also solid teak.

Because of its cost, the amount of teak used should be cut to a minimum. This can be done by making the basic lid of a piece of 1/2″ plywood, then covering it with 1/2″ or 3/8″ teak. Great care must be taken when countersinking and screwing down these pieces, for their thinness makes them very prone to splitting. Use flat head screws carefully, and try to leave as much space above them as possible so the plug will have adequate seating. Use resorcinol glue for both the teak-to-plywood and teak-to-teak adhesion. Trim out to cover the plywood's edge with 1/2″ × 1″ wide trim having 3/8″ bullnosed edges. The shallow frame part of the lid will act as a strong back on the plywood and keep it from warping. The two hefty handholds on either side (see "Grabrails") will actually act as a sort of coaming to keep the helmsman from sliding away on a heel.

The backrest is a solid piece of teak supported by a pair of galvanized pipes in through-bolted bases.

THE FINELY FITTED YACHT

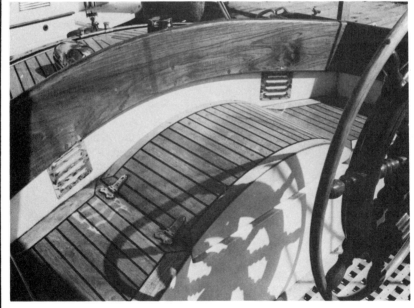

THRONES

The Curved Seat

This is by far the most comfortable seat for a helmsman when driving windward. Its fabrication is uncomplicated, especially if one is willing to forget the idea of a locker beneath it. The width of the seat will need to be at least 20″ if a rise of 4″ is to be achieved. A lesser rise will be too gentle to be of much help. Conversely, a much steeper rise will yield the sensation of sitting on Mount Everest. In any event, the overall height must be carefully watched to make sure you don't end up with the helmsman's feet dangling helplessly in the air. Cut the front and back curved pieces from 2″ × 6″ fir stock (or teak if you can afford it) to the shape decided upon, and let in the inside edge of the curves as shown 1/2″ high and 3/4″ deep, to provide a shoulder for the plywood seat base to fit into. The plywood itself will have to be laminated, for it's impossible to bend a 2′ long piece of 1/2″ plywood to form a 4″ deep arc. So start by securing the fir pieces to the existing seat much as explained in the "Angular Seat," then lay in the first piece of 1/4″ plywood, glue, and screw it to the shoulders. Cover the first piece with waterproof plastic resin, lay your next 1/4″ piece over it, and screw it down into the shoulders. In both cases, do a dry run first so you can mark in the bevels that will be required at the ends of each plywood to form a suitable fit with the seat. Now, lay 1/2″ thick teak stock milled to 1¾″ wide strips (anything wider will rock on the curve) over the plywood, glue, screw and plug. Use the same precautions and the same glue as described for the angular seat.

Under no circumstance should you use teak that's less than 1/2″ thick, for this seat must not be varnished or it will turn into a uselessly slippery slide. Without varnish, however, the teak will have to be cleaned periodically, and this cleaning will result in the eventual erosion of the wood to the point where the frighteningly frail teak plugs (frail because of the thinness of the teak stock which has to house a screw head with a shoulder below and a plug above) will unanimously crack and pop out. Sure, you can pull the screws, countersink, deepen, and re-plug, but you can only do that so often before you come through the bottom.

At any rate, if you find you're dissatisfied with the results, grab a chainsaw, trim off a few things, then install a tiller and have a good time.

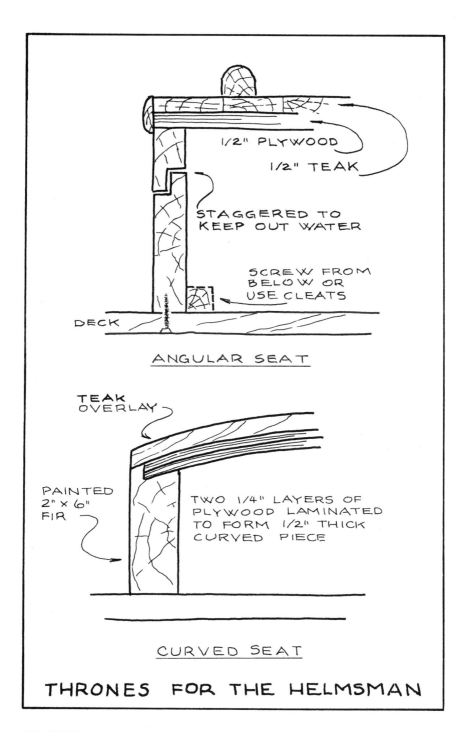

1/2" PLYWOOD

1/2" TEAK

STAGGERED TO
KEEP OUT WATER

SCREW FROM
BELOW OR
USE CLEATS

DECK

ANGULAR SEAT

TEAK
OVERLAY

PAINTED
2" × 6"
FIR

TWO 1/4" LAYERS OF
PLYWOOD LAMINATED
TO FORM 1/2" THICK
CURVED PIECE

CURVED SEAT

THRONES FOR THE HELMSMAN

COCKPIT

19

COCKPIT INSTRUMENT COVER

Many valiant attempts have been made by manufacturers and individuals alike to construct some sort of opening instrument panel cover that will be waterproof and still leave access to switches within, yet I have never seen one that worked. The best solution seems to be to put things needing constant handling into an opening portlight (see that section) and seal all the *read-out* instruments under a waterproof plexiglass cover. Crowd all your instruments into as tidy an area as possible. Be sure to include here the oil pressure sound alarm, for as well as providing protection, the plexiglass will somewhat muffle that shrill, nerve-wracking little sound.

For the frame, use 3/4″ × 3/4″ remnants that any good plastics place will have available. If you have any instruments with faces that protrude from the cockpit wall more than 3/4″, you have to make your frame to suit.

The cut plexiglass frame can be adhered with plexiglass solvent to a sheet of 1/8″ thick plexiglass which is to be the protective cover. This will create a completely waterproof unit. Radius all corners and sand all edges. Caulk and screw the cover into place. Don't forget to put a drop of caulking compound into each screw hole. The screws should be spaced no farther apart than 3″, for the plexiglass will want to work with temperature variations, causing seal breaks, causing leaks.

Next, breather holes must be drilled to keep any moisture that ventures in from settling and staying. One 1/8″ hole just inside each corner should suffice nicely. The holes should be drilled from inside, that is, through the cockpit face itself. The humidity is bound to be less belowdecks, unless of course you're the proud owner of a six-ton sieve.

THE FINELY FITTED YACHT

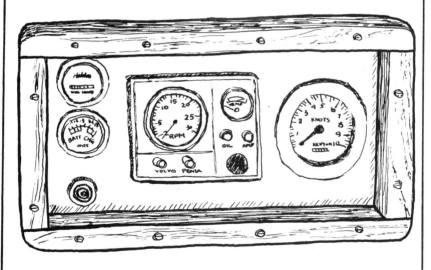

COCKPIT INSTRUMENT COVER

PORTLIGHT FOR COCKPIT SWITCHES

An endless array of new production boats, as well as limited edition beauties, appear with exposed ignition switches in the cockpit. These, without variation, take on water, which at best causes a temporary short, at worst, after a two-week cruise with the key always in place, freezes the key irremovably. A simple solution exists — that of installing an opening portlight in the side of the cockpit. Besides protecting the ignition, it will also provide a quick access, all weather home for essential switches which are best next to the helmsman. A switch for the spreader lights would enable the helmsman a quick glance at the sails at night, or allow verification of deck conditions without having to disturb the crew down below. A switch for the instrument panel light (preferably with a dimmer) would also be most handy here. If the portlight is well located and the switches mentioned are mounted inside on a small sheet of plexiglass, badly needed light can be supplied to the engine room or stowage area beneath the cockpit.

Locate the portlight out of the way of legs and install it inside out (dogs accessible to cockpit). Be sure the hinge is on top so the natural position of the port will be *closed*. The sleeve of the portlight should be long to provide adequate space for the keys and switches. Try to crowd everything on as small a piece of 1/4" plexiglass as you can, leaving open as large an area as possible for belowdecks ventilation. Cut the plexiglass to the outside diameter of the portlight ring and attach it with the same through-bolts that hold the portlight in place. Bed everything in polysulfide.

Replace the usual cotter pins in the hinge rod with rings to leave as much skin as possible on legs and knuckles.

Once you've got it installed, you'll never understand how you could have ever lived without it.

THE FINELY FITTED YACHT

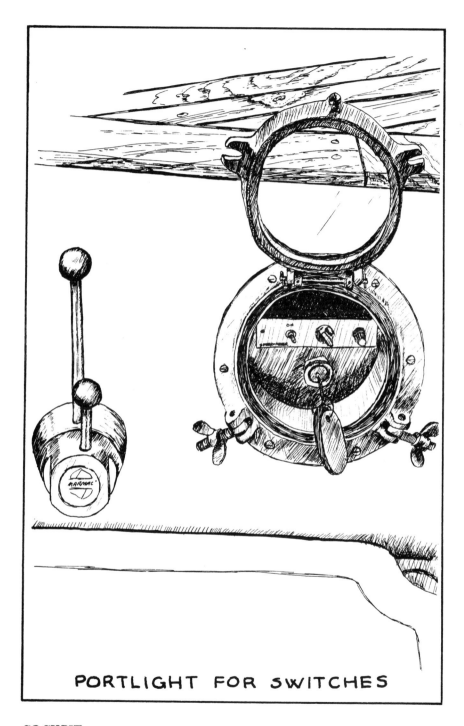

PORTLIGHT FOR SWITCHES

COCKPIT

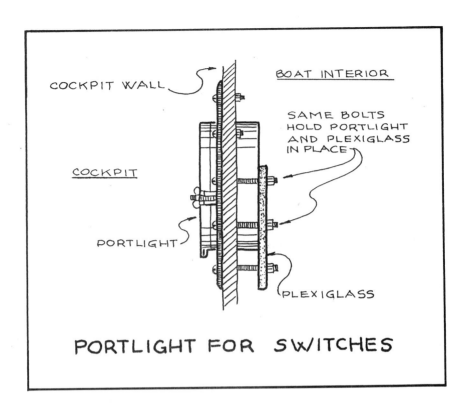

COCKPIT WALL

BOAT INTERIOR

SAME BOLTS
HOLD PORTLIGHT
AND PLEXIGLASS
IN PLACE

COCKPIT

PORTLIGHT

PLEXIGLASS

PORTLIGHT FOR SWITCHES

WHEEL AND COMPASS GUARD

Spoke-handled ship's wheels have a nasty habit of clouting a relaxed cockpit crew in the elbows and knees. Since a wheel of this sort is quite often accompanied by a binnacle compass which needs protection from falling bodies and winch handles, installation of a multi-purpose steel guard like the one in the photo would seem to be a very good idea.

In addition to the above functions, it makes an excellent handhold for the helmsman in broken seas, as well as giving the crew in the foreward part of the cockpit a good leaning and bracing place, and a handhold.

It should be fabricated of 1″ diameter stainless pipe and, of course, it will have to be bent to the proper radius by a metal shop. To furnish them with sufficient information, give them: a) the diameter of your wheel (handles included), b) the width of your cockpit, c) the depth of your cockpit, d) the distance from the cockpit sole to the top of a handle at 12 o'clock, and e) the amount of space you would like between the top of the wheel and the bottom of the guard. Have them run the straight pieces that make up the feet of the guard clear to the cockpit sole. Drill at least three holes in each, and bolt through the cockpit sides with 3/8″ bolts.

COCKPIT

COCKPIT GLASS LINER STOWAGE

I took a sampling at some boat shows and found the following engineering oversight on many fiberglass production boats. Although great pains have been gone to, to build comfortable cockpit coamings with wide enough tops for winch mounts, most of this lovely hollow space is unused. From below, it's merely a dead air area in either the engine room or quarter berth, and while it goes begging, genoa and mainsheets lie about in the cockpit hopelessly entwined. Dumb. These areas should have access cut to them from above and should be sealed off from below, and used as a perfect place for reams of sheets to keep them from tangling around ankles and engine controls.

The cutting should be done by drilling a 1/2″ hole within the surface to be cut away, and then with a very sharp hacksaw blade in a saber saw, the whole piece should be removed. Do not leave the hole too large or too close to anything structural like a cleat, or you'll weaken the whole arrangement. The saw must be sharp and have very fine teeth, or great bits of gelcoat will chip away and necessitate frustrating repairs. Next, with 100 grit sandpaper, round all new edges thoroughly or the above-mentioned chipping will occur on first contact. The insides of the edges should be done as well to save lines and skin from catching. Next, rough cut pieces of plywood to act as temporary sides and bottoms of the new space. Put judicious amounts of mold release wax on these, for they will be removed as soon as the fiberglass has set up in the pocket. You'll see why in a moment. Wedge, or if need be, tack these into place. Using two layers of mat with a layer of cloth between, lay up the new sides and bottom of the pocket. Be sure to seal off all corners and holes. Overlap generously onto the existing glass. (If the underdeck was painted, the paint has to be removed with paint remover before bonding.) Work all loose strands flat while the resin is still soft. When it has set up, remove the plywood baffles. Put a couple of coats of clear gelcoat over the outside of the pocket. For drainage, drill two 1/4″ holes in the face of the liner as close to the bottom of the low spot of the pocket as possible. Test with a cup of water to determine this. You now have: a) a perfect place to heave your mass of sheets, and b) a lovely source of natural light to brighten up some dingy belowdecks area.

THE FINELY FITTED YACHT

COMPASS GUARD

The compass guard is nearly a must in most yachts, for anxious winch handles are apt to be flying about. The notion that one doesn't require a guard because one usually uses great care can be compared to leaving the life ring on shore because you're not falling overboard today anyway. Loss of the compass is not only a very costly bit of misjudgement, but can cause severe discomfort on a long ocean passage.

The most desirable guard is, of course, a second transparent shield which would permit an unrestricted view of the compass card at all times. This is simplest to adapt to a vertically mounted compass. The sides can be left open for cleaning access, the upper part of the face can be made from 1/8″ plexiglass to limit light refraction as much as possible, and the lower part can be of 1/2″ plexiglass. It should be noted that the lower part exists not to protect the compass per se, but to avoid having a protruding, very kickable blade of plexiglass exposed which would be the case if the top were simply extended to the bottom of the compass. The point where the faces meet should be rounded as much as possible, hence the need for using 1/2″ thick glass on the lower face. Attachment to the bulkhead can be made by cutting 1/2″ × 1/2″ plexiglass on a bevel and using the two pieces as you would cleat stock. See drawing.

Another type of guard can be made of small stainless or brass tubing. The "T" shape indicated in the illustration is the simplest to use, requiring only one weld. The ends of the tubes can be flattened with a hammer, rounded, then drilled to accommodate attaching screws. No flat metal stock should be used as a substitute for the tubing for unavoidable sharp edges will result. The horizontal or main part of the guard must be so designed that it will fall well under the compass card to avoid any possible visual interference.

For horizontally mounted compasses, the solution would involve fabricating a shallow all-plexiglass or plexiglass-teak combination box. Again, leave access for cleaning and ventilation to avoid condensation.

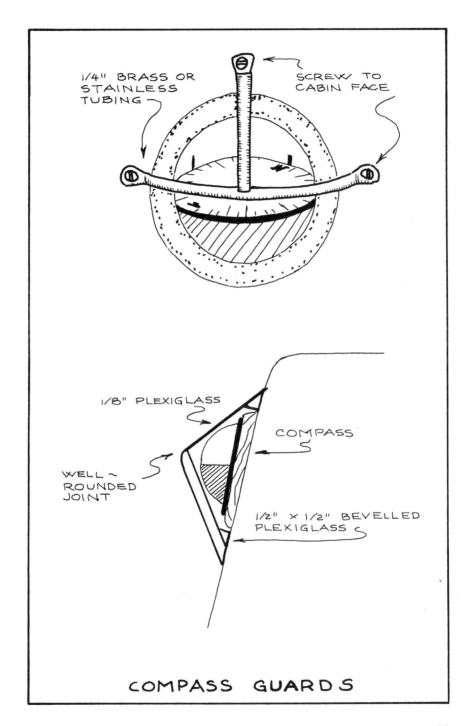

1/4" BRASS OR STAINLESS TUBING

SCREW TO CABIN FACE

1/8" PLEXIGLASS

COMPASS

WELL ~ ROUNDED JOINT

1/2" x 1/2" BEVELLED PLEXIGLASS

COMPASS GUARDS

COCKPIT

COCKPIT STOWAGE BOX

If no other way exists to increase stowage in the cockpit, then, as a final solution, a wood box can be built and fitted into a little-used area of the cockpit — like aft just under the tiller or forward where it can act as a step to the bridge deck. The box can be a conservative size, say 8″ × 20″, so it will rob the cockpit of as little space as possible. Only solid 13/16″ teak or mahogany should be used for all parts except the bottom, where a piece of 3/8″ plywood will suffice. The height of the box should be no more than 16″, otherwise, it will become nothing but another garbage bin. If kept small and well organized, it will ·be a perfect place for a flashlight, engine and boat keys, a thermos for the helmsman, winch handles, a bilge pump handle, fire extinguisher, etc.

Cut your sides and your front to size. Cut drain patterns in the bottoms of all three pieces, for sooner or later, water will get under the box and somehow it must get out. Cut the drain patterns at least 1½″ high so the space beneath them can be cleaned and lost things retrieved. If you have a dovetail jig, by all means use it; if not, use a piece of cleat stock in the corners. Merely butting will not suffice here, since bodies will be flying and giant feet stomping, always in the wrong places. Put cleat stock along the aft edge of the sides to act as mounting pieces onto the cockpit walls, eliminating the need for a solid back to the box. If you have a removable cockpit sole, fabricate a permanent back onto which the hinges for the lid can be screwed, then the box can be mounted by means of the wing nuts and bolts inserted on the belowdecks side of the cockpit walls. In this way, removal will be quick and non-destructive.

Assemble the sides and bottom using resorcinol glue, screws, and plugs. If installing a backless box, cut the bottom 1/4″ short of the cockpit wall, for the lid will be hinged from the wall, and water will inevitably be draining down same; so cut the bottom short and let it drain in peace. Put caulking under the legs of the box and install with 1″ sheet metal pan heads.

The lid can be fabricated from a single piece of 13/16″ teak, overhanging the box by about 3/4″ front and sides. Bullnose all around and, about 3/8″ from all the edges, cut a shallow 1/8″ drip groove along the bottom. Nothing will keep all the water out, but this will help a bit. Install two strong backs to prevent warping. Attach the box to the cockpit wall with brass or stainless butt hinges.

THE FINELY FITTED YACHT

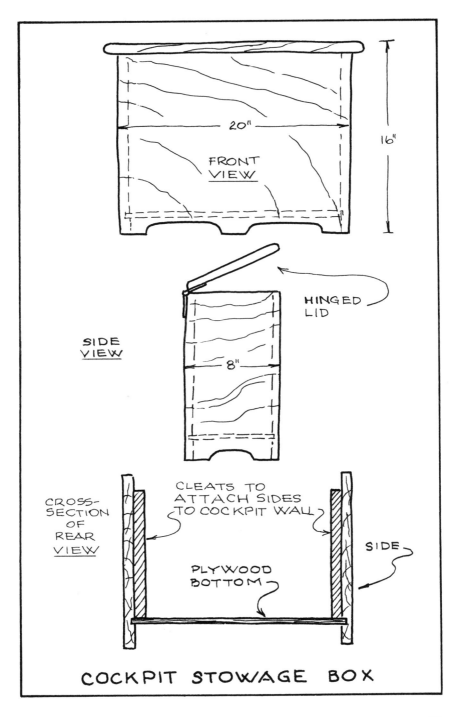

FRONT VIEW

20"

16"

SIDE VIEW

HINGED LID

8"

CROSS-SECTION OF REAR VIEW

CLEATS TO ATTACH SIDES TO COCKPIT WALL

SIDE

PLYWOOD BOTTOM

COCKPIT STOWAGE BOX

SLATTED COCKPIT SEATS

Many fiberglass, steel, and cement boats have very cold, very slippery, cockpit seats made of the above materials. Since cushions are not always practical, especially in foul weather when things get the most slippery, a very fine solution is the use of fixed or hinged (depending on whether a locker lid makes up the seat or not) teak slats. These are widely used from the Dutch Trintella line of yachts to *Wanderer IV*.

They are no more complicated than they sound to construct, and they add much warmth and friction in exchange for a handful of dollars. Rip 13/16″ teak into 2″ wide slats, and bullnose the top edges. You will be leaving 1/2″ spaces between the slats, so calculate the number you'll need accordingly. If you come up with an odd measurement that would require your ripping a slat to half width, don't. Instead, either increase or decrease your spacing.

Next, from the same stock, rip 1½″ pieces that will act as ribs to which the slats will be screwed. Bullnose the *bottoms* of these. You will need one rib at each end and one about every 12″. Assemble, using a 1/2″ plywood spacer, resorcinol glue, and slightly countersunk 1″ pan heads, drilling and screwing from the *ribs*, of course, so the screw heads won't show. There is no need to plug them here, just be sure they're deep enough so they won't act as pivots. If you are hinging the seat, let in butt hinges about 24″ apart, and attach to the cockpit coaming.

If you are installing the slats permanently, just run a bead of caulking on each rib and drop them into place. This is no place to get carried away with caulking. If you do, you will have the stuff squishing out all over, and cleaning it up between the slats will be no small task. Two 1″ pan-head screws through *each rib only* should be enough to hold in any circumstance.

I once saw an attempt to simplify this slat operation by eliminating the ribs and screwing the slats directly onto the tops of the seats. Unbelievable. The space between the slats became a holding ground for water, crumbs, bugs, and dirt, all of which congealed into a kind of greenish goo. I, as obedient humble crew, was obligated to sit atop it all with my clean white tennis shorts. I burnt them the next day.

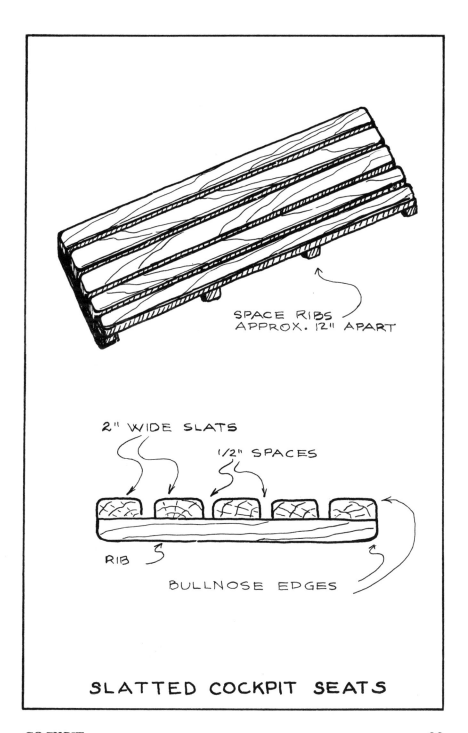

SPACE RIBS
APPROX. 12" APART

2" WIDE SLATS

1/2" SPACES

RIB

BULLNOSE EDGES

SLATTED COCKPIT SEATS

SIMPLE BOOM CRUTCH

Probably no two boats exist with similar boom gallows, and that's quite as it should be. Most are masterpieces of design, incorporating holders for life rings, davits for dinghies, bases for ship's bells, and brackets for outboards, but if you want to make a very functional removable boom crutch without the trimmings, here it is. It will fit any boat with a raised cabin. It consists of two brass pipes, one of slightly greater diameter than the other, to allow a telescoping assembly, and a hefty head piece to house the boom.

First, secure brass pipes of about 1½" diameter for one, slightly less or more for the other. The length of the larger piece will be determined by the height of your cabin; the lower end being as close to the deck as possible, the upper end being about 2" below the cabintop, so it will not be a protruding weapon when the crutch part of the pipe is removed. Through-bolt these to the face of the cabin about 3" from either end with 1/4" round head bolts, making certain that you do not distort the walls of the tubing with undue pressure. If you do, you will never be able to insert the removable pipe.

If your deckhouse face slopes, as most do, cut a teak shim block about 3" square, to achieve perpendicularity. To be sure the pipe sits on the block snugly, file a hollow seat 1/4" deep with a shoe rasp.

The length of the pipe that fits into the crutch should be measured from the boom when it's in a resting position. It should be cut to reach the top of the fixed pipe, plus 6". The last 6" will be the part to slip into the fixed piece. Next, you will have to cut a slot in the removable tube to accommodate the top bolt. Cut it with a hacksaw and then bend it out until it breaks.

For the wooden head, cut a 6" square piece out of 2½" teak stock, and shape it as in the illustration. The star is optional. To affix it to the tube, drill a 2" deep hole to fit your tubing, clean the hole and tubing, and apply a nice coat of thickened epoxy to both, and unite. Perform this last step with the tubing firmly in place; you can then align the head perfectly by actually setting the boom in it to determine the most ideal angle. If you try to do this last step on some distant work bench, you'll find the head piece permanently askew, correctable only by chopping down the mast and planting it on your starboard caprail. Weird.

THE FINELY FITTED YACHT

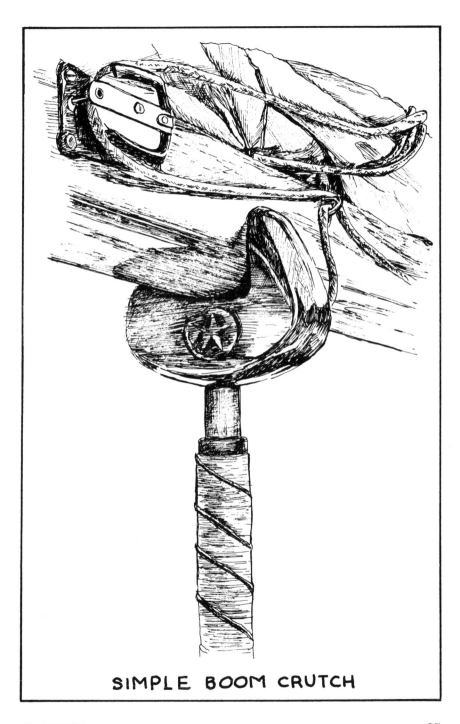

SIMPLE BOOM CRUTCH

COCKPIT TABLE

In spite of what you may have been told, beer cans jammed into cockpit scuppers, salami resting on hairy knees, and coffee cups squeezed between quivering thighs, is not the most civilized way of conducting lunch above decks. An improvement is a portable wood cockpit tray which can be taken below to be loaded up with goodies, then can be fixed firmly in the cockpit with the simplest of attachments.

The tray should accommodate four mugs; some people advocate four *cans*, although I've yet to see one of them sip coffee or tea from a Coors can. It should have separate areas for two small plates or containers for food, and one small space for serviettes and cutlery. The whole thing need be no larger than $10'' \times 20''$.

A $3/8''$ piece of plywood cut to the above dimensions is the starting point. Surround this on all sides by searails. The aft and foreward searail can be solid, but the two short ones on the ends should be the hand-holed variety (see "Searails"). The corners can be enclosed, for the tray is portable and can be turned upside down for cleaning. Glue, screw, and plug.

The internal partitions may be made of solid stock or plywood. Cut two pieces of $3/8''$ plywood to a width of the diameter of your favourite mugs plus $1''$, and a length of the *interior width* of the tray. With a hole saw, cut your holes, leaving at least $1/2''$ of wood all around. Next, from $3/4''$ solid stock, cut four $1\frac{1}{2}''$ wide pieces, whose lengths are equal to the width of your mug-hold inserts. Glue and screw these to the aft and foreward searails, and glue and screw the mug insert onto them. Note: do not enclose the space you've just created below the mug holders. If you do, and anything spills or sticks in there, cleaning it out will be a horror show. Repeat the above on the other side.

Next, cut another piece of $3/8''$ plywood that will fit into the remaining central space. Scribe onto it the outlines of the containers or plates you will be most often using, cut them out with a jigsaw, and glue the plywood directly onto the inside of the tray bottom.

Now, purchase two sets of dinghy gudgeons and pintles, attach the pintles to the aft searail of the tray about $3''$ in from the ends, and attach the gudgeons onto the aft or foreward face of the cockpit. Slip the tray in place and bon appetit. If this doesn't beat stuffing pepperoni in your pant cuffs, I don't know what does.

THE FINELY FITTED YACHT

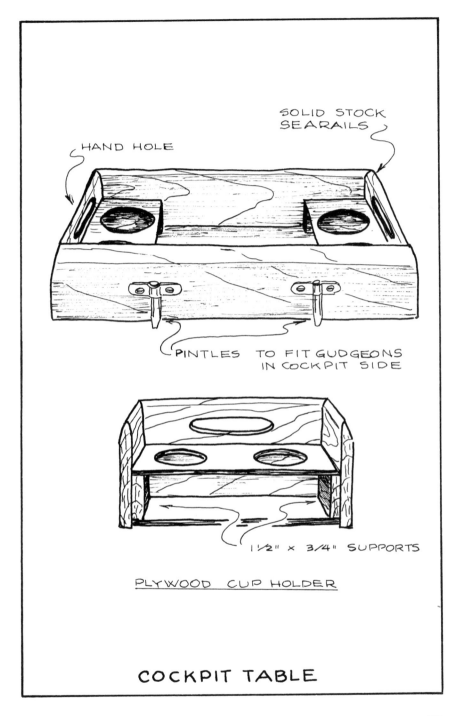

HAND HOLE

SOLID STOCK
SEARAILS

PINTLES TO FIT GUDGEONS
IN COCKPIT SIDE

1½" × ¾" SUPPORTS

PLYWOOD CUP HOLDER

COCKPIT TABLE

WHEEL WRAPPINGS

The slick steel wheels of modern yachts look very fast and racy, but can become frighteningly slippery when covered by drops of rain, or the sweat of fear. In northern climates, they can also be inhospitably cold for the hands.

To overcome the above traumas, you can do one of two things: wear gloves, or put a fine whipping of cotton twine around the wheel. The first solution is more practical, but does pathetically little to enhance the beauty of the wheel.

Begin by laying about 4" of the end of a ball of cotton line along the wheel, then proceed by taking the ball around the rim and tying a series of half hitches. Continue each half hitch the same way by passing the working end through the loops from right to left. If you make all your hitches the same, you will develop a nice spiral pattern because each knot (where the line passes over itself) will fall automatically in order.

To finish off the line at each spoke, leave the last hitches fairly loose, then pass the line back through them, draw it tight, and trim. Continue on to the next arc of the wheel.

An alternate to the above is the straight whipping, where the line is passed around the wheel's rim without the half hitches. This is just as functional, although somewhat less decorative.

To mark the set of the wheel at the point where the rudder is dead fore and aft, fit a Turk's-head over the rim. If you say that's too much bother and why not just wrap a piece of electrician's tape over it, then you're probably the kind of person who puts ketchup on his escargot.

COCKPIT   39

WINCH HANDLE HOLDERS

For instant mounting, little maintenance, and general all around practicality, one is hard pressed to recommend anything but the soft molded plastic winch handle pockets available at your ship's chandlery, with the exception of the blatantly obvious solution in the photo. Instead of spending about $15 for a pair of white molded beasties (one at the mast and one at the cockpit), one can simply purchase a length of soft plastic tubing with an ID of about 2½″ and simply cut it as shown. Total cost for two will come to a whole dollar. Do cut the top as shown to enable the handle to slide into the most accessible position. Round off the edges with a knife or file, for sharp edges can cause nasty paper cut-like wounds. Besides the low cost, these units have the unquestionable advantage of having their bottoms completely open, making the entire tube accessible and cleanable. The store-bought ones have a joke of a drain hole which plugs up with the first available nasty goo, forming an inaccessible damp pit where all sorts of slithering, slimy things propagate.

One caution. I have seen some people use aluminum tubing or hard PVC tubing for the holders. This is a mistake. Their hard edges will become shin hunters of the first magnitude.

COCKPIT 41

COCKPIT CUTOUT

Vast unused space can be found between the solid molded walls of most fiberglass cockpits as well as many old plywood ones. Aside from being inaccessible from the outside, these areas are usually barely accessible from within. Such a condition is ideal for a cutout box for winch handles. The length of the opening you cut should be just less than the length of your handle and the height should be 4″. In solid fiberglass or plywood, the drilled hole and jigsaw method should be used. Pencil in the cutout marking 1″ radius corners, and drill a 1/2″ hole anywhere within it. Through this, insert your jigsaw blade and cut away. Make the cut as perfect as possible. Now construct a box from 1/2″ plywood. Make the interior measurements 6″ high, 5″ deep and 3″ longer than your handle. Slope the bottom 10° for drainage. You'll notice that the box will be considerably larger than the opening, and so it must be so that the lip on the bottom (2″ high) and a little at each side can act to keep the handle in place. Butt and glue and screw all joints. Trim the perimeter of the front of the box with 3/4″ cleat stock. You will be using this to attach the box to the cockpit wall. Fiberglass the entire inside with cloth and matt tape to make the box waterproof. Fasten it to the cockpit side with #10 R.H.S.M. screws. Use a very generous uninterrupted bead of polysulfide between the cleat stock and the cockpit and screw tightly. Drill a small 1/4″ drain hole in the cockpit wall just above the sloped floor for drainage. In a plywood cockpit, this hole should have a light copper tubing inserted and bedded in polysulfide to prevent water from seeping between the veneer laminates and causing dry rot.

Trim in teak. Bed the teak trim solidly to prevent any water retention.

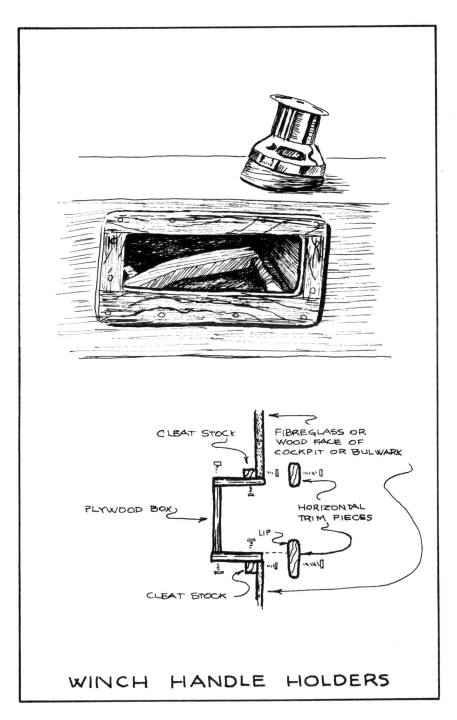

CLEAT STOCK

FIBREGLASS OR
WOOD FACE OF
COCKPIT OR BULWARK

PLYWOOD BOX

HORIZONTAL
TRIM PIECES

LIP

CLEAT STOCK

WINCH HANDLE HOLDERS

COCKPIT COAMING

In many vessels (*Warm Rain* included), the seating accommodations in the cockpit are considerably less than luxurious. Even if a coaming of some sort does exist, it's usually just high enough to torture the small of your back. *Scorpio*, a lovely teak ketch from Venezuela, has had a beautifully designed and fabricated extension installed above the original coaming. Aside from enhancing the yacht's appearance, it has created a safer and infinitely more comfortable cockpit. Even a quick glance at the photo, however, will tell you that this is a major undertaking, so unless you have access to a steambox and have a goodly collection of clamps, don't even begin.

The material required will be a single piece of 1″ teak, or mahogany stock, about 4″ wide and as long as you desire to make it. Now, find the thinnest blade you can for your table saw, or alternately, take your piece of wood into a furniture or door maker and have him rip the 1″ stock down to 1/8″ thick by 4″, wide strips. Next, carefully measure off the cockpit coaming, curves and all, or better still, make a paper pattern of it. Using this pattern, set up a series of blocks on a workbench or a piece of old plywood. Nothing elaborate needs to be done here; just use pieces of 2 X 4 and screw them down temporarily per diagram. Ten-inch blocks will do quite nicely, unless you want to run two full length pieces for the long stretches. The space between the inboard and outboard blocks should be about 1/8″ more than the total thickness of your planks. When your blocks are secure, gather up all the clamps you have (the wood handscrews are the best for this purpose). It would be good to place one every 6″-8″. Steam a 16″ area of a plank where your curves are to be, then lay it out, and brush glue over its surface. Be sure you use resorcinol glue. Teak is impossible to laminate with anything else. Place the plank into the blocks, then quickly glue up both sides of the next plank and slip it inside of the first one. You'll find the use of discardable rubber gloves most helpful here. If you have a friend who could help to clamp and to hold, so much the better. When you have all the planks in place, use a mallet to hammer them all down as evenly as possible, and clamp as suggested. If you're not using clamps with wood jaws, slip wood pads (scrap plywood about 2″ X 3″ is fine) between the metal and the teak to prevent pressure marks. When all the clamps are set, wipe off all excess glue with a damp cloth. Allow it to set overnight. In the morning, trim the edges off with a minimal setting on your table saw and sand thoroughly. Varnish or oil. Next, have a shop make up three stainless or bronze brackets. If your cockpit coaming is sloped, have them bend the bracket to suit. Through-bolt, using carriage bolts inboard and cap nuts outboard. Bed your bolts in a caulking compound. Now, just sit back and relax. Slouch if you like.

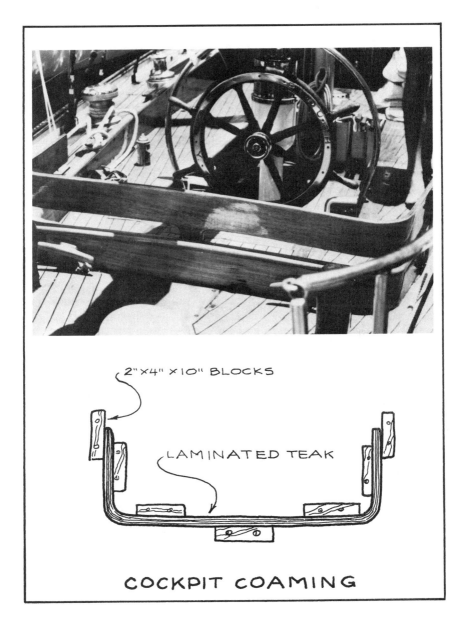

2"X4"X10" BLOCKS

LAMINATED TEAK

COCKPIT COAMING

TEAK COCKPIT GRATES

A cockpit grate or, at least, cockpit slats are mandatory in many of the modern yachts whose cockpit soles, whether all fiberglass or steel, or glass over wood, are often too inadequately textured to be sufficiently effective as a non-skid surface when substantial amounts of water are taken on board. Besides, grates look pretty.

This grate differs vastly in complexity from the lighter construction stowage-grates. It requires two interlocking sets of dadoed 3/4″ X 3/4″ stock, glued and screwed at every joint, as well as a substantial framework (tapered adequately along the sides to suit the cockpit), which will have to be attached to the end of each strip with the use of dowels.

First measure the cockpit to establish how many and what length of each dadoed strip you'll need. Three vital points must be taken into consideration:

(a) The grating grid itself must end up having perfectly parallel sides. All tapering and fitting adjustments will be made to the solid surrounding frame.

(b) The surrounding frame should be made to be at least 2½″ wide at the narrowest point, meaning that in a severely tapering cockpit, you may end up with a 5″-7″ frame piece on the beamier part of the cockpit.

(c) The arrangement of the grate grid should be calculated so that a full space always adjoins the frame (see diagram). This will be needed so that each dowel will have an undadoed full 3/4″ X 3/4″ stock end to go into.

Now, with the number of short and long pieces determined, select 3/4″ teak boards so that the least amount of waste will be necessary, i.e. the length should equal the combined lengths of one short plus one long or two shorts and two long, etc.

Next, divide the length of your board into 1½″ intervals with a short and exact mark, then set your 3/4″ wide dado blades to remove half thickness (3/8″). Do a test run on a scrap piece of wood to verify the settings. The dadoing can be performed on either a table saw or radial arm saw. The radial arm has the advantage of a longer table and non-moving board, but if care is used, a table saw will do the work just as well. Begin dadoing at the first mark and continue for the length of the board.

Next, set a single carbide blade for a 3/4″ wide cut and rip your grate slats. Be sure to use a good stiff blade to guarantee a perfectly straight and vertical cut. After every three or four cuts, recheck the

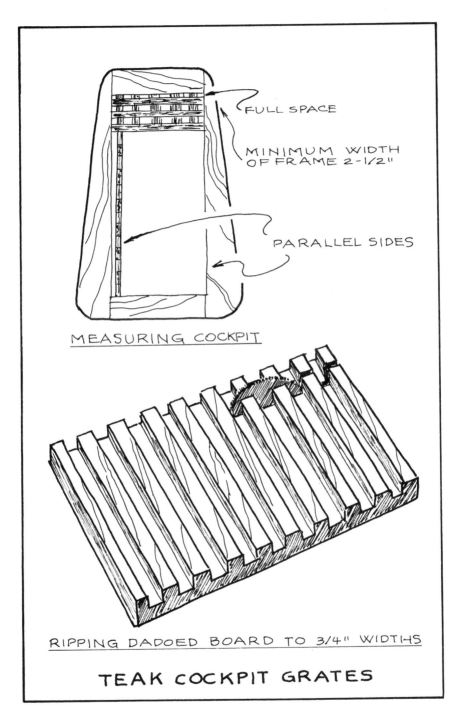

FULL SPACE

MINIMUM WIDTH OF FRAME 2-1/2"

PARALLEL SIDES

MEASURING COCKPIT

RIPPING DADOED BOARD TO 3/4" WIDTHS

TEAK COCKPIT GRATES

blade settings by fitting a couple of the cut stock together. Now, cut your strips to length making sure you end up with a full 3/4″ × 3/4″ block at each end.

Next, take your athwartship pieces, turn them dadoed side down, and with an appropriate drill bit and countersink, drill holes *above* each gap to fit a #6 F.H. screw. Now, brush a bit of resorcinol in the dadoed areas — very little indeed or the stuff will squeeze out, and: a) stain the wood, and b) necessitate your scraping excess glue out of a half million little square holes — and assemble the entire grate with screw holes up. Pop in your screws, set them gently with a hammer, then screw down. Use caution; remember that the little wedge-shaped shoulders of screws can split wood. Plug each hole using resorcinol glue, and let it set for a few hours.

While you wait, cut out your frames leaving a good 1/8″ all the way around to facilitate removal. If you have a lip of any kind around your cockpit seats, you'll have to allot for that with more perimeter space. Make the fore-and-aft pieces of the frame full length, fitting the athwartships ones in between.

Run a light bullnose of 1/4″ radius around both upper and lower edges of the outside of the grate to prevent splintering.

Next, with a chisel, remove the bulk of the plug heads (see "Detailing"), then belt-sand off the rest.

To attach the frames to the grate grid, set all the pieces in place, and using a small square, draw a line from the center of the end of each grid piece right onto the frame in that position, and also a couple of marks joining the ends of the frames to each other. These marks are for centering your dowel holes. Code all your pieces for easier identification.

Now, clamp each of your pieces (frames and each grate side) one at a time, to a workbench, and, using the doweling jig (see "Tools") with a piece of tape on your drill bit as governor, drill each hole to a depth of a half inch plus a hair. Be sure your jig is perfectly centred on the lines you've drawn. Drill all holes in all frames and the grate, then, using 1″ dowels dipped in resorcinol glue, assemble. The fastest method is to fill one piece with dowels, drive them to seat with a mallet, then tap the whole thing in place into the corresponding piece. Bar clamp the whole grate firmly, using two bar clamps on top to clamp the ends and two on the bottom to clamp the sides. Allow it to set overnight. Then fit it into place and do final adjustments.

Some people like to elevate their grates to facilitate drainage. To do this, rip runners to 3/8″ height from 3/4″ wide stock to the length (minus 2″) of your grate and secure it to the grate on either side plus every eighth fore and aft grate strip.

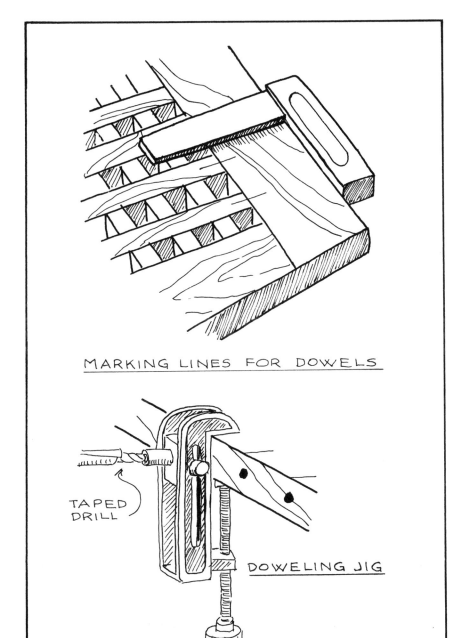

MARKING LINES FOR DOWELS

TAPED DRILL

DOWELING JIG

TEAK COCKPIT GRATES

COCKPIT

49

on deck

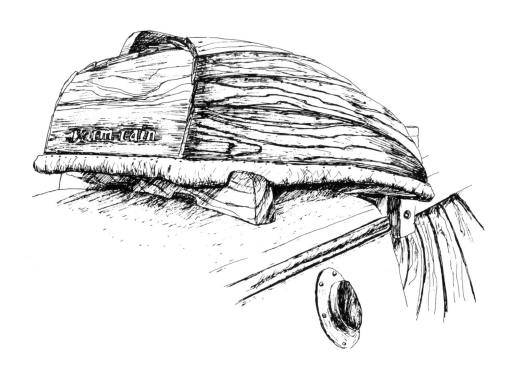

SKYLIGHTS

I can say without exaggeration, that the greatest single interior change *Warm Rain* underwent, was when we cut a 21″ × 20″ hole in the coachroof of the salon. Until then, the most pleasant places aboard were the forepeak, with four portlights and a deadlight in the foreward hatch, and the galley area where light poured in through the open companionway hatch. The salon, up to that point, was a rather gloomy place with a pair of settees. The hole in the coachroof changed all that. With ample light, the nooks and crannies were brought to life, the beautiful grains in the teak tongue-and-groove were finally visible, and the settees became great places to read or visit or just watch the sky.

We proceeded to weatherproof the hole with a traditionally shaped, but vastly redesigned, skylight, which then added as much life to the topsides as the hole in the roof did belowdecks. The major aspect of the redesign was to make the entire skylight one piece, eliminating the traditional hinged wings which on many yachts leak so ferociously. The skylight now functions very much like a foreward hatch, with a pair of cast hinges, and a thread-lock.

The glass in the skylight is tempered, which makes it very resilient to blows from dropped winch handles. Tempered glass was chosen over plexiglass, because the latter will scratch and become quite unsightly regardless of how careful one is with it. If you don't mind a few scratches, by all means go ahead and use it, for it is much less trouble to fabricate (you can cut it with a jigsaw as long as the protective paper coating is still on it), and it's truly unbreakable once you get into 1/2″ thickness, which is what you need for a skylight of any size. With the plexiglass, you obviate the need for protective bars which do look handsome, but are rather a pain to install. For all that, you can actually bypass the gabled skylight and construct a slightly curved one to match the camber of your coachroof, using only a single piece of plexiglass and an elegant, but simple, frame of four pieces of teak (see photo). The time saved on such a simplified version could easily add up to 40%.

Whichever you choose, design the skylight to be as low as possible for both aesthetic and practical reasons.

The following design and construction methods will be interchangeable up to the coamings, after that, each skylight will be covered separately.

THE FINELY FITTED YACHT

Warm Rain's skylight.

Hatch type skylight.

Building the Hole

There is, of course, no particular size the opening of a skylight should be, but I've always thought that 22″ × 22″ is a good size, for it allows a body or sailbags to pass through. For more light and more air, a skylight as large as 36″ × 22″ could be built using four separate pieces of glass in a much reinforced frame, as was on *Nightingale* (see photo). When measuring for the cutout, remember you'll be losing 1½″ in both directions to coamings. Putting the skylight between two deckbeams is most advisable. Once you begin to tamper with structural beams, the reinforcement required to replace them will become discouragingly complicated. Check to make sure you won't be cutting into wires, then drill a 1/2″ hole anywhere within the perimeter of the skylight, stick your jigsaw blade through the hole and cut away. Make your cuts as true as possible to avoid any potential gaps and subsequent leaks. Next, from 13/16″ stock, cut four pieces for your inside coaming, to a width 2″ greater than the thickness of your coachroof. Wipe the sides of your opening thoroughly and lay a generous bead of caulking (Dolfinite will do) all the way around the edges and install the four pieces, one at a time, so their lower edges come flush with the inside of the coachroof (see diagram). Countersink and screw the frames to the coachroof, making sure you screw right into the centre of the plywood core. Brush a bit of resorcinol onto the ends of the frames that will butt against the other frame pieces and screw them to each other as well.

Trim out the coachroof-to-coaming interior joint as in Diagram B. You will next have to install the outside coamings as in Diagram A. Both pieces can be cut from 13/16″ stock; the lower one to a width of 1″, the higher one to a width of 2″. Cut the corners to 45°. Screw both of them directly into the coachroof, leaving a 3/4″ gap between the outside and inside coamings. Use generous amounts of bedding compound on coaming-to-coachroof joints and a bit of resorcinol on coaming-to-coaming joints. Lightly round all edges with sandpaper to prevent splintering.

The coamings are now complete. The only thing left to do is to build the skylight itself.

The Flat Plexiglass Skylight

Mill the frame for the hatch as shown in Diagram C. Lap and screw, dovetail, or cut on 45°, and dowel the corners. When together, make some very exact interior measurements for the plexiglass and cut it to size with a good hacksaw blade in your jigsaw. An ordinary blade would make too rough a cut. Very slightly round the outside edge with sandpaper and dry-fit it into place. Drill countersunk holes

THE FINELY FITTED YACHT

Nightingale's skylight.

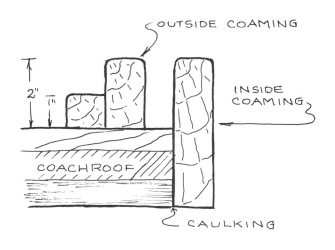

OUTSIDE COAMING

2"

INSIDE COAMING

COACHROOF

CAULKING

DIAGRAM A — DOUBLE COAMING

SKYLIGHTS

for 1″ #10 F.H.S.M. screws every 4″ into the plexiglass. Countersink so the screw head will come flush with the surface of the plexiglass. Run a bead of silicone sealer around the 1/2″ rabbet, set the plexiglass in place, and screw it down. Don't try to wipe off the excess sealer now; you'll just smear it and make a mess. Wait until it's dry, then you can easily scrape it off with your fingernails.

The Gabled Skylight

First, determine the amount of rise you'll want. Something like Diagram E is a pleasant amount. Cut your foreward and aft frame pieces from 13/16″ stock. Skip the rabbet. Cut your side log frames from 1½″ stock, and rabbet the bottom, and slope the top to the angle of your end (foreward and aft) pieces (Diagram D). Butt them and glue and screw. No need to get fancy here.

Next, from 13/16″ stock, cut 3½″ wide pieces. Cut three long ones to overhang the frame by 1″. Remember to allow for a 1/2″ rabbet at both ends of each of the short pieces; see Diagram F where they lap into the long pieces. Run the 1/2″ rabbets the full length along the inboard edges of the outside long pieces and on *both* edges of the central long piece. The angle of its rabbet will have to be adjusted to the gable of the skylight. Run the 1/2″ gable on the inside edges of the four short pieces, as well as their ends, as previously mentioned. Set them all in place, glue them, and screw them to the frames, i.e., glue and screw Diagram F into Diagram E and D. Whew!

Now comes the easy part. Measure in your glass (or plexiglass) areas, then install the plexiglass, as in the flat plexiglass skylight. If you'd rather use tempered glass with a little tinting in it, just take your measurements to a glass shop and have them fabricate the pieces for you. Be sure your measurements are exact because after the glass is tempered, it *cannot* be cut. Now, just run the silicone around the rabbet and press the glass into place.

If you want the brass rods running fore and aft as in photo, fabricate four identical end pieces as in Diagram G. Cut your rods to the *same* length as the glass. Assemble with the rod supports, and screw the supports into the frame, one screw per end, with #8 screws. Use glue. If you've done everything properly, your rod supports will overhang the glass by 1/4″ at either end, just in case the silicone fails. Don't hold your breath.

If possible, double hinge the hatch (a set both foreward and aft). To hold the hatch open, use a chopstick. I do.

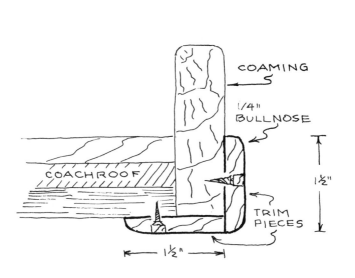

COAMING

1/4"
BULLNOSE

COACHROOF

1½"

TRIM
PIECES

|← 1½" →|

DIAGRAM B — INTERIOR TRIM

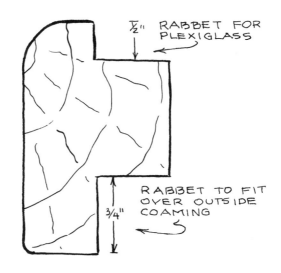

½" RABBET FOR
PLEXIGLASS

RABBET TO FIT
OVER OUTSIDE
COAMING

¾"

DIAGRAM C
SIDE LOG FRAME — FLAT SKYLIGHT

SKYLIGHTS

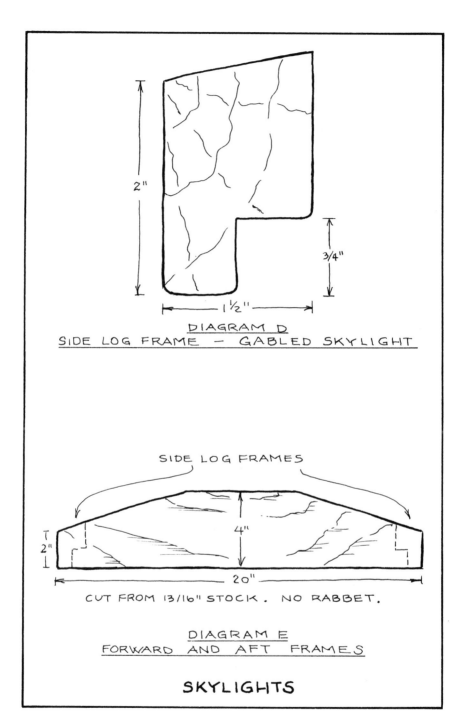

DIAGRAM D
SIDE LOG FRAME — GABLED SKYLIGHT

SIDE LOG FRAMES

CUT FROM 13/16" STOCK. NO RABBET.

DIAGRAM E
FORWARD AND AFT FRAMES

SKYLIGHTS

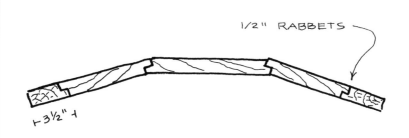

1/2" RABBETS

⊢3½"⊣

DIAGRAM F
END VIEW OF GLASS FRAME

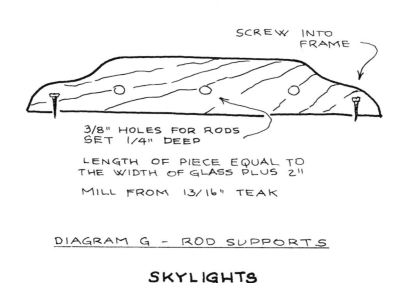

SCREW INTO
FRAME

3/8" HOLES FOR RODS
SET 1/4" DEEP

LENGTH OF PIECE EQUAL TO
THE WIDTH OF GLASS PLUS 2"

MILL FROM 13/16" TEAK

DIAGRAM G - ROD SUPPORTS

SKYLIGHTS

DORADE VENTS

If you've sworn to have no teak at all on your boat, please relent and sacrifice an hour's maintenance annually and make yourself a beautifully varnished teak dorade box with a glistening brass or stainless cowl that has its inside painted the same colour as your sheer stripe. Once it has funneled the cooling air below and teased the eyes above, you'll send me letters of thanks. (Post cards will do.)

The best throat diameter is $3''$ and up, the problem of course being that monstrous vents will require monstrous boxes. In spite of what you frequently hear, "bigger" in the box itself is not at all "better". Commonly thrown about formulas, such as box height must be twice the diameter of the throat, are naïve. Surface areas must be discussed here and not heights. The box as shown in the diagram should have air passage capacity equal to the number of square inches available in the throat, e.g., $3'' \times \pi r^2$ is equal to the surface area that must be provided as an opening in the box. This, of course, is not only designated by the height and width of the box, but also by the height of the baffles inside it. To make a box with greater area capacity than the throat would be damaging to the system, for it would provide an expansion space where the air can eddy and disrupt the flow into the cabin.

The box should be made of $3/4''$ solid teak with butted ends glued and screwed. Semi-circular drain holes should be cut on either side just below the cowl in case water finds its way into it.

The lid of the box has also been a matter for controversy, with many people advocating the use of $3/4''$ plexiglass instead of solid teak to allow more light belowdecks. This seems initially quite a pleasant idea, but just as successful a system can be achieved without depriving the yacht of a lovely teak box lid. Into the foreward part of the box just above the vent hole in the coachroof (same diameter as the throat of the vent), a similar hole can be cut and a bronze ringed deadlight inserted. Since the hole in the coachroof is only of $3''$ diameter anyway, plasticizing the entire lid of the box for light would be quite redundant.

For tropical use, one should consider a second threaded ring (the same one the cowl usually sits in) instead of a dead light. Now, a $3/4''$ piece of plexiglass can be cut to act as a plug in the ring. It would have to be taken to a machine shop to have appropriate threads cut into it.

The inside base of the box should be lined with cleat stock. The whole thing should then be bedded in Dolphinite or polysulfide and

THE FINELY FITTED YACHT

DORADE BOX

the cleat stock drilled and screwed to the deck. One last thing before you install the lid. Futile attempts of all sorts have been made to install adequate circular mosquito nets into the deckhouse hole after the system has been built. Thoughtless and regrettable. Now is the time to act. Acquire a fine brass screen, and using Monel staples or light tacks, attach it over the inside of the hole *on the lid*. You'll now be permanently bug-proofed.

Here, perhaps, a word on the type of cowl to be used. Cowls range from soft squishy plastic to cast bronze you couldn't dent with a hammer. Advantages of the soft plastic ones are obvious: they are less likely to foul lines, they cause less damage to falling bodies, and they are inexpensive. But boy, are they ugly! They oxidize and stain rapidly and very little can be done to bring them back to life. The heavy stainless or bronze ones come with solidly cast rings into which fit solidly cast plugs for winter sailing when even a breath belowdecks is too much.

A point here about installing the threaded ring. When marking the screw holes for it, be sure the cowl is in it tightly. Have the cowl face forward and now mark the holes and drill.

To add a finishing touch to thick cabin tops made up of fiberglass, plywood, and insulation — all of which are visible belowdecks once the hole is cut, a thin sleeve of light gauge brass or copper should be formed into a ring and held in place inside the hole with three or four brass tacks. This will provide that slight accent that differentiates the master from the hacker.

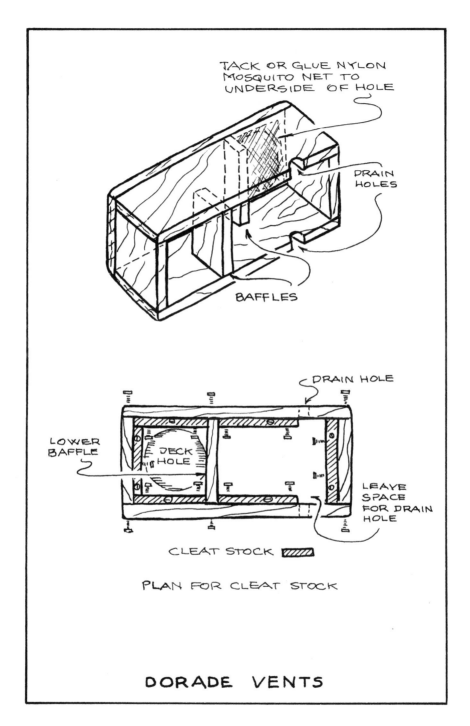

TACK OR GLUE NYLON
MOSQUITO NET TO
UNDERSIDE OF HOLE

DRAIN
HOLES

BAFFLES

DRAIN HOLE

LOWER
BAFFLE

DECK
HOLE

LEAVE
SPACE
FOR DRAIN
HOLE

CLEAT STOCK

PLAN FOR CLEAT STOCK

DORADE VENTS

SIMPLE BOOM GALLOWS

The range of potentially functional gallow designs is so great, that I feel it would be futile to even begin discussing it, especially because most make use of complex steel fabrication, incorporating them into stanchions, or davits, or stern pulpits.

One very fine traditional set, using a very simple concept, that can be adapted to most yachts, whether on the aft deck or the coachroof, has been given rebirth by the nautical hardware firm of Merriman-Holbrook. The set consists of two corner fittings and two bases. Both can be slipped into brass pipes that make up the uprights. The bases should be bolted through the deck or cabin top and backed up belowdecks with either a single plate of the same diameter (1/8" thickness is fine) or a set of washers. The single plate is, of course, the preferred alternative since it gives the most aesthetic finish and the most even reinforcement as well.

The location of the gallows will have to be decided in order to establish the length of the wood cross member. The coachroof just at the companionway hatch has been a favourite of many yachtsmen, for there the uprights can be made quite short and, consequently, quite stable. The obvious drawback of this arrangement is that the wooden cross member interferes with foreward vision.

Most yachts have the gallows on the aft deck and this, indeed, is a great friend for the helmsman or night watch to lean against or hold on to. The problem, of course, is how to secure the gallows in this position since the height of the uprights will often reach a rather wobbly four feet. The cleanest and most functional solution I have seen was the use of guy wires (see diagram). The wires used were sheathed stainless, the same as used for the lifelines, with a single turnbuckle in each piece for aligning and tensioning the gallows. Since the sloped aftmost wire is pinched in at the stern (especially so on double enders and canoe sterns), a very stable guy system is established. Padeyes or eyebolts can be used aft for the wire bases.

The wooden cross member is most easily made up of a single piece of 1½" teak cut to the shape in the illustration. It should have three nests for the boom to facilitate aft deck traffic, regardless of whether the yacht is docked port-to or starboard-to. For the most even job, cut the nests with a hole saw with a radius equal to 1/4" more than the beam. Bullnose all edges. To protect the boom's paint or varnish, line the nest with a piece of leather and tack its edges with brass tacks to the foreward and aft face of the cross member.

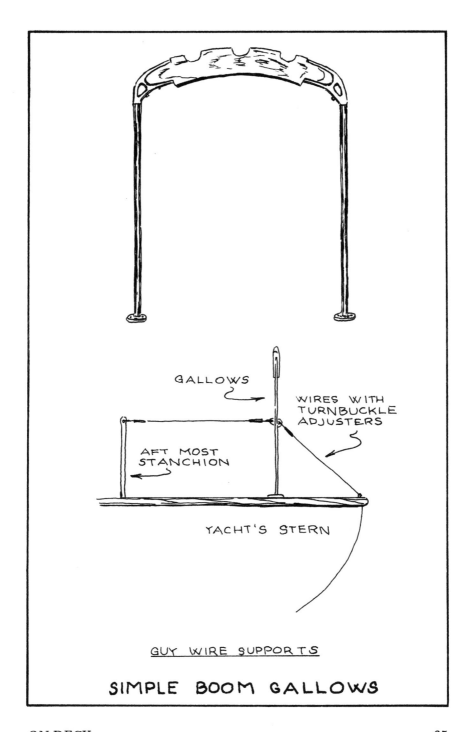

GALLOWS

WIRES WITH
TURNBUCKLE
ADJUSTERS

AFT MOST
STANCHION

YACHT'S STERN

GUY WIRE SUPPORTS

SIMPLE BOOM GALLOWS

GRABRAILS

Since grabrails are, in most cases, a matter of life and death, or at least a good lengthy swim, their installation should be one of the first major undertakings. When the dust clears after all arguments, only two sensible alternatives remain. One is the traditional looped wooden rails, and the other, the brass eye with rope line rails. A third variety, a solid rail with a concave detail for grip, has many supporters, but this seems to me sadly inadequate, for although it is undeniable that a ready hold can be gained in any given spot, that hold is tenuous at best, being literally of the hanging-by-the-fingernails variety.

Looped Rails

The first thing to do is determine the placement and length of your rail. Running parallel to the cabinsides, about 6″ inboard from the edge, is ideal. If you have good thick laminates in your cabintop (for example, 1/2″ plywood core with 1/8″ glass on either side), you need no precautions, for you can simply screw into the cabintop with #14 sheet metal screws. If your cabintop is of a weaker construction, or has a foam or balsa core, you will have to through-bolt, in which case you better be certain there are no fittings or fixtures belowdeck that would impede your work.

Milling should be from 1″ solid stock, to a width of 2½″. Fabricate a single loop jig out of 1/8″ plywood, and use this as a pattern to guarantee that all your loops will be identical. The loops should be on 10″ centres with the footings between at least 2″ to make a solid base.

Divide the 2½″ width evenly between wood and space. Be sure not to taper the tip of the last loop too drastically, for it will become frail, and splinter with changes in the weather. Once cut, bullnose the loops and the top of the rail with a 3/8″ router bit. Next, pre-drill your grabrail, and countersink to a depth of 1/2″. The size of your drill bit will depend on whether you screw or through-bolt. If screwing, use #14 PHSM screws; if through-bolting, use stainless steel round heads. Try to calculate the exact bolt length needed, allowing 1/4″ to protrude belowdecks, for then you will be able to use cap nuts, which look much more pleasing than a regular nut which has a bit of the bolt sticking through. In neither case should you use flat heads, for these have wedge-shaped shoulders and wedges split wood, and if you want to split wood, get a job in a shingle mill.

THE FINELY FITTED YACHT

Next, using the rail as a guide, drill your first hole and screw it gently to the deck. This is a dry run; do not use caulking. Drill and screw the entire rail into place, then remove all screws and clean the drilled out rubble between the rail and deck. Place a good ring of caulking around each hole and re-insert screws. If you're through-bolting, you'll need a person belowdecks to place washers and nuts. Tell him to tighten gently. Remove any excess bedding compound with a wooden scraper. Plug, making sure you use resorcinol glue. Let set overnight before you lop off the heads of the plugs.

Brass Eye and Line

The most difficult part of using this method is finding the looped brass fittings. Once found, they should be screwed or through-bolted to the deck with the same precautions as above, on 20″-24″ centres. A good length of 1″ dacron should then be secured and spliced and whipped, as in the photo, onto the fore-most and aft-most fitting. Do not use poly line, for it becomes a bit too hard with weather, and much too rough on the hands.

As seen in the photo, this makes for extremely attractive and almost flawlessly functional, grabrails. Upkeep is non-existent, initial expenditure of time and money minimal. The one major drawback is that it cannot be used as a foot brace while fumbling around the mast or boom, but then you can't have everything.

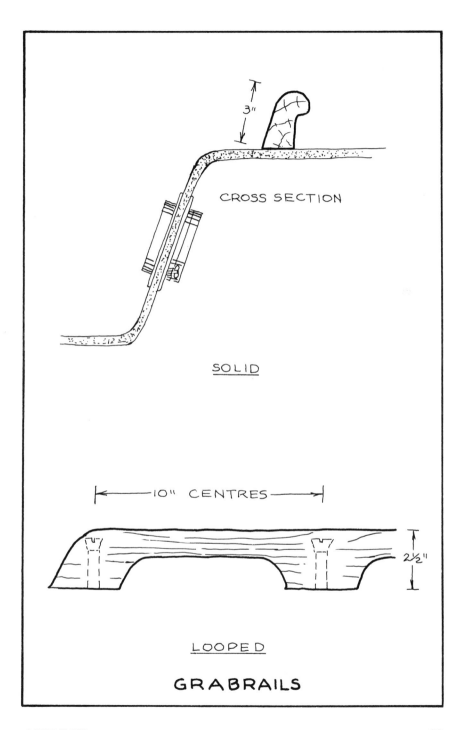

3"

CROSS SECTION

SOLID

|← 10" CENTRES →|

2½"

LOOPED

GRABRAILS

DECKHOUSE STEP

On many motor sailors and power yachts, the height of the cabin makes commuting from deck to cabin top rather treacherous. A cabin side step on the cabin's aft face (not on the narrow side deck where it could endanger shins and knees) can be of great help.

The location of the step in the photograph is not the most ideal since it protrudes past the corner of the cabin.

The step and the support should be of 13/16″ teak. A piece 6″ wide and 12″ long will be enough for both. Cut the piece into two 6″ long portions. The depth of the step can be left at 6″ if space on the aft deck allows, but 4″ is quite serviceable and 3″ is better than nothing. Two inches isn't.

Fit the knee support against the cabin side. With the aid of a small level, scribe a horizontal line onto it and cut it. Eyeball in the curved shape of the knee, then scribe, and cut, and bullnose the curved edges. Next, place the knee in position on the cabin (usually at the halfway point between the deck and cabin top) and after making sure it doesn't rock either vertically or horizontally, scribe a line around it onto the cabin. Now, go below and measure in the location, and make sure that when you drill through from the outside, you will be doing so in an unobstructed area. Drill two holes 2″ apart in the area you scribed. The hole should be for #10 S.M. screws.

Next, ask a friend to hold the knee in place, then go below, and using the holes you've just drilled as guides, drill into the knee to a depth of 1¼″ to 1½″, then clean the knee and cabin surface and cover one or the other with bedding compound. Now, ask the friend to hold the knee most securely and very exactly in place, then, from below, insert your screws, choosing such a length that will allow 1½″ deep penetration into the knee.

When the knee is installed, lay the piece for the step on top of it, and scribe the edge parallel to the house. Bullnose all non-contact edges. Cut and refit just to check, then install in identical fashion, but adding a bead of resorcinol glue and a couple of 1″ # 10 P.H.S.M. screws to fix the step onto the knee. Plug all screw holes.

If you elect to varnish it, sprinkle a bit of very fine silicone, for friction, on the stepping surface while the second coat is still tacky, then brush off all excess silicone and go on with successive coats.

THE FINELY FITTED YACHT

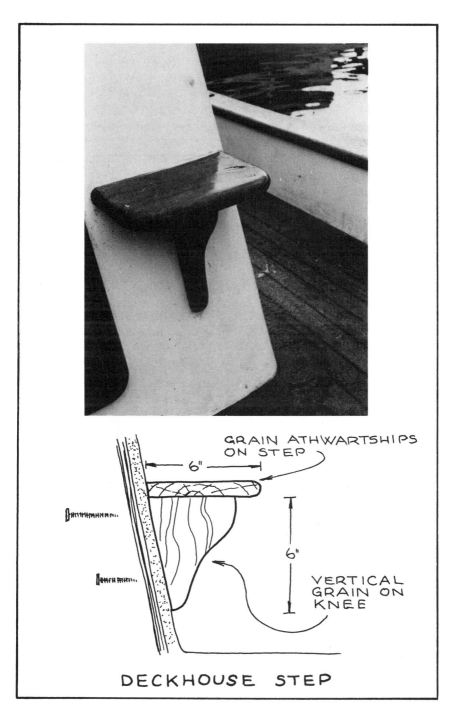

GRAIN ATHWARTSHIPS
ON STEP

6"

6"

VERTICAL
GRAIN ON
KNEE

DECKHOUSE STEP

TEAK TURTLE HATCH

This is a very practical item on most vessels, for not only does it keep the main hatch totally dry when driving hard to windward, but it also makes for a good base for the mainsheet travellers and dinghy chocks. Furthermore, it provides a good firm place to stand when reefing or wrapping up the main sail; the main hatch on its own tends to slide when stepped upon.

The turtle hatch should, if possible, reflect the look of the main hatch in both material and construction, although there is basically nothing profane about mating a teak hatch with a fiberglass turtle hatch, or vice versa.

In most cases, the simplest method of installation will call for bolting the turtle hatch directly to the deck and if this is indeed feasible, then you will be involved, basically, with building a three-sided, bottomless box.

The three sides should be milled from 1¾" stock, cut to a width 2" greater than the overall height of the side of your hatch (see diagram). This is to allow for a 1" rabbet into the inboard top edge, into which the top can be laid, plus some sort of an aft piece to support the aft edge of the top, plus about 1/4" clearance between the hatch and the turtle hatch to avoid binding.

Run the rabbet clear along the side pieces but terminate it 7/8" from the forward end so the rabbet ends will not interfere with the dovetailing or lapping of the frames. For dovetailing, use a dovetail jig (see "Tool" section) and for lapping, use common sense and Diagram A. Assemble the frame with resorcinol glue and clamps.

Since most hatches (and consequently turtle hatches as well) have some sort of a camber, the 1/2" layer of plywood, which is to be the foundation layer of the top, will have to be made up of two 1/4" sheets. This is to avoid having to force-bend a 1/2" piece into place. So, lay in your first 1/4" plywood and glue it (resorcinol glue) to the frames, slipping in a screw every 8" and carefully countersinking it just below the plywood's surface. Next, cover the first layer of plywood with glue and lay in the second layer. Screw this into the frame at 8" intervals, but staggered between the screws holding down the first layer. Next, rip teak to a 1/2" thickness and 2" width (or the width of the hatch slats if they are teak). A width greater than 2" will require that you double screw each piece (two screws side by side) or the edges will forever curl up. Unless you must have a caulked turtle hatch to match your main hatch, just butt the slats

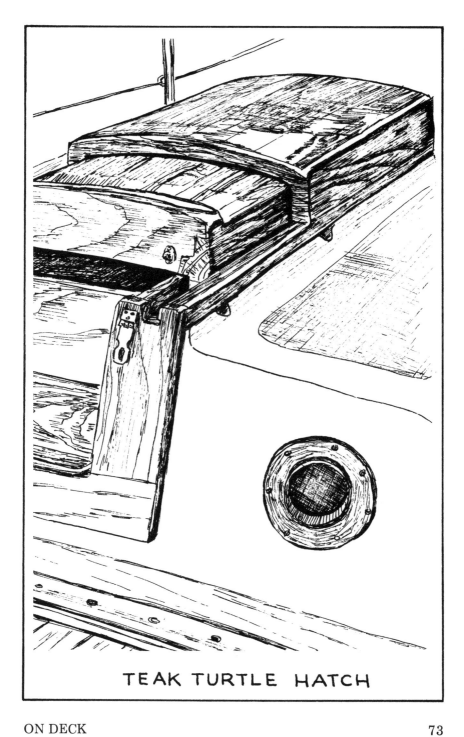

TEAK TURTLE HATCH

side by side as tight as you can. Use resorcinol glue and very carefully countersunk and most carefully tightened #8 flat heads. Plug, sand and varnish or oil.

Next, saturate the underside of the turtle hatch (the plywood) with a good wood preservative like Cuprinol to prevent any mildew from forming. Remember, you won't have any access to this surface once the hatch is screwed down.

Lastly, to install, set the turtle hatch in place, pencil in its outline and drill pilot holes right through the deck. Now clean both the deck and the bottom of the turtle hatch thoroughly, then run two beads of polysulfide around the hatch frame and put it back over the holes. Ask a friend to sit on the turtle hatch and not move while you run below and secure it in place by running #10 or #12 pan head screws into it through the cabin top. Be sure to use screws of such a length that will penetrate at least 1½″ into the hatch frame. Space them about 6″ apart.

Clean off the excess caulking and enjoy.

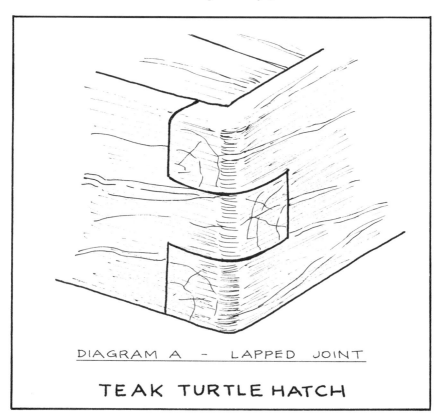

DIAGRAM A - LAPPED JOINT

TEAK TURTLE HATCH

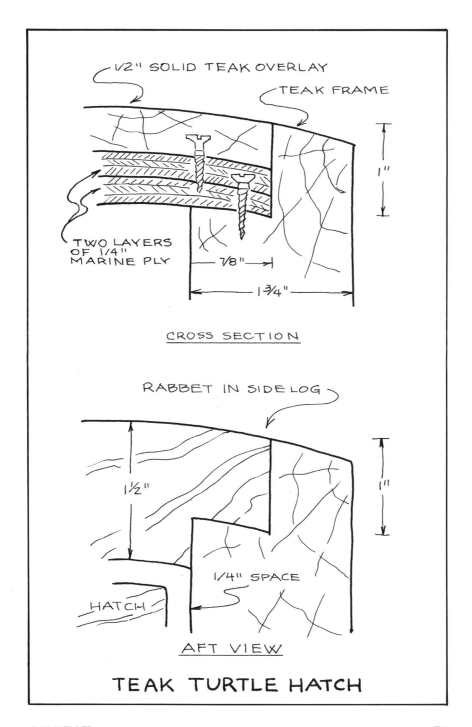

1/2" SOLID TEAK OVERLAY

TEAK FRAME

TWO LAYERS OF 1/4" MARINE PLY

7/8"

1 3/4"

1"

CROSS SECTION

RABBET IN SIDE LOG

1 1/2"

1"

1/4" SPACE

HATCH

AFT VIEW

TEAK TURTLE HATCH

KEVEL

This is most practical for those with pirate-phobia, although it can be a useful tidbit aboard most vessels with bulwarks. As shown in the diagram, it has its own enclosed fairlead. To determine the size of the kevel to be made, one would be well advised to obtain a cast or spun hawse pipe fairlead first. Then, from 1″ stock, cut the kevel to the shape shown, being sure to leave at least 1″ around the hawse pipe.

For a typical 12″ kevel, the horns (past the point of fastening) should be 3″ long. Drill 3/8″ holes for mounting bolts. Bullnose all edges. To mount, cut vertical spacers from 1″ stock to fit snugly between the cap rail and the deck. If required by the cap rail overhang, taper the spacers to fit snugly. Bed the verticals in beads of caulking, set them in place, and, using the kevel as a pattern, drill the mounting holes. There is no need to fasten the verticals separately to the bulwark, for the kevel mounting bolts should be enough.

Mounting should be done with 3/8″ carriage bolts to minimize head exposure and, for the same reason, cap nuts should be used or nylon bushinged lock nuts. Any protruding bolt end should be trimmed flush with the nut with a hack saw.

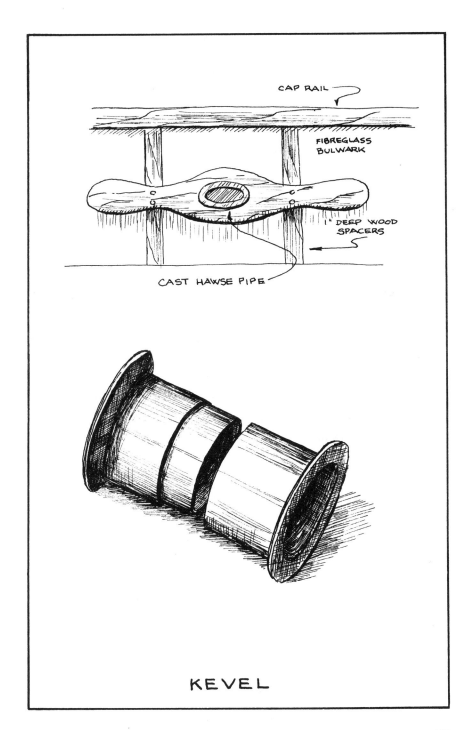

CAP RAIL

FIBREGLASS
BULWARK

1" DEEP WOOD
SPACERS

CAST HAWSE PIPE

KEVEL

WOOD CLEATS

Good wood cleats can last as long as bronze or alloy ones and are infinitely easier for the average sailor to fabricate. Cleats should be very hefty, made of oak or teak, and extremely well-rounded to avoid chafe at all points. The dimensions given in the diagram are for a 10″ long cleat. They can be adjusted proportionately for any cleat.

Draw the profile of the cleat onto a piece of 1¾″ stock, drill the 1/2″ holes to give a nice smooth bite, then cut out around the holes with a jig or band saw. Next, holding the cleat in a vise, drill the 3/8″ bolt holes. Bevel the sides on a table saw (see end view diagram), then settle down with a little shoe rasp and start forming, shaping, and rounding. Bullnose all edges and round the throat. Finish with sandpaper, then oil. Varnishing cleats that are used with any frequency is rather futile, since a line will eat the varnish off in little time.

When the cleat is finished, ascertain that the base is clean and even (as is the surface upon which it is to be installed), then, using the cleat holes as guides, drill the mounting surface, wipe it clean, then coat both the cleat and mounting surface with polysulfide bedding compound (squirt a little into the holes just to be sure), and then bolt it into place. The best underdeck reinforcement is, of course, a single steel plate with two holes. Lacking this, utilize the largest washers you can get your hands on. Use nylon bushinged lock nuts, or a dab of polysulfide on a common nut, to avoid its working loose. Check the nuts once a year just to be sure.

THE FINELY FITTED YACHT

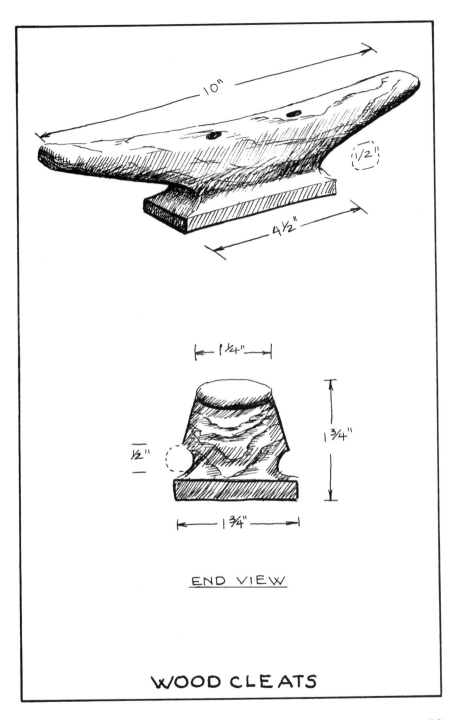

10"

1/2"

4½"

1¼"

1¾"

½"

1¾"

END VIEW

WOOD CLEATS

ON DECK

79

RECAULKING OLD TEAK DECKS

On mature yachts, the seam caulking of teak decks will have to be redone eventually. The manufacturers of "black death", Grove Caulking, suggest a thorough study of procedure before beginning.

Preparation

Old deck seams require careful preparation to achieve years of protection. The old caulking compound, which must be removed, may be hardened or gummy. In either case, it should be taken down to the cotton in a "V" seam, and to the wood in a rabbetted seam. All traces of the old material should be cleaned from seam edges as well.

For hundreds of years, shipwrights have used a variety of simple, handmade tools for removing seam compounds. In the amateur's hand, these "reefing" tools are far superior to power equipment for there is less chance of damaging adjacent wood surfaces.

The tail of an old file may be heated, bent at a 90° angle, and ground to sharpness along the edges to the shape of the seam (Diagram B) or an old, good quality steel screwdriver may be similarly adapted. Linoleum knives are often used also.

Bear down on the tool while pulling it toward yourself, working to the bottom of the seam in the process. After the bulk of old material has been thusly "reefed", the tool is carefully pulled along both seam edges to scrape away crusted material. This is important, as the new bond really starts in that area (Diagram C). Be sure all burrs and splinters along the seam edges are removed also. Sliding a rasp along the seam grooves does this easily.

Electric power tools can be adapted for seam reefing without too much difficulty. The face plate on a router or circular saw can be altered by drilling, tapping and inserting small studs of desired seam width, behind cutting bit or blade. By hand reefing a few inches, the blade and studs may then be inserted into groove. The blade then cuts out old material while the studs act as a guide. Considerable time may be saved by this method but more care must be exercised to avoid damage to planks. Hull seams can be reefed in this manner as well.

Carefully search lapped seams for wood deterioration and repair as necessary. Renew slack cotton caulking as necessary, but leave at least 1/4" for the Deck Caulk. Check for loose plugs and renew as necessary. If refastening is needed, now is the time to do it. Seams

THE FINELY FITTED YACHT

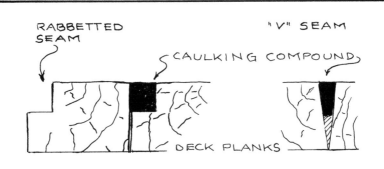

RABBETTED SEAM

"V" SEAM

CAULKING COMPOUND

DECK PLANKS

DIAGRAM A

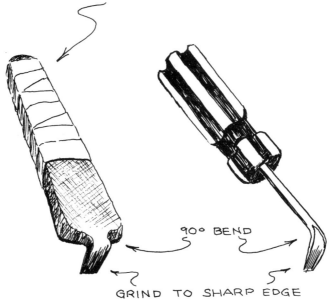

WRAP FILE WITH TAPE
TO HOLD COMFORTABLY

90° BEND

GRIND TO SHARP EDGE

DIAGRAM B

RECAULKING OLD TEAK DECKS

should be thoroughly vacuumed to insure dust and debris-free surfaces. The worst is now over!

Caulking

Fill your cartridge and caulk the seams from the bottom up. Be sure to leave excess for sanding later (Diagram D). If decks will not be sanded, however, seams may be masked, then caulked. When applying to masked seams, leave a slight excess above the deck surface. Then, hold a putty knife almost horizontally and pull it along the filled seam with a slight downward pressure. This will allow a slight extrusion of material behind the blade so a slight convex surface will be left. This usually creates enough excess to compensate for minor shrinkage during the curing process. Deck Caulk starts its cure or "tacks up" quickly after application, permitting immediate removal of the masking tape. While masking and filling is satisfactory, the results will by no means approximate the "newness" you will have created by filling and sanding.

DIAGRAM C

ALLOW CAULKING TO OVERFLOW

DIAGRAM D

RECAULKING OLD TEAK DECKS

DINGHY CHOCKS

The initial decision apart from "where" to stow the beastly dinghy is whether to stow it upside down or right side up. You may think that pondering this is a rather prosaic expenditure of time, but I assure you that the following considerations are of great value:

(a) Visibility — an upright dinghy is of course broader at the top; it therefore blocks out, on the average, about 30% of forward vision.

(b) Readiness — an upright dinghy is a most inviting stowage box collecting everything from fenders to apple cores, which require relocating before the dinghy can be used. Of course a beautifully fabricated cover will obviate this problem, but then time will be required to remove (and later put neatly back in place) the cover itself. The "upright" undeniably has the one advantage of not requiring flipping; an operation that is oftentimes awkward and strenuous.

(c) Protection — I've found the upside down dinghy on the foredeck of *Warm Rain* an invaluable friend. On rainy nights when portlights must be kept closed, the forepeak hatch, which is below the dinghy, can be left open to let in great quantities of fresh air. During rough days, the dinghy becomes a reassuring leaning place when headsails need to be changed. If you have a slow, manual windlass like we have, then you'll find the dinghy a lovely seat from which to contemplate the scenery while you relentlessly haul in 200 fathoms of chain. For the efficiency-minded sailor, the foredeck dinghy becomes a "sail weight," under which a headsail can be temporarily jammed while the other is being hanked into place. The removed sail can then be bagged after the new one is aloft.

A dinghy on the foredeck blocks a smaller area of your vision than a dinghy amidships, but it is of course more vulnerable to large headseas.

After pondering the above, the choice is obvious: all dinghies should be stored in torpedo tubes. If you haven't one on your current vessel, here's a dinghy chock to tide you over. I have always been a firm believer in simplicity, so I feel the one-piece chock in the illustration the most sensible.

Rough cut a 4″ wide piece of 1½″ teak, oak or mahogany to length, allowing 4″ to overhang the dinghy's bulwarks on either side. Lay it on the cabin top where it is to live, and scribe the cabin's crown onto it and cut. Scribe and cut the upper edge to match. Next put it back in place, and put the dinghy on top of it and mark in the

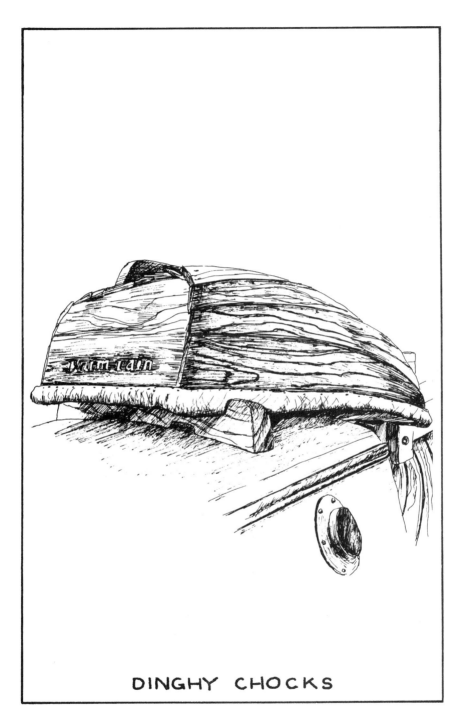

DINGHY CHOCKS

cutouts in which the dinghy will rest. Allow 1/4" on either side, to make placement and removal easier, then cut to a depth of 1". The inch will be enough to keep it snugly in place. On the lower side cut two drain spaces about 3/4" deep and 3" long. Bullnose all upper edges. Next, fit the bottom edge of the chock to the cabin top to perfection, then bed in polysulfide and, with two carriage bolts, bolt it to the cabin top as shown. On the forward face of the chock overhang, install a 3/8" shaft padeye (diamond base will provide the best screw configuration for this application) to act as the aft tie downs for the hold-down straps. For fabrication of same, see "Canvas" section.

If your dinghy has a pram bow, and you're using the half-round rubber bumper along its bulwarks, you can bypass a forward chock and let the bow rest happily on the deck or bowsprit end. The chock and the hold-downs should prevent most fore and aft movement of the dinghy, but since you have a painter anyway, you may as well use it and tie it firmly to a samson post or bow cleat or something.

About a third of the way aft of the dingy's bow (or wherever they'll be most out of the way) install two eyebolts to act as bases for the forward ends of the hold-downs.

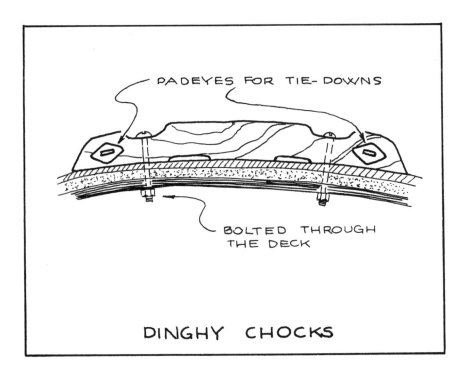

DINGHY CHOCKS

THE FINELY FITTED YACHT

TEAK DECKS

Teak decks are the epitome of decadence on a fiberglass boat, application or exclusion of which can be decided only after lengthy deliberation between you and your ego. I have always thought it would require a babbling moron to take a perfectly solid non-skid, waterproof and rot-proof fiberglass deck, spend $900 on teak and fasteners, then drill a thousand holes to hold the wood down, then spend $300 on caulking and bedding compounds to seal and waterproof the thousand holes he has just drilled.

Needless to say, we put teak decks on our boat at the expense of almost 200 hours of screamingly frustrating labor. But they are beautiful and they are non-skid and we do love them and I wouldn't trade them for a brand new Porsche ... well, maybe a silver one. Here's how it's done.

Type Of Deck and Wood Selection

Try to pick the straightest, least knotty pieces of wood you can find. The longer, the better. If need be, shop around for long clean pieces. One of the worst jobs in doing the decks is butting ends together, so try to avoid too many joints. Knots look beautiful down below if oiled or varnished, but topsides they'll just weather and pop out, or if you are bending your planks, they'll surely snap in two at the knot.

If you do have to have joints, be sure to place them in the area of least curvature. Even if your planking is milled as narrow as an inch and three-quarter it will be almost impossible to bend the last foot of teak, so try to get your joints to stagger and try to put them amidship where the curvature of the deck is at its least.

Predetermine the width of the planking you intend to use. If you are running your decking straight fore and aft without bending, the width of your planks can be unlimited. Running them in this fashion is a traditional procedure and it is very simple to do, but only if your cabin sides themselves are uncurved or only slightly curved. If their curve is drastic, an attempt at straight decking can only result in a myriad of short, unsightly, slivery pieces. If you intend to have a curved deck with either a king plank or herringbone foredeck, using planking wider than two inches will lead to grave problems during bending unless the boat is of great length and very slight of beam. If it is, perhaps you could push the width of the decking to 2-3/8″ or to 2½″. I mention this tradeoff here because it's good to know your intended plank width before you buy your teak stock so that you will select only those widths which will lend themselves economically to your purpose.

The thickness of the stock should not fall below 3/4''. Anything thinner will be very difficult to plug as well as be more inclined to warp and crack with constant weathering. If the plug thickness ends up being less than 1/4'', the plug is guaranteed to crack and pop out before the year is over.

Milling

Whether you use straight decks or curved ones, you should mill a caulk groove into the edge of each plank. You will need this groove into which to pour polysulphide sealant after your deck is laid. The caulking not only seals the deck and keeps water from entering into the plywood core through the screw holes, but it also remains flexible to allow the decks to shrink and swell without causing the wood to buckle or crack. The caulking groove need not exceed 1/4'' X 1/4''. I have seen some teak decks without grooves, but I have never known how they survive. The grooves can be milled into the planks with either a dado or two cuts of a table saw.

Covering Boards

To determine the shape of the covering boards, you will have to scribe them to fit the cabin and/or your bulwarks. To be sure that you don't waste expensive teak, cut templates for each board out of 1/8'' thick veneer. The length and width of each board will be dictated by economy. The wider and longer you make your covering boards, the more scrap you will have. Boards 3½'' wide look wide enough to seem intentionally different from the 2'' planking and yet are narrow enough to be fairly economical. The length of each board will depend on how drastically curved your cabin sides or your bulwarks are. If they are curved as much as ours, the boards cannot economically exceed five feet.

Making and fitting covering boards will probably be the single most time-consuming task in your decking. They should be cut with a band saw (if one is not available a saber saw will do) out of wide planking. I managed to cut ours on a table saw; if you set your blade at a height barely sufficient to cut through your wood and no more, you will be able to do it too if you concentrate.

A side note: if you want teak decks, I think it practical to mill and lay them before you do any small projects. The amount of large scraps from milling the decks is phenomenal, and all this scrap can be utilized for corner trim, searails, etc.

If you have an extremely small radius at your cabin-side-to-deck or deck-to-bulwark turns, fitting the boards flush against the cabin or bulwark will be simple. If, however, you have a substantial radius, you must choose one of two alternatives. You can: a) begin your decking at a distance from the vertical side where the curve will have no consequence, or b) hand plane the bottom edge of the covering boards to accommodate the radius in the fiberglass. The joints for the covering boards can be made using any number of traditional scarfs. The structural integrity is virtually identical; thus, your choice will have to be based on taste alone.

Do not mill caulk grooves into the covering boards. For the long sides,you can use the groove in the first plank; as for the scarfs, it is preferred that you bed and screw the boards down in their final position first, then belatedly chisel in the grooves. This way, if your butting or alignment is not perfect (and they never will be even though the screw holes have been dry fitted), you will be able to cheat a little and chisel a nice parallel-sided caulk groove.

The King Plank

I am not sure that a single logical argument exists in favour of a king plank except that it is pretty. To do one is time consuming and painstaking. If you can get the pattern for it from someone with a sister ship you will be far ahead; but if not, you will spend many hours drawing in the lines and routing them out.

The fastest procedure involves laying the planks with roughly hacked off ends. The angle at the ends is irrelevant and the fit unimportant for the ends will later be overlapped by the king plank. Once the planks are all down, make a pattern out of thin veneer or cardboard for the king plank. The width of the plank and the angles you use will be of your own choosing. Cut out the king plank from a solid piece of teak, lay it over the deck, and draw its shape onto the over-long planks. Now take the router and set it exactly to the depth of your teak decking. If anything, leave it 1/32" shallower, because then you can easily penetrate the last bit of wood with an old chisel and remove the excess. This way you won't have your expensive router bit dulled by the fiberglass.

Now you can drop in your king plank and see how it fits. Don't worry about it being in perfect alignment. As long as your mistake is no greater than a sixteenth of an inch,you will be able to correct it when you rout in the caulking groove between the king plank and the other planks.

Herringboning

This method is less demanding. It is quicker than a king plank, because it involves only the first stage in laying the deck. You must use more caution, however, in scribing your angles on the end of each plank to make certain you don't wander too far off the centre line. But again, remember that a one-sixteenth or even a three-thirty-second mistake is allowable. You will then only have to rout in a centre line caulking-groove to notch out the mistakes and complete the job.

An absolutely vital note, whichever method you employ, is to have the straight bit for your router sharpened just before you start working on your teak decks. If you can get a carbide-tip bit, so much the better; whatever else you may have heard, teak is a brittle wood and prone to chipping if anything but the sharpest of tools is used.

Deck Laying

The first step in laying a deck should be shaping and fitting the covering boards. Dry fitting should include the placement of each board into its final position and putting at least a few screws into their final places.

When it seems you have done everything you can to make the covering boards fit perfectly, take out the screws you have just put in and lift up the covering boards. You will find little mounds of white fiberglass powder surrounding the mouth of every hole. Some of the powder will have stuck around the screw hole on the wood too. This powder must be wiped off completely or the board won't set evenly and may teeter over the little mound, eventually causing it to crack. This procedure of dry fitting and cleaning off the dust mounds should be observed with every teak-to-glass joining to guarantee better joints. Once the dust has cleared, you can permanently install the boards.

The first step in installation is to lay two unbroken beads of black polysulphide about one inch from either end of the plank onto the fiberglass. Many people have used Dolphinite as the bedding compound, but Dolphinite has the tendency to expand and ooze oil in very hot climates even a few months after laying. I've heard of some decks buckling because of the expansion. Even if buckling doesn't occur, the seam-caulking may be pushed away from the wood, allowing water to penetrate.

At any rate, lay down two beads of polysulphide, and just for safety, pop a drop into each screw hole. If you think that's being over-anxious, just try not doing it and see how you sleep at night. I

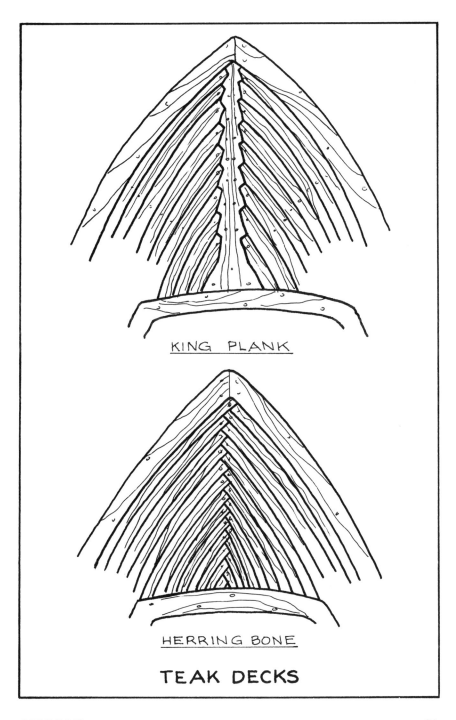

KING PLANK

HERRING BONE

TEAK DECKS

didn't do it originally, only to end up four days later taking every fastener out of the deck, screw by screw, and popping in a belated drop of sealer, then putting the screws back in. That's being over-anxious.

Once the covering boards are in their final place, the fun begins. Use your table saw to cut about ten pieces of $3/4''$ thick by $4'' \times 4''$ plywood blocks. Now gather up all the oak, ash, and teak scraps you have and cut them into wedges ranging from $4'' \times 10''$ to $1/2'' \times 5''$.

The harder the wood you use, the better, because you will be smashing these blocks with a hammer and you will want the wedges to last as long as possible under this onslaught.

Wedging teak planking to form curves.

Next, establish the athwartship points where you will be putting screws into the planks. The screws should be no more than 12" apart; if the bends are radical, use closer centres. At these 12 or whatever inch points draw a straight pencil line athwartships on the fiberglass. Nothing looks prettier than perfectly lined up plugs, and the pencil lines will help you prettify.

Now get your first plank, cut it to length, then take the 3/4" ply blocks you have just cut and screw them into the deck 4" or 5" from the covering boards and about 12" apart. Use one screw only and use it in the centre of the block so that the block can swivel when you insert different shaped wedges. Drive in this one screw deep, or the force of the wedges will cause the screw to bend, and it is almost impossible to pull a crippled screw out of fiberglass.

Now lay double seams of caulking down the length of the deck where the first plank will go. Spread it evenly and thickly. Be sure to put a bead right next to the covering board to seal the edges. Don't scrimp. It's easier to wipe off the mess that squeezes out than to try to fill the voids under a screwed down deck. Also, have a couple of rolls of paper towels ready along with a can of acetone to wipe the goo from your hands, tools, and your left ear lobe. Rags are passable, but too frequently, you'll end up wiping old goo onto your hands, instead of wiping the new goo off; so, use paper towels and throw them away. It's only money.

Now, summon the bulkiest friend you have and secure his loyalty for the next four days. You will need every ounce he carries. The longer his reach, the better.

With a screw gun and drill motor, some 1" pan head sheet metal screws (remember flat heads split wood) and a couple of hammers, you will be set. You will also need about 30 tubes of polysulphide. Have them handy, for it's very ulcerizing to run out when you're raring to keep going.

Now, with the goo spread evenly and with the large friend hanging onto the other end of your plank, bend the plank and place it behind the blocks. Once it's down behind the blocks, don't ever take your weight off it. Be sure to hold down both ends and both centres, and tell chubby not to lose his balance or the plank will spring up like a steel coil and smash his face in.

Now comes the critical point. Insert wedges between each block and the plank; begin to tap each wedge gently and evenly, one tap each at a time. Give your helper a hammer too, but tell him to be gentle and never to take his weight off the plank. As the plank is stressed more and more, the more vital this constant pressure becomes, because the greater the tension, the greater the tendency of the plank to spring up and smash in the aforementioned face.

Be certain, also, that all wedges *advance* evenly. If one proceeds or lags behind the others by too much, the plank will crack and literally explode. Teak shatters in the most frightening fashion, taking its toll of skin and blood as it does. Try to keep the leading edge of the plank somewhat off the fiberglass. If the plank is squeezed down completely tight, you will be scraping off all of the preciously spread polysulphide; so, keep hammering gently until the plank is butted tight against the covering board.

Once in place, screw it down and screw it down tightly immediately. Drill your countersink holes about halfway through the 3/4″ plank. If you drill any less, you will not have a deep enough hole for your plug; as mentioned before, if the plug is less than 1/4″, it is guaranteed to crack and pop out very shortly.

If, by some chance, you hear a nasty cracking sound before you wedge the plank into place, don't start bashing in the nearest portlight in anguish. As a matter of fact don't even move. Take a bit of resorcinol glue (which you should have sitting around ready mixed) and pour it generously into the obviously cracked wood. Now hammer the wedges home and, as if nothing has happened, screw the plank into place. You may have to disturb the straight line of the plugs and put a couple of screws out of sequence to make sure the crack won't open up. Wipe off the excess resorcinol glue and try to forget about it. You may now get off the plank.

Move your blocks back about two inches, screw them down, and start the whole process over again. Some people advocate not cutting the planks to length until they are laid in their final place. This idea is probably very good, for then you won't have to worry about ending the planks in exactly the right location. While you are attempting to bend them, it's almost an impossibility anyway.

On the other hand, it's simple to set in a board, set it and screw it, then just whack the end off with a good sharp chisel. Use only the sharpest chisel or you will split the teak. Don't try to hack the whole end off in one oafish blow. Penetrate no more than 1/8″ per blow; then chisel out the groove and do the next vertical penetration. Don't use this chisel to go right to the fiberglass. Nothing can ruin a good chisel quicker than a few blows at a steel-hard deck. Have a duller chisel at hand to cut through the last 1/16″.

Other Things

There are a few problem items with teak decks, like nibbing, which I prefer to making wedges, where the sheer line no longer

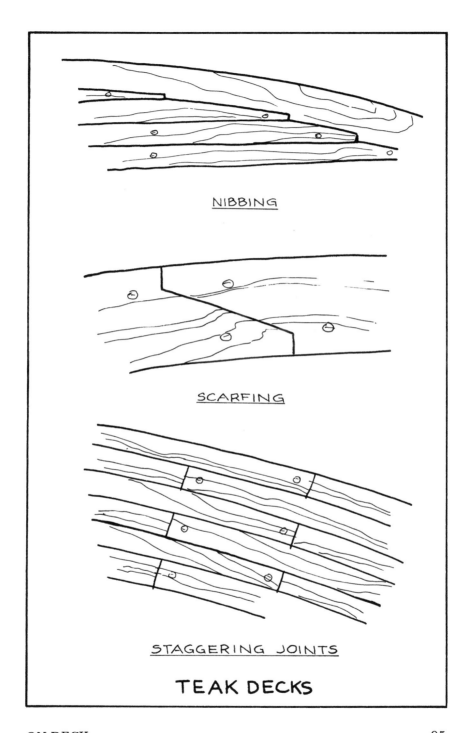

NIBBING

SCARFING

STAGGERING JOINTS

TEAK DECKS

parallels the cabin sides. Nibs can be angled and lengthened to taste. Other problems like corners, deck fills, cockpit trim, etc. are shown in the photographs.

Once you have finished laying the deck, the fun is just beginning. Your next job is to plug the 1,000 screw holes. Make sure you align grains of the plugs and tap them in good and deep. It is preferable to use a clear epoxy glue on the plugs instead of resorcinol, for resorcinol is a very dark red colour which leaves a very dark brown ring around the plug, no matter how great your care.

Now go back, and with a chisel whack off the tops of the plugs. Don't bother to get them flush at this time. Just get rid of the bulk, so that if someone kicks one, it won't break off and require replacement.

Caulking

Get the most powerful vacuum cleaner you can find and clean all the scrap and dust from the caulking grooves. Make sure you unlodge every piece of junk you find.

Now go shopping and take a lot of money. For a 30' boat, you will need about three gallons of "Detco" two-part polysulphide. About 1/2 pint of hardener comes with each 3/4 gallon kit, and each 3/4 gallon kit costs about $65. You will also need to buy about 40 empty caulking cartridges, a quart of Detco teak primer, a gallon of acetone, and a lot of paper towels.

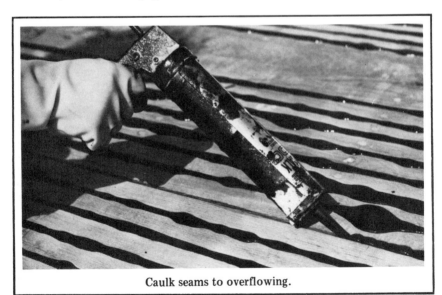

Caulk seams to overflowing.

The one item you may have difficulty finding is the empty cartridges. I did, and when I found them I was so happy that the atrocious price of 55¢ each (for an empty cartridge??!!) gave me heart failure for no more than 49 seconds. You will get used to highway robbery like this throughout your boating career. At any rate, secure about 40 of these tubes early and have them ready.

Now, using a small acid brush, primer all the immaculate caulking grooves thoroughly. Don't worry about getting primer on top of the teak deck itself. It will be sanded.

Caulk right away. To be economical time-wise, you will have to mix a gallon of caulking a a time. Mix in the catalyst thoroughly. This is a demanding task, because the polysulphide is as thick as tar. Fortunately, the catalyst is a light brown colour, so its path is easily traceable.

Stir the catalyst in completely, but *slowly*, or you will trap a jillion air bubbles which will stay in the thick caulking compound. They will be transferred and trapped in the caulking grooves only to pop when you are sanding the hardened caulking. Once you sand off the top of the bubble, you will be left with gaping holes which you will have to open, clean out, and fill with more "black death." To this end save a quarter of a gallon of polysulphide and a bit of hardener. You will need almost that much for repair work.

Don't be afraid to let the polysulphide fill the grooves to overflowing. When it hardens, it will shrink and settle. It is a lot easier to cut off the excess than to fill the voids. Once the poly has gone off, trim off the overflow rubber with a sharp chisel. Then get a belt sander and about four 50 grit sanding belts (anything finer will have its pores filled in no time) and grind the caulking right down to the wood. If you find any air holes in the seams, fill them now.

You will find if you curve your decks that the edges of some drastically curved planks will have a tendency to turn slightly upward, necessitating very extensive belt sanding to bring it to an even level. After you have leveled the deck with the 50, use the 80 grit paper to get out the cross-grain gouges, and finish off with 100. Then oil or let bleach or whatever you like.

You can see from the foregoing that laying a teak deck is not something you can leave for a dull Sunday afternoon. It does take time (as mentioned, approximately 160 hours) and quite a bit of money to do a satisfactory, lasting job. If you can afford it, by all means don't hesitate, for there are very few sights to a sailor quite as heartwarming and satisfying as the sight of a freshly scrubbed, bright teak deck. . . . Anyway, it's probably the best non-skid you can find.

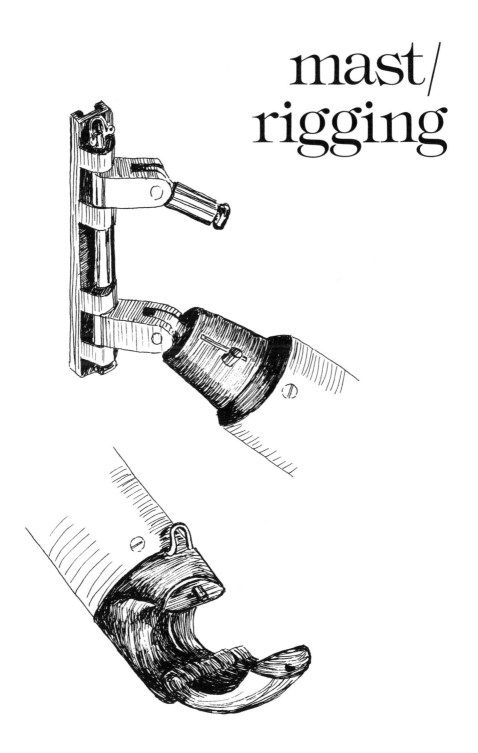

mast/
rigging

MAST STEPS

Personally, I think mast steps are a terrific thing, but only on other people's boats. I find that I have more than a sufficient number of things on my mast, as it is, to snag halyards. The old cast bronze steps one finds on some yachts seem to be the most harmless, offering little chance for a snag, but even less chance for a good footing. Since your feet literally perch on a tiny foothold, your knees automatically clutch the mast with all their might, so that by the time you reach the spreaders, gangrene will have devoured your lower limbs. The new stainless loop steps have the advantage of providing secure footing, but because they are cut from light gauge strapping, they cut into your hands so effectively that you are periodically tempted to let go, and let the corpse fall where it may.

The aluminum rungs are of the same basic design, but being cleverly extruded from tubular material, have the advantage of offering more surface and fewer sharp edges. So take your pick. Whichever you choose, be forewarned that the only thing harder than climbing mast steps, is installing them, unless you pull the mast and set up your little side-show on the dock. Dangling forlorn from the bosun's chair, trying desperately to drill true holes, then tap truer threads for machine screws, is not for the faint of heart. But if you must do it, drill and tap with great accuracy and care. Drill just barely through the mast wall, otherwise, you might be stripping the casing off wires within. Tap true, and use the shortest screws possible. If you can find 1/4″ machine screws of about 3/8″ length, terrific, for then you won't have about a hundred long bolt stems inside your mast for your wires to chafe against. In a wood mast, you will, of course, be using bronze or stainless steel wood screws. In either mast, the steps and screws must be thoroughly bedded in polysulfide or corrosion/rot will be a guaranteed result.

When measuring for steps, be as ascetic as possible; for the fewer holes, the less work; the fewer holes, the less weakening; and the fewer steps, the fewer snagged halyards. If you have average legs, one step every 14″ (alternate sides of the mast) will be ample.

Before you drill the first hole, have a drink and think it over, then take the steps back to the chandlery, buy a good bosun's chair with the refund, and spend the rest on the ladies. *Sic transit gloria mundi.*

THE FINELY FITTED YACHT

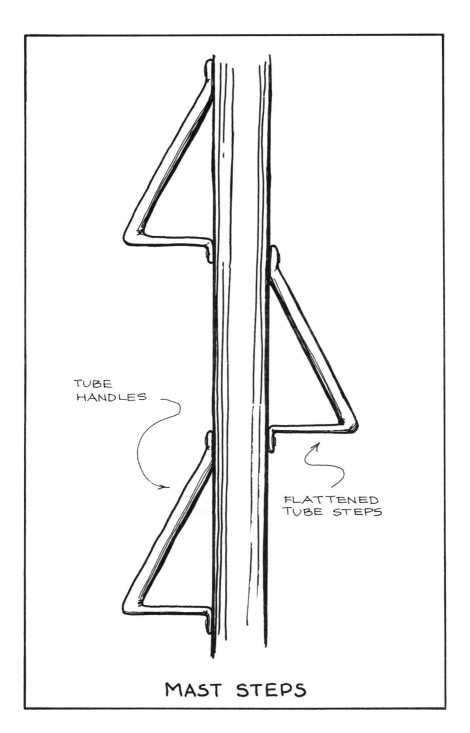

TUBE
HANDLES

FLATTENED
TUBE STEPS

MAST STEPS

MAST AND RIGGING   101

THE PROPER MAST STEPS

Now that you've rested up after a night with the ladies, you are emotionally cleansed to the degree where you can undertake some serious mast step construction. Up to the spreaders, ratlines of rope should be installed, as described in that section. From the spreaders up, your new project begins.

To be succinct, it's a long and narrow rope ladder with 13/16″ teak rungs. A lovely advantage of this ladder is that it stows in a conservative amount of space, and since it is stowed, it's out of the way of halyards and wind. The flat steps make for relatively good footing, and the rope sides make for excellent hand holds. The ladder will be hoisted by a halyard to the masthead, and it will be held taut by having the lower end tied to the halyard's other end and it, in turn, made fast to a mast base cleat. As can be seen in the illustration, the rungs are cut to hug the mast and eliminate that leaf-on-the-vine feeling. The rungs should be patterned to fit the *foreward* part of the mast (unless you have cutter rig with an obtrusive forestay), for the most likely mast emergency requiring the ladder will involve the mainsail with a jammed or broken track, which will obstruct the sail and keep it from coming down. In such a case, a ladder fitted for the aft face of the mast would be of precious little value. If you do have a cutter rig, and have to run the ladder aft anyway, it would behoove you to attach a slide on every second step, and run the slides in the track for added security.

The line used for the sides should be 5/16″ three strand. It will be run on the aft, as well as the foreward, part of each side of each run for maximum stability. If only a single line were to be used on each side, the steps would pivot and make a nerve-wracking operation into an almost unbearable one.

The rungs should be cut 6″ deep and 6″ wide, with the wood grain running athwartships. I once had an acquaintance who tried to do otherwise, only to find his cedar rung split in half as soon as weight was applied. Radius all corners well, especially the pointed ones nearest the mast, to reduce any chance of splintering. A note on materials. Teak is the ideal wood to use, but since the ladder will be exposed to weather only infrequently, any good short-grained wood like ash, oak, or mahogany can be used. Do try to stay away from soft woods, like fir and cedar, for although they are lighter and less expensive, they tend to split as they dry with the years, and may cause a descent from the mast at a rather breathtaking speed.

Once the rungs are cut, mark your holes at least 3/4″ in from any edges, and drill a 1/8″ pilot. To prevent breaking out and

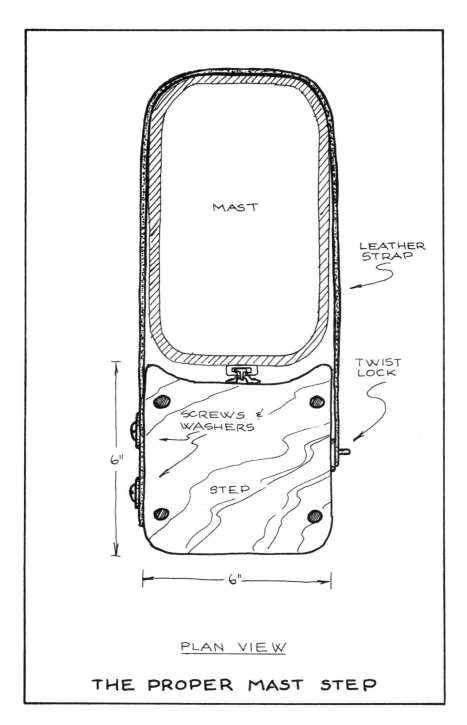

THE PROPER MAST STEP

splintering on the other side, drill with caution, especially when your drill bit is about to come through. To further prevent said splintering, drill your 5/16″ hole from each side, meeting in the middle, then ream thoroughly to make sure no ridges are left within to cause chafe on the lines. Round the edges of the holes with sandpaper. Next, ascertain the total length of your ladder, and cut a single piece of line about four times that length plus a few feet for mistakes. Weave your line through a hole of the lowest run, then through a matching hole in the rung above, and so on. Above the top rung, leave a loop of two-foot length, and begin a descent of the rungs on the opposite side. If done properly, you will have four lines parallel, with crossovers under the bottom rung and in the two loops over the top rung. Only two knots will be utilized, thereby cutting the possibility of failure to a minimum. Both will be under the first rung, so if the knot fails, you will fall only half the height of the mast. Terrific consolation, yes?

Next, bring the two lines on one side (port or starboard) together, as close above and below each rung as possible, and secure them to each other with round seizings. See diagram. Do these seizings as if your life depended on them. Seize the tips of the two loops together above the last rung as well. In the bottom rung, through-bolt a swivel ring, with the ring beneath and countersunk nut on top. The downhaul end of the halyard will be attached to this.

Next, cut three lengths of 3/4″ wide leather strapping, the length of which should be determined by measuring from the centre of a side of a rung, then around the mast, back to the centre of the other side. Fix one end of the strap to one side of the rung with two screws and finishing washers. On the other end, affix a metal loop for a twist lock. Fix the twist lock itself to the centre of the side of the rung, determining the exact position by holding the rung in place on the mast. Repeat this procedure with the centre and topmost rungs as well. The straps will be activated to hold the ladder firmly against the mast. Oh yes, don't forget to unsnap these on the way down.

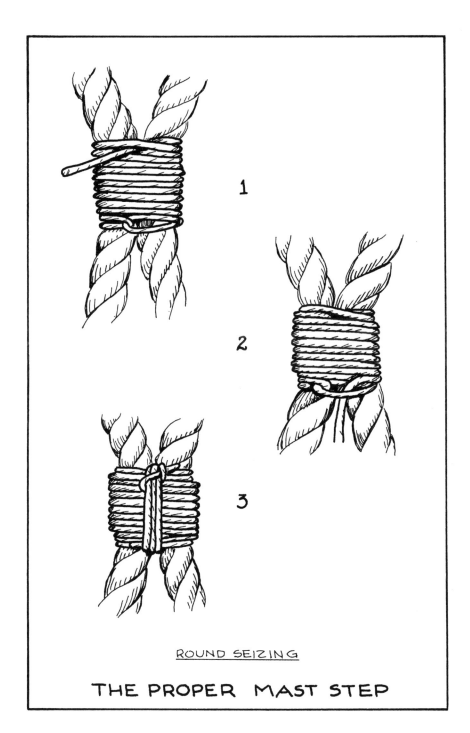

ROUND SEIZING

THE PROPER MAST STEP

RATLINES

I dislike mast steps for the reasons mentioned in that section, but ratlines have always appealed to me, first for their appearance and second for their usefulness. It is of course true that they will carry you only to the spreaders, but that to me seems a very nice spot to go, to look out for reefs, logs or rocks, or just to sit and relax and hug your favourite mast.

Wood Ratlines

These can be fabricated in much the same way as the rails for the in-shroud belaying pins, but of course the stock used can be scaled down to 13/16″ laid on edge. One and one-half inch width will be plenty. A great problem with wood ratlines is that they protrude past the shrouds and chafe the mainsail on a run. Since they are also more difficult to make than rope ratlines, I see little reason for their use except that, because of their rigidity, they do add that feeling of security lacking in the limp ropes.

Rope Ratlines

Susan and Eric Hiscock have used theirs on *Wanderer IV* for some years, and feel that they have served very well with minimal maintenance.

The ratlines can be spaced anywhere from 12″ to 18″ apart depending on the length of your legs and your skill with seizing and splicing. If you're not very handy, make them as few and far between as possible. Three-strand rope will have to be used for the rungs so neat eyes can be spliced into their ends. Hervey Garret Smith advocates splicing the eyes so they barely meet the shrouds but some people prefer to make the rung somewhat longer to create a built-in sage in the rope to act as a safe "crotch" for the feet. Whichever you decide, splice all your eyes neatly, then using racking seizings, fix them to the shrouds.

When I discovered a black tarrish compound peeking out between the seizings, I asked Eric Hiscock if that was a special compound he used to prevent the rungs from slipping down. He said, "Quite." And his eyes sparkled mischievously. "Friction tape."

SPREADER TIP GUARDS

Many people contend that because they don't own large head sails which sheet flat against spreader ends, they have no need for tip guards. Quite false. Sooner or later the main sail will make its way out there on a sloppy day with the boom well out, and it only has to happen once in a rolling sea and rip; a lovely new main sail goes back to the sailmakers. Many fine commercial tip guards are on the market, ranging from the old-fashioned "T" shaped wire hugger to the new above-the-spreader wheel. The former has many varieties, most of them having an identical flaw, that of pressing too tightly around a spreader creating a non-venting space where water settles and rots wood or corrodes aluminum. The wheel, on the other hand, sits above the spreader on a spacer, and although it looks rather unsightly, it does avoid the above-mentioned problem. But a pair costs about $15, which seems silly, because if you want something unsightly up there, you can use old tennis balls that are usually free. A more aesthetic, more economical solution exists. Small bits of sheepskin can be quickly cut and wrapped around the shroud above and below the spreaders. A scrap piece bought for about $3 will last for years on spreaders and other chafing areas. The one terrible drawback of sheepskin is that it creates the same rot and corrosion encouraging condition as the old rubber case, so care must be taken that they are kept away from the spreader itself, at all times. If they get soggy and filthy, they can be removed and replaced, using care to allow the spreader to vent.

In tropical areas with much rain, the greatest invention is still the wheel.

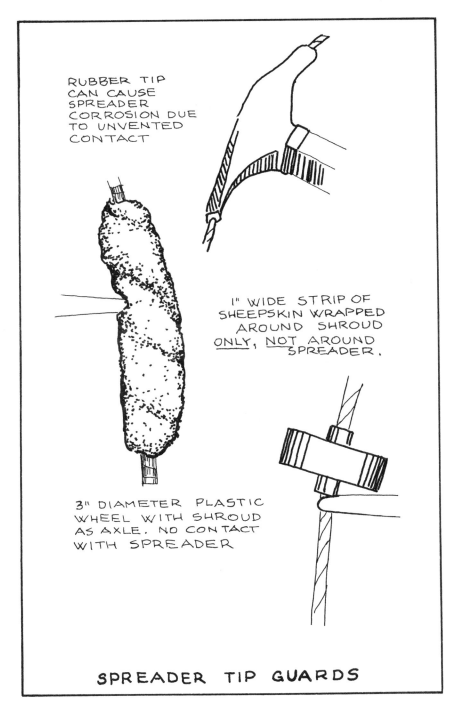

RUBBER TIP
CAN CAUSE
SPREADER
CORROSION DUE
TO UNVENTED
CONTACT

1" WIDE STRIP OF
SHEEPSKIN WRAPPED
AROUND SHROUD
ONLY, NOT AROUND
SPREADER.

3" DIAMETER PLASTIC
WHEEL WITH SHROUD
AS AXLE. NO CONTACT
WITH SPREADER

SPREADER TIP GUARDS

REACHING POLE

Far too often, far too many people end up using their engines in light breezes or rolling seas for lack of a reaching pole. The excuse given by most is the prohibitive cost of these beasts, and that is, of course, true, but only in a myopic sort of way. Now that diesel is edging its way to a dollar a gallon, a good pole would pay for itself in a couple of years, and just think of the pleasure you'll have had, the eardrums you'll have saved, and the vibrations you'll have avoided.

I shall try to avoid a lengthy discussion on end fittings, suffice it to say that in this case, the more expensive the better. Of inboard fittings, the best is a socket end which locks onto a mast toggle which, in turn, is attached to a mast car; the worst is Gertrude clutching the boat hook under her arm. A socket/car arrangement is about $150, whereas the hospital bill for Gertrude can be limitless. The socket pin is in all ways superior to the piston-lock, because the former can effortlessly swivel 360°, while the latter can bind and snap. Outboard ends range from $30 piston ends to the spring-jaw type racing end at $160. We bought the latter. I must have been out of my mind.

It is basically difficult to save money on the fittings, but about $60 can be saved on the extrusion for the pole. All kinds of raves are made about the quality of extrusions to justify the price of $100 for a 15′ pole of 3½″ diameter, when a similar piece of tubing can be bought from any major irrigation firm for about $1.50 a foot. The things to watch for are: even wall thickness and absolutely no dents or dimples. The following tube-diameter-to-tube-wall ratios should also be insisted upon: 1″ to 2″ tube − .065″ wall; 2½″ to 3″ − .085″ wall; 3½″ and up − .125″ wall. A couple of thousandths either way will change nothing. The tube must, of course, fit snugly onto the fitting so it is best to take the fittings with you when you buy the tube. Assembly is done with four 1/4″ machine screws at either end. The holes will have to be tapped. Coat the end fittings with polysulfide or silicone to prevent water from settling in and causing rapid corrosion. If you have an internal trip line, a Harken wire block fitting will be needed about 18″ from the inboard end of the pole. Now, wrap and tape your end fittings and hustle the pole down to an auto body shop and have it primered and painted your favourite epoxy colour. Then just settle back and watch that genny pull and listen to the silence.

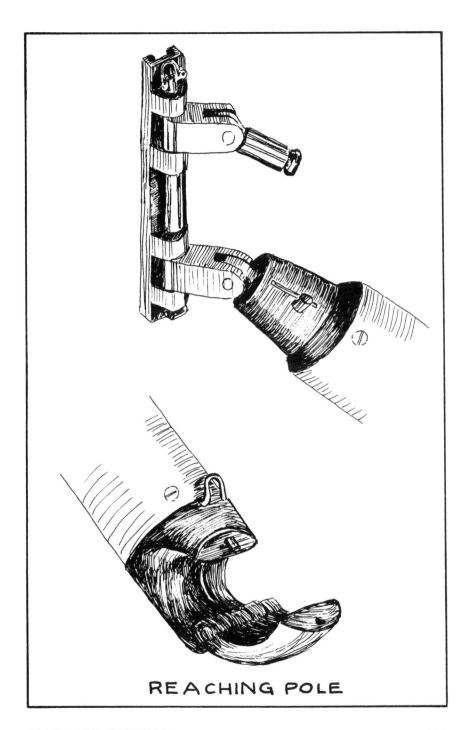

REACHING POLE

PIN RACK FOR MAST BASE

Apart from the fact that they remind you instantly of Captain Blood and pirates and parrots, and make you feel like you could be a kid again forever, I can't see a single good reason for having mast base pin racks. True, they are out of the way of sheets, unlike their shroud-mounted counterpart, but it is also true that, used in conjunction with a mast of any height, which according to somebody's law means halyards of at least twice the length, tensioning of the halyards will be almost impossible, so they will forever bang the mast.

Stock used should be 1″ for the rails and 1½″ for the uprights and pins. A 3″ width for the rail is adequate. When measuring for length (which, of course, depends on the dimensions of your mast), allow at least 2″ between the inboard edge of the rail and the mast. That, along with the extra clearance you'll gain from the narrower pins, will give you sufficient room for your knuckles to work around the lines. The rail ends will have to be lapped. Since most force on the rail will be upward, have the pieces aligned fore and aft, shorter on top than the ones aligned athwartships. This way you will not be pulling apart on the laminates, but rather pulling them together. If you can't quite follow the reasoning, don't worry about it, just do it. Use resorcinol glue and clamp them overnight. If you wish to fabricate fancy uprights, do it on a lathe, otherwise, just rip your 1½″ pieces to 1½″ squares (8″ in length will be plenty) and bullnose all edges with a 3/8″ bullnose. When your rails are set, bullnose them also, inside and out.

For size and kind of pins, see "Pin Rails in Shrouds." The one difference here is that the pins need not be fixed to the rails, and cast bronze pins can be freely used, since the rails are well inboard, considerably lessening the chances of a pin-overboard situation.

To affix the rack to the deck, you will have to drill an extremely straight 3/8″ hole down the center of each leg, at the allocated spot of each corner, as well as the deck. Use caulking on all joints and assemble with a length of 3/8″ all-thread and sizable washers and cap nuts, both above and belowdecks.

If you want to protect the edges, line them with a strip of brass as in photo.

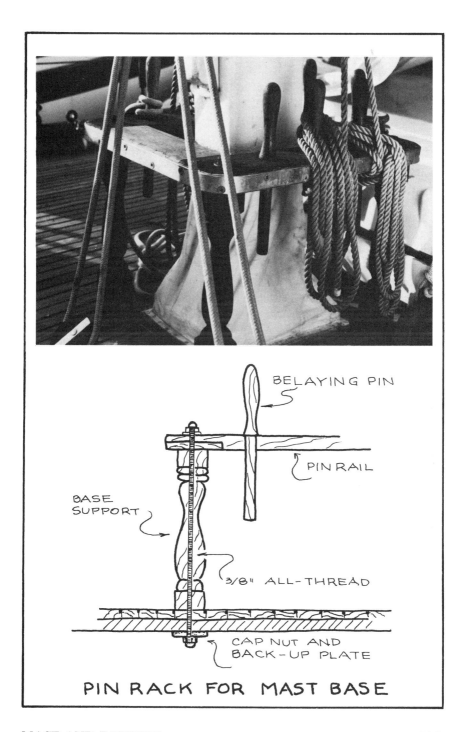

BELAYING PIN

PIN RAIL

BASE
SUPPORT

3/8" ALL-THREAD

CAP NUT AND
BACK-UP PLATE

PIN RACK FOR MAST BASE

MAST PULPITS

I am told that this is an essential piece of cruising equipment, without which one may fall overboard or worse. I have not been able to ascertain precisely what the "worse" could be, but it sounds comparable to a steady diet of gut-bomb burgers, so it must be avoided at all costs.

The one obviously positive feature of the contraption is that it makes for a perfect base for pinrails away from the standing rigging and pleasantly close to the mast where the most frequent need for them arises. It's a pretty looking piece of engineering, but one which will have to be fabricated almost entirely by a machine shop. The height should be designed to personal measurements, more specifically, the top should brace you half way up the back of the thighs for good balance and mobility, and still permit you to lean well back on a heel and use your weight to good advantage. The spread between the bases need be no more than 20″. One and one-half inch pipe should be utilized and bent from a single piece. A crossbar welded to two uprights would have two horrendously sharp corners resulting in charley horses the size of an average Clydesdale. Have 3″ diameter base plates with four 1/4″ holes in them welded onto the legs. Get a second set of these plates with matched mounting holes to use as backup plates belowdecks. Individual washers will not provide the strength of a single plate. About two-thirds from the bottom of the pulpit, have two 2″ X 2″ flanges welded. Upon these, you can mount the pinrails. For construction of these, please consult "Belaying Pin Rack." Bypassing the pinrails would be quite acceptable here, for the horizontal piece of the pipe could be used to secure the halyards, although tying and untying them would require a bit more time than using belaying pins.

Mounting the pulpit about 20″ outboard of the mast would seem a good compromise, allowing unhindered mobility, but still providing reassuring support. This last measurement is flexible with personal preference and should be decided upon only after a friend holds the boat hook behind your thighs and you go through your basic mast related eccentricities on different angles of heel.

THE FINELY FITTED YACHT

MAST PULPITS

RADAR REFLECTOR

It's odd that so many people are willing to part with ten precious dollars for three hunks of aluminum with slits.

The cost for a piece of salvaged light gauge 12″ × 36″ aluminum should not run more than about 90¢. Nor is the project labor intensive. The two vertical pieces are identical, thus can be shaped at the same time by laying one on top the other. Use a couple of C-clamps or a vise to hold them together while fabricating.

You will find that you will need two side-by-side cuts to make the slits, but don't panic, remember aluminum is soft and the hacksaw blade in a saber saw will go through it as if it were butter. To remove the slit piece, simply bend it back and forth a few times; it will break off quite willingly. If you're fussy, clean up the crotch with a fine file.

Cutting the horizontal piece requires a bit more finesse, in that you'll have to drill a series of 1/8″ holes as close to each other as possible, then join them together by gently maneuvering the drill bit back and forth until it erodes the thin partitions. Now slip in your hacksaw blade and cut away.

Clean off all rough edges, then drill the four holes in each vertical plate — 1/8″ holes will do nicely. You will just be running light bits of wire through them to hold the pieces together.

The beauty of the thing is its stowability. By pulling out the bits of wire, the pieces can be collapsed and stowed anywhere. When needed, they can be assembled in a minute and run up to the spreaders on a burgee halyard. When doing this, one would do well to tie both top and bottom of the reflector to the halyard to make it as stable as possible. It sure beats yanking your pots and pans aloft in the fog.

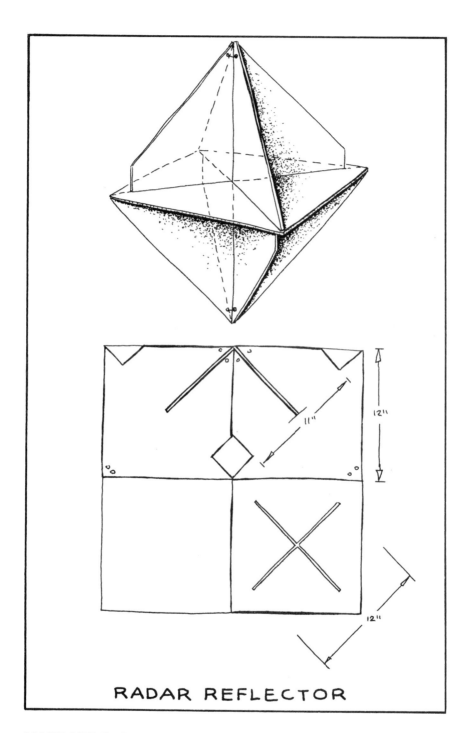

RADAR REFLECTOR

BAGGY WRINKLES

I'm not sure why baggy wrinkles carry as much connotation of romantic voyages as they do, but apart from this quite sufficient reason for their existence, they constitute some of the most functional chafing gear ever conceived. In their most limited use, they make perfect spreader ends where sails would otherwise become victims of stitch chafing and cloth tearing. On a larger scale application, four or five 10" lengths spaced evenly over the upper half of the aft lower shroud will prevent general chafing when the main lies hard against a shroud on a run. It is true, of course, that the use of vangs can largely reduce the pumping action of the boom which comes upon every roll of a running yacht, but *largely* doesn't mean *completely*, and if the baggy wrinkles add only another year or two to the life of a main, I feel they have done their duty. A 400-square-foot main at $3.00 a foot buys a lot of bananas. Some people claim that baggy wrinkles cause too much windage aloft, but then, so does the mast and if you were to discard *it*, you'd have nothing to hold up your shrouds.

The best material to use is old synthetic ropes. Organic ones, like hemp, can be rather stiff and tend to retain moisture for an excessive period of time. The moisture has little bearing on chafe gear used on shrouds, but at the ends of spreaders, it can cause corrosion in aluminum and rot in wood.

Peel the old rope apart into individual strands and cut them into lengths of 3" to 6" depending on how baggy you like your wrinkles. Next, sit up on deck on a fine sunny day and halve a piece of 10' line over a stanchion, tying the two loose ends behind you a few inches apart so your fingers will have room to work between them; then take an individual strand you've just cut and lay it under the two lines. Bring the two ends over and down in between them and slide the strand down within a few inches of the stanchion. Proceed in a similar fashion until you have finished the length you wanted, remembering that on a quarter-inch shroud, three to four feet are required to make up one foot of finished baggy wrinkle. Now, knot the two pieces of line. If you choose, you can trim the ends of the strands to even lengths, or be adventuresome and leave them rough. Now, wrap the baggy wrinkle around the shroud, strand ends out, and tie top and bottom with your leftover line.

They make beautiful silhouettes in the sunset.

THE FINELY FITTED YACHT

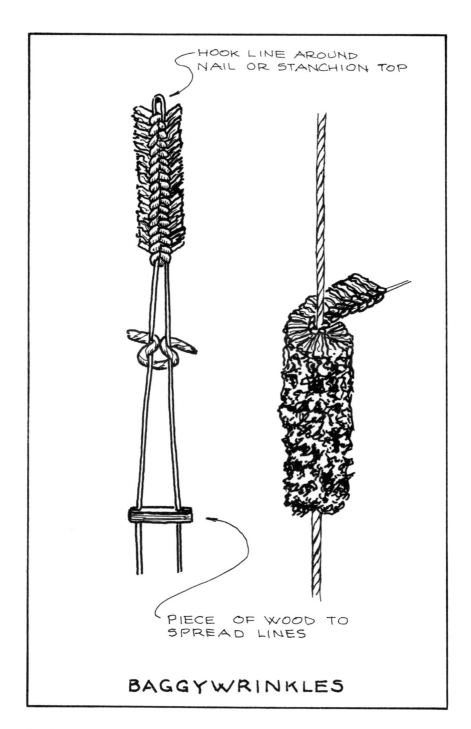

HOOK LINE AROUND
NAIL OR STANCHION TOP

PIECE OF WOOD TO
SPREAD LINES

BAGGYWRINKLES

MAST AND RIGGING   119

VANGS

A skipper sailing his vessel on a run or a reach without the aid of a vang, is not only losing efficiency and chafing his sails unnecessarily, but in an active sea, he's begging for a scalping.

If a sail has slugs in its foot, the only equipment required will be a piece of rope, a place to tie it to, and a rubber snubber. The snubber I feel to be a mandatory part, for without it, unnecessary loading will be put upon the middle of the boom. On a violent roll, booms have been known to break because of poorly assembled and handled vangs, vangs that did not have a rubber snubber to absorb the shock of the crew's mistake. The snubber can be slipped through the slot between the sail and boom (see diagram), then the length of line run through its bronze loops, while the line's outboard end can be made fast to a padeye, eyebolt or stanchion base. *Warm Rain* has her stanchions bolted through the bulwarks with 3/8" carriage bolts so to facilitate a footing for the vang, we simply used a longer bolt and slipped a 1/4" thick stainless steel tang over its end, thus avoiding the need for additional holes in either deck or bulwark. To accelerate engagement and removal of the vang, the lower end of the line can be fitted with a snap shackle. The rubber snubber will usually yield sufficiently under manhandling so that the line will slack, enabling the shackle to be disengaged.

A problem does arise, however, when the crew sits back and enjoys the exhilaration of the run too much to notice the freshening of the wind. Attempts to disengage the vang will become difficult as knots tighten and lines strain. To prepare for such an occasion, *Warm Rain* has been fitted with a fine (and expensive) block system. The lower one is a becketed fiddle block with a cam cleat and built-in snap shackle, the upper is a single sheaved fiddle block with a snap shackle. With ample line and the cam cleat, very rapid adjustments and releases can be executed even by the least muscular of crews. To stow out of the way, the block is snap shackled to the foremost mainsheet boom bail and the line hauled tight.

On vessels with boltropes instead of slugs on the main, a boom bail will have to be fitted. Generally, a good location is six to eight feet aft of the mast. On all but the smallest of craft, a bail with a three-bolt hole pad should be used to lessen the possibility of its being torn out.

THE FINELY FITTED YACHT

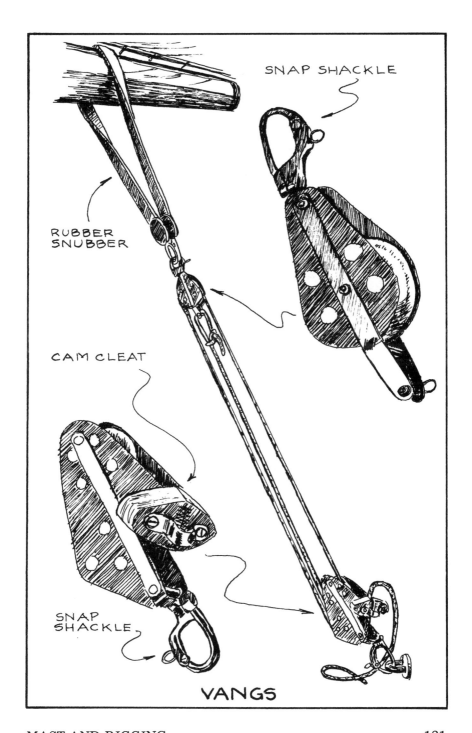

SNAP SHACKLE

RUBBER
SNUBBER

CAM CLEAT

SNAP
SHACKLE

VANGS

MAINSHEET TRAVELLER BRIDGE

The overall trend in modern yachts has been to move the mainsheet traveller off the bridgedeck and onto the cabin top in the region of the main hatch. Although this method lacks the classic simplicity of its bridgedeck cousin, which usually consisted of a piece of aluminum or stainless track simply bolted through the deck, it does have some major points on its side. First, it removes the whole apparatus from the heavy traffic of the companionway mouth where the mainsheet forever tangles around arms and legs. Second, it makes fairleading to a winch quite simple. Indeed on a cutter, one can simply lead the sheet to the leeward staysail winch, although if the approach angle is too steep, jamming can easily occur. Third, because the arc travelled by the boom becomes smaller the closer you get to the mast, and because the traveller on the cabin top is at least 15″ higher thus much closer to the boom, considerably less line will be required to operate the traveller, although one will have to use a bit more muscle. Fourth and last, with a bridgedeck traveller, it's almost impossible to avoid mainsheet chafe on the aft cabin corners when the yacht is generously boomed out on a run. With the cabin top version this problem is averted.

But. You can't just take a piece of track and bolt it simple-mindedly through the cabin top, for quite often hatches and grabrails will be in the way, necessitating construction of a bridge. As you can see from the illustration, the fabrication of the bridge is fairly straightforward, involving only four blocks for support and a laminated span, but the difficulty arises in securing the bridge to the cabin top. More about that later.

First, establish the fore and aft location of the bridge, remembering that any distance less than 7′ from the average mast, will decrease your leverage to where tremendous forces will be acting on both bridge and gear. The most ideal positioning would of course be directly over a deck beam which would help distribute all forces over the entire width of the cabin top.

Second, establish the length of your bridge. In most instances a three to two ratio can be used as rule of thumb, i.e. at a point 7½′ from the mast, a 5′ track would be the maximum needed. Common sense factors like positioning between grabrails etc. should also be taken into consideration. Once the length has been determined, rip teak and mahogany, or teak and ash, or any decent hardwood for that matter into 1/2″ thick by 2½″ wide pieces. Your final product will be 2″ wide when finished, but the spilled glue, and some slippage

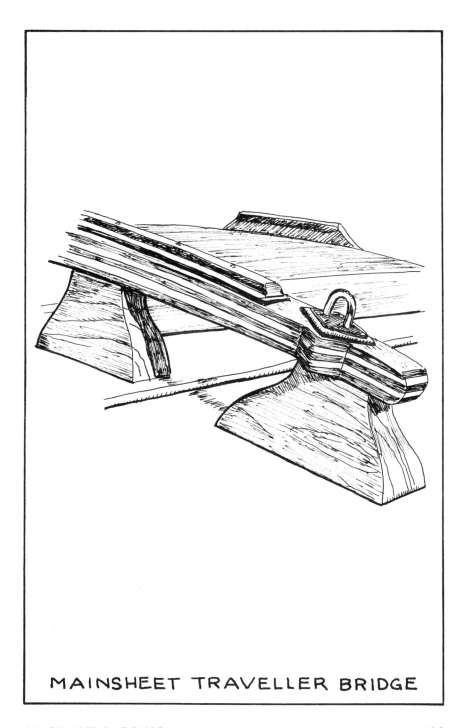

MAINSHEET TRAVELLER BRIDGE

of the laminates during clamping, will require that you trim off 1/4"
on either side.

Next, determine the camber of the cabin top by running a
horizontal string from one proposed end of the bridge to the other
(points "X" on diagram) on the aft edge of the cabin, and measuring
the two points "W" and "Y". Transpose those measurements to a
workbench and cut blocks from scrap material, on top of which the
laminates can be clamped (see illustration) to establish the proper
curve. Use resorcinol glue and as many clamps as necessary to insure
that all laminates make contact at all points. Let set overnight.

Meanwhile, cut at least four blocks to act as supports. Your
blocks can be shaped to your personal taste, but remember that any
variety of a truncated pyramid will provide much more stability than
just a squared block of wood whose fore and aft dimensions simply
equal that of the span itself. Since the blocks will be subject to much
weathering and strain, teak would be the best choice for material.

When the resorcinol has set on the laminates, run them through
the table saw to trim the fore-mentioned 1/4" from each side, sand
the edges lightly, and get the whole rig on deck. From below decks,
drill through the deck beam that's to act as backup to the bridge as
perpendicularily *to the beam* at that point as you can. Remember,
that's right angles to the beam, not to the cabin sole or anything else.
Drill a single 3/8" hole for each block, then have a friend centre the
blocks above each hole and drill again, this time right through the
block, and, lastly, repeat with the span in place. Countersink the span
to let in a 1½" washer and the head of a bolt. Below decks the
aesthetically cleanest thing to do would be to run a 1½" wide brass
strip (an 1/8" thickness is ample) along the length of the deck beam
and tighten the bolts down with bronze cap nuts.

Finally, the track can be installed on the span. Here you can
either use 1¾" #14 F.H. sheet metal screws or you can through-bolt.
The latter is of course the more structurally sound thing to do.

Be sure to use ample bedding compound (Dolfinite is the easiest
to clean up from teak) between the track and span.

A last word. If you use the flat genoa-track-type track, under no
circumstances should you use plastic track ends. If the track car ever
slides over with any power at all, the plastic end can shatter and the
car can fly off the track. I'd like to see anyone sail a 40 footer in a
blow with an ungeared mainsheet in his hand.

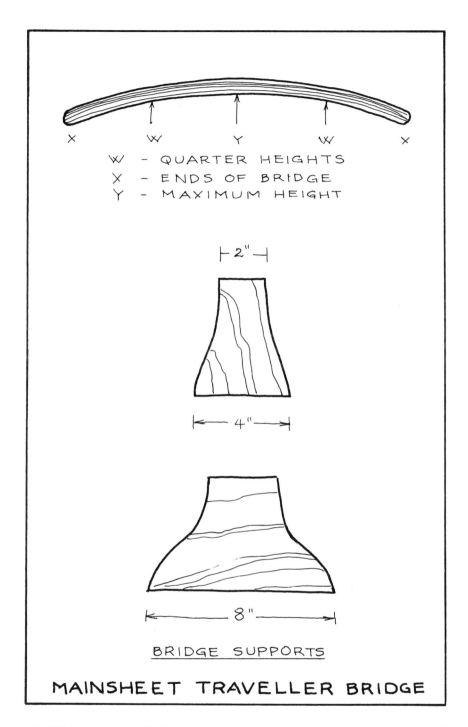

W — QUARTER HEIGHTS
X — ENDS OF BRIDGE
Y — MAXIMUM HEIGHT

BRIDGE SUPPORTS

MAINSHEET TRAVELLER BRIDGE

IN-SHROUD PINRAILS

Aside from adding character to most yachts, pinrails provide marvelous places for stowing halyards. Carefully designed and fabricated, they can be of great value; shoddily assembled and mounted, they will endlessly foul sheets and nerves.

The size of your vessel (distance between lower shrouds) will determine the length of the rail, but simple general guidelines are available. The rail should fit between the shrouds 30″-35″ off the deck, depending on whether you're Mickey Rooney or John Wayne.

Use 1¾″ stock ripped to 3″ in width. This width should not be compromised, for every bit of it will be needed as mounting support. I'll explain later. The rail should overhang the shrouds, on either end, by 1½″. Cut a groove in each end to the exact thickness of your shroud, to a depth of 1½″, and no more. Perform this with two cuts of your bandsaw. To get the proper angle, clamp a piece of wood across the bandsaw table (in front of the blade) with two C-clamps. This piece will act as a fixed guide. That the ungrooved part of the rail be equal to the distance between the shrouds is mandatory, for it is this length of the rail that will keep it from riding upwards when tensioned by halyards.

Next, scribe and cut a curve from the bottom to the top of the rail at the point where the shroud runs through it. The scribed area should be shaped as in the diagram — very fine at the bottom and wider at the top. Near the top, it should incorporate the full 1½″ overhang of the rail. You are now ready for the pins.

For these, either wood or bronze can be used. If you can rustle up an old set of bronze ones, great; if not, a wood or metal shop can turn out a set for you. The number of pins to be used should be carefully contemplated. Pins should be set no less than 5″ apart, otherwise lines will foul and knuckles bruise. A good pinlength, of either material, is 8″-10″. The shank diameter should be 1/2″ for bronze and 3/4″ for wood.

The pins can be made to be either permanently fixed or removable. If removable, the base of the pin's grip should be clearly flared, to prevent the pin from wedging in the hole, inhibiting quick removal and line release, which is the only reason for having removable pins in the first place. If your pins are stationary (glued or side-screwed) the flaring is not important. One word on removable pins: as quick as they are to operate, as handy as they are for cracking nuts and skulls with, they do have a nasty habit of jumping overboard. Remember, bronze does *not* float!

THE FINELY FITTED YACHT

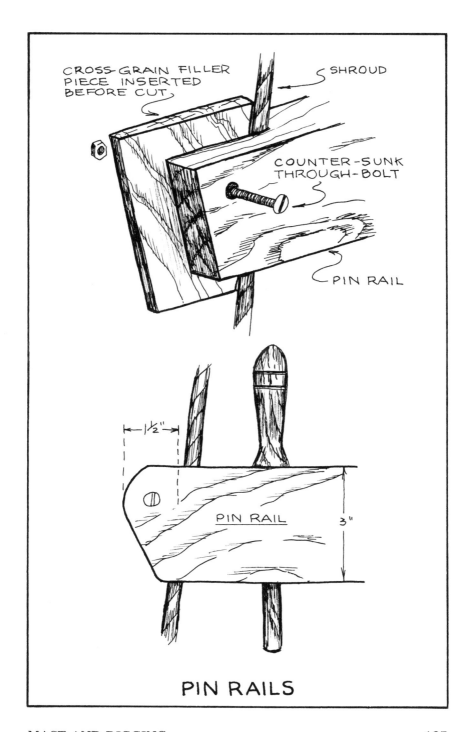

CROSS-GRAIN FILLER
PIECE INSERTED
BEFORE CUT

SHROUD

COUNTER-SUNK
THROUGH-BOLT

PIN RAIL

1½"

3"

PIN RAIL

PIN RAILS

Once you have drilled the holes for your pins, you will be ready to mount the rail. Fit it into place and insert into each slotted overhang a piece of wood (fitting very snugly), filling up the entire slot right to the shroud. This piece should run crossgrain to the rail to help prevent cracking or splitting. It should overhang the rail everywhere. Remove the piece, cover both its sides with resorcinol glue, and slip it back into place. Drill a 1/4" hole through the center of the widest part of the overhang, countersink from both sides to a depth of about 1/4", and through-bolt. When the glue has set, jigsaw off the excess stock. To make sure you don't nick the shrouds, slip a piece of tin between the shroud and excess wood to act as a stop.

You can, of course, follow a safer procedure by trimming *before* gluing, or even shaping, of the rail's end. To do this, rough-fit the rail and the filler, drill the 1/4" hole, remove the rail from the shrouds, and fit the bolt to hold filler piece firmly in place. Now, shape the rail (with filler piece in it) with a jigsaw, on a nice solid surface, such as a work bench. Sand and detail, then reassemble, and glue and bolt into the shrouds.

Whichever way you did it, you're done. The rail will slip neither up, nor down.

THE FINELY FITTED YACHT

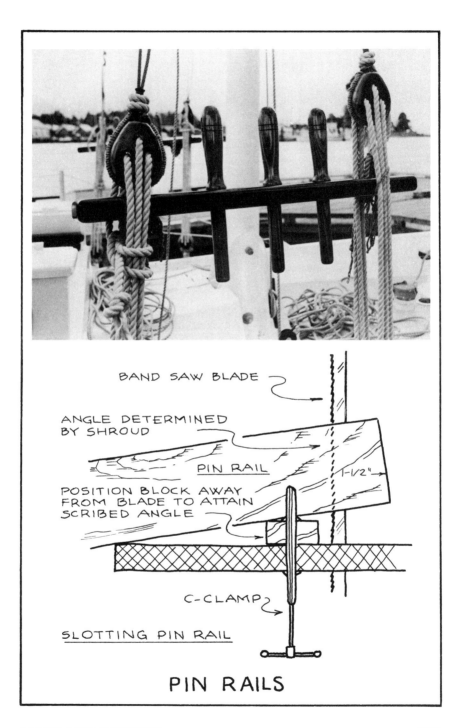

BAND SAW BLADE

ANGLE DETERMINED
BY SHROUD

PIN RAIL

1-1/2"

POSITION BLOCK AWAY
FROM BLADE TO ATTAIN
SCRIBED ANGLE

C-CLAMP

SLOTTING PIN RAIL

PIN RAILS

safety

BOATHOOKS

Much too frequently I have seen injuries to both yacht and limb for lack of a simple, but sturdy, boathook. In today's harbours, where the numbers of both vessels and half-wits is on an irreversible upsurge, a proper boathook should be considered a tool of basic self defense. The collapsible aluminum backscratchers have only one positive point in that they are light, so that when you're standing with smashed caprail and crumpled little boathook, you can take it and heave it a long long way.

Even sadder than crushed caprails are crushed hands and feet that have been thrust between yacht and piling, or yacht and yacht in last minute, helpless desperation. None of the above would have occurred had a good boathook been well used.

The Pole

The best poles are of spruce. Granted they are heavier than aluminum, but they do have two major advantages in that: a) when wet they are less slippery, and b) if dropped overboard they will not fill with water and sink as their aluminum counterparts sometimes do.

The traditional diameter of 1¼" seems to be one easily handled by most hands. The length is another problem. We have on *Warm Rain* one that's just over 10' long, and I must say I have needed every inch of it plus some on numerous occasions, ranging from peeling kelp from the self steering vane, to taking accurate soundings in very shoal bays. Many will argue that a pole of such length and weight is unwieldly and impractical, but to those I say that most poles can be easily handled by anyone after a few practice runs. Everyone has man-overboard drills and abandon-ship drills, the need for which occurs much less frequently than maneuvering in close quarters, so why not have "half-wit abeam" drills as well.

The Tip

The ideal boathook tip, I feel, is one with a hook and a spike. The spike will get firm footing on wet rocks or slippery pilings, while the hook of course will grab mooring lines and fallen caps. The fear that a spike will gouge another boat's hull or brightwork can be eliminated if proper use of a pole is learned. Both the rigging and lifelines of most boats are very strong points and one can, with a bit of finesse, snare either in the crotch of the pole between the hook and the spike. Lifelines are especially handy, for the pole can be slipped along them as the vessel progresses.

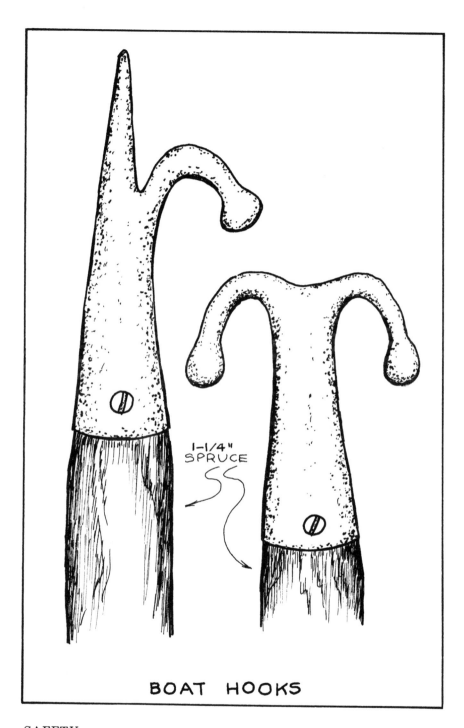

1-1/4"
SPRUCE

BOAT HOOKS

NAVIGATION LIGHT BOXES

A little bit of character doesn't hurt any yacht, and if it can be derived from a functional piece of equipment, so much the better. Wood navigation-light boxes can be made very easily, and, if well situated so they do not interfere with any running rigging, they can be a feast to the eyes for years to come. They have traditionally served as home to kerosene lamps, one green, one red, but they look just as good if any of a variety of handsome electrical fixtures are installed upon them. Traditionally, they were installed in the shrouds, but I feel that this is a somewhat treacherous location for they're in the way of genoa sheets. At any rate, a teak navigation-light box is the perfect thing to carry the yacht's name smartly engraved. Not only does this look handsome, but the light emanating from the lamps may just be enough to illuminate the yacht's name. Of what conceivable advantage that could be I'm hard pressed to imagine, but it sounds good.

Four-inch wide 13/16" teak stock is ample here. The sides and the ends can be cut to a 4" radius to reduce bulk and the look of severity. The bottom piece can be cut away drastically (see diagram) retaining bulk only aft, and that only to house the lamp. Butt the three pieces together and glue, screw and plug. If you had thoughts of carving the boat's name into the box, you would be wise to do so before assembly just to give your hands a bit more room to work.

I have seen very smart installations on bow pulpits (where wires can be run relatively inobtrusively along the pulpit frame) but the most imaginative implementation I've seen, was the incorporation of the light box into the base of a dorade vent (see diagram). This method obviates the need for the one long side, requiring only a narrow base and a back. The most convenient thing with this method is that the wires can be run out through the dorade box so they'll remain at all times hidden from sight and weather.

THE FINELY FITTED YACHT

IN SHROUDS

WITH DORADE BOX

NAVIGATION LIGHT BOXES

BOW NETS

On most cruising boats, especially ones with bowsprits, bow nets are an almost indispensible item. They are a great help in keeping lowered headsails and headsail handlers out of the water. On *Warm Rain,* they also serve to hold in dinghy oars and boat hooks.

Some beautiful handcrafted nets have appeared over the years (*Warm Rain's* was fabricated by dear Candace in about three days), but the most utile, least expensive, and least time consuming nets are those cast away by fishboats. The very fine herring nets are, of course, of little or no use, but the old woven hemp and the newer acrylic nets with substantial strands, make perfect boat netting.

The cleanest method of installation utilizes a single line reeved, or really stitched, over the bow pulpit for the top, while a similar line can be reeved through small padeyes attached every 8" or so to the sides of the bowsprit platform. This single line method enables one to remove the net with ease for washing, varnishing, etc.

Acrylic nets should be cut with a hot-knife to seal the strands and prevent them from unravelling.

Normally bow nets terminate at the first set of stanchions, but I've seen numerous cruisers with small children or dogs (sigh) run netting completely around their boats. If this procedure is to be followed, one must cut lead holes in the netting for genoa sheets. To avoid the tearing or chafing of the net, a frame of dacron tape should be sewn around the holes.

I have found bow nets most useful when used in combination with shock cords to hold down folded sails. The shock cord can be hooked into any loop of the net, hastening all foredeck activities by eliminating the need to search out and snare miniature padeyes hidden somewhere beneath 500 square feet of genoa.

Nets not only help to keep sails and people aboard, but they make dandy stowage places for oars and boathooks.

RUDDER STEP

This is beneficial only to vessels with aft hung rudders, but for them it is of such great value that it can be called *vital*. On a mundane level, it serves very well in replacing the boarding ladder which is, at the best of times, awkward to stow. It will not have the charm and comfort of a craftily made teak ladder, but it doesn't take ten hours to make either. The vital aspect comes in life saving. It's all fine and well to have magnificent life rings and man overboard poles and strobe lights, but getting the man back on board should be given some thought as well. Almost anyone can help himself to some degree given at least a footing of sorts, and it is exactly this footing that the rudder steps provide.

In its simplest form, it can be made from a teak block cut to a modified wedge shape, with the fore and aft parts beveled to reduce drag, and the outboard face cut to a wedge, to halve the possibility of it being torn off in case a stern plunges in heavy seas. Two through-bolts per step should be used for mounting. It is mandatory that the rudder be pre-drilled, cleaned, and the holes and the step sopped in polysulfide, otherwise headaches will forever be caused by leakage. Because salt water will tend to dry out the blocks, they should be well oiled at least twice a year.

As a substitute, the old bronze mast steps can be used, one on each side. When selecting them, care must be taken to choose the one that has the most holes, to reduce resistance as much as possible. Where you can find these nowadays is beyond me.

Whichever steps are utilized, one should be installed just above the boot stripe and the other about 14″ higher.

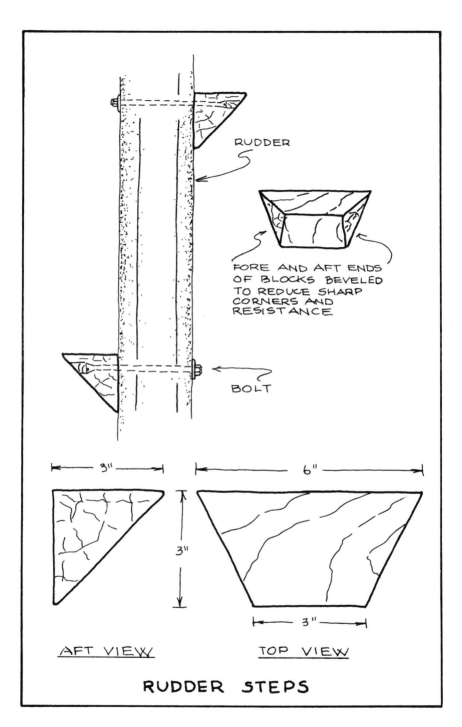

RUDDER

FORE AND AFT ENDS
OF BLOCKS BEVELED
TO REDUCE SHARP
CORNERS AND
RESISTANCE

BOLT

3"

3"

3"

6"

3"

AFT VIEW

TOP VIEW

RUDDER STEPS

LIFE RAFT STOWAGE

A life raft should be totally accessible and quickly releasable. Its ideal location has always been a matter of debate, some advocating as a matter of primary importance, proximity to the cockpit, others, proximity to the stern, to keep it on deck in storms. Still others advocate keeping all areas around and above the raft completely clear to prevent the possibility of its wedging or entrapment when half inflated.

Wherever you do put it, think it out well, then proceed to secure it with the help of the following chocks:

From 13/16″ stock, cut four triangles with 3″ legs. Round all three corners to prevent splitting. Using one of these as patterns cut four "L's". The radius of the "L's" crotch should be determined by the corners of your life raft cannister. With resorcinol glue and 1″ #10 P.H.S.M. screws (drilled and inserted from the triangle into the "L" to obviate the need for plugging), assemble the two pieces as shown. Bullnose all upper edges. The triangles will serve to elevate the cannister off the deck, preventing accumulation of moisture and dirt beneath it.

Now, install the chocks with two screws each into the cabin top, not forgetting to use polysulfide generously for bedding. Plug the screwholes using resorcinol glue on your plugs.

Since the cannister will have about equal forces on it athwartships as fore and aft, a cross system of securing would be most advisable. Many cannisters come with hold-down gear. If yours doesn't, fabricate your own. This requires four 2½″ open padeyes, one on each side of the cannister. Mark the locations for the padeyes, and drill the screw holes and install the padeyes dry. Now, acquire good quality 2″ dacron strapping, and cut four pieces for straps. To determine the length, measure from the inside of the padeye to within 2″ of the center of the cannister. Add on twice four inches for the fold-under loops at each end. Now, for optimum strength, sew the folds in the pattern shown, leaving 1″ loops at either end. Slip a padeye through each loop, and screw the pads firmly onto the deck. You will notice a 4″ square space formed by the apparently short straps in the center of the cannister, and so it should be, for now you can run a 5/16″ lanyard through the loops to join them. Just pull the lanyard tight and make it fast with a perfect bowline. This will provide an instant, one-knot release.

Just pray that you'll never have to untie it.

THE FINELY FITTED YACHT

Chocks can be large and bulky, as above, or just corners, as below.

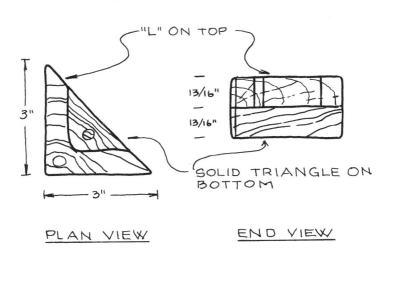

"L" ON TOP

3"

3"

13/16"

13/16"

SOLID TRIANGLE ON BOTTOM

PLAN VIEW   END VIEW

LIFE RAFT STOWAGE

MAN OVERBOARD POLE

The marine industry has a nasty habit of occasionally over-pricing items, and the man overboard pole seems to be a jewel in their high cost crown of lifesaving devices. It retailed, at time of writing, for about $90, which is somewhat prohibitive for a glorified fishing pole which can be made for a total cost of $10 and two hours work.

For the basic pole, use either a fine 10' bamboo pole or a hefty but cheap 1/2" ID CPVC pipe. CPVC is a hard, yet flexible, product used for indoor plumbing. It costs less than copper pipe and is available in lengths of 10' which is what's needed here, and comes in orange, beige and blue. Next, secure a block of rigid urethane foam about 4" X 4" X 12". Round the edges and corners neatly with a file to make them less fragile. For the tapered bamboo pole, measure the diameter of the pole two feet from the wide end and drill a vertical hole through the centre of the foam, having a diameter of 1/16" less than your newly acquired measurement. Slide the foam down from the thin end til it fits snugly. Next, using light fiberglass mat, bond over the whole foam and over a few inches of the pole directly above and below it. Be sure there are no leaks. Trim the ends of the wet mat on the pole with a razor blade before the resin sets. Paint it a bright non-gloss color. (Non-gloss will hide the flaws in the fiberglassing.)

Alternate flotation can be gotten from two float beads of cork or wood, the type that fishermen use on their nets. They may have to be reamed with a round file or drill to fit. Use 1/4" stainless steel bolts drilled through each float and the pole as well to hold the rig together.

Now for the counterweight. The bottom end of the pole must be heavily weighted to maintain verticality while in the water. Procure two pounds of lead shot from your local gun shop, and after having cleaned out the bottom 20"-25" of your bamboo pole with a long drill bit, or of your CPVC tube with an acetoned cloth and a stick, mix the shot into a batch of resin. Stir and stuff the mush into the pole. Fill it flush. A rubber end from a crutch makes a nice, safe cap.

For the top of the pole, sew and affix a red and yellow flag 12" square, red triangle top right, yellow triangle bottom left. This is the international signal for the letter "O" and "man overboard".

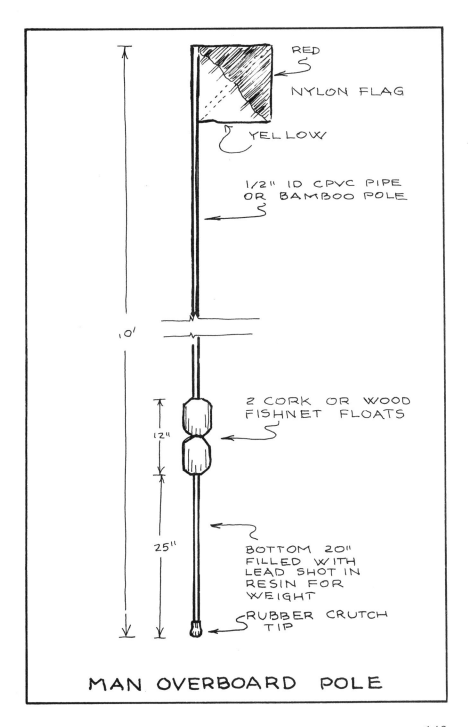

RED

NYLON FLAG

YELLOW

1/2" ID CPVC PIPE
OR BAMBOO POLE

10'

2 CORK OR WOOD
FISHNET FLOATS

12"

25"

BOTTOM 20"
FILLED WITH
LEAD SHOT IN
RESIN FOR
WEIGHT

RUBBER CRUTCH
TIP

MAN OVERBOARD POLE

SAFETY

MAN OVERBOARD POLE STOWAGE

Whether the pole is purchased or self-fabricated, proper stowage arrangements must be made to make it readily accessible in case of emergency. Since most yachts, at most times, travel forward, leaving the person overboard behind, the aft section of the vessel makes for an ideal stowage area. To be more specific, the backstay with two small attachments makes for a very secure support.

The base of the pole can be rested in a length of white PVC tube of 10″ height that has a diameter large enough to allow for a quick draw. Some people advocate the use of metal flag pole fittings, but I find these a little too shallow to be relied upon. The tube can be fastened to the backstay with rope lashings top and bottom. To keep these from wandering about vertically, file deep notches in the areas which they are to occupy. Stainless steel hose clamps make adequate substitutes, but they do look rather unsanitary, reminding one of radiators and sewage pipes.

At the top end, a narrow sleeve of canvas will house the pole and protect the flag from the sun. A length of 16″ will suffice. To fabricate, cut a piece of canvas to 18″ × 8″, double fold all edges and hem. Fit snaps at 4″ intervals along the long edge, and one snap in the middle of the long end. This will be the top of the sleeve and will keep it from slithering down the backstay. Stitch 1″ of the top corner shut to keep the flag and pole inside, otherwise the flag will forever protrude and get sun bleached and ugly. Be sure the sleeve fits snugly, but not snugly enough to impede sliding the pole up the backstay, which is what you must do to remove it from the tube base.

Some yachtsmen prefer having the pole slung into brackets or hung from snapped canvas straps from the lifelines. This often results in unscheduled man overboard pole overboard practices, which is not at all a bad idea since very few people have adequate manners to fall overboard at the properly scheduled times anyway.

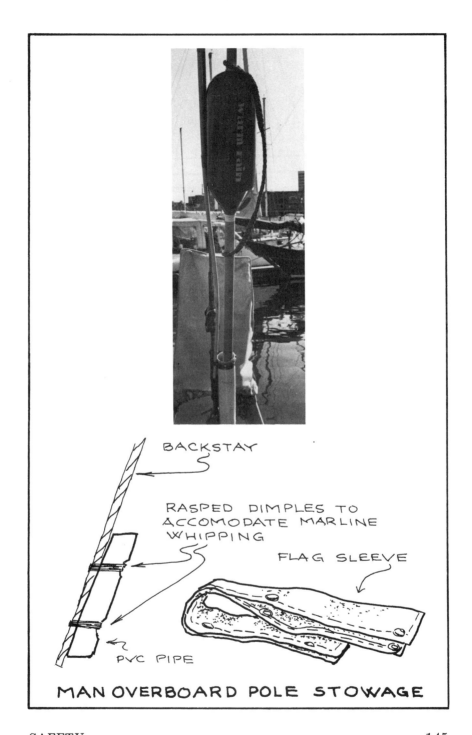

BACKSTAY

RASPED DIMPLES TO
ACCOMODATE MARLINE
WHIPPING

FLAG SLEEVE

PVC PIPE

MAN OVERBOARD POLE STOWAGE

MAN OVERBOARD SYSTEM

The advent of Hank Searl's novel *Overboard* emptied chandlery shelves of most safety systems and probably just as well, for with a little patience and ingenuity, one can duplicate a system which retails for $250 for about $90. The two items too difficult to build at home are the strobe light and the whistle. I have doubts whether one can produce the horseshoe buoy for any less than they sell for on sale (about $25), but everything else can be done by even the clumsiest among us.

The Strobe Light

I dislike absolute remarks, but consensus has it that the most functional and reliable distress strobe light is the ACR model 565. This is a self-activating unit which is stored upside down, righted immediately as it hits the water by its own counterweight, and activated by gravity, i.e. the battery's own weight causes contact. It puts out about 250,000 peak lumens per flash which is visible for about 15 miles on a clear night. It operates on the one battery non-stop for about 40 hours and costs about $1.40 per hour. Not a bad rate for saving a life.

The Overboard Pole

A good size overboard pole with flag is another integral part of the system. It can be constructed at a cost of about $10. (See "Overboard Pole" for details.) If built to a proper length of 11 to 15 feet and equipped with the prescribed flag, it can be seen at great distances from the deck of a boat in all but the wildest seas, long after the head of the swimmer has become invisible.

Dye Marker

A small plastic bottle of highly concentrated fluorescent dye (available at commercial art stores) should be tied to the buoy. There's no need to get excessive and weigh down the thing with a five gallon jerry can, for one pint will cover a tremendous area that will catch and reflect sun and searchlights from a goodly distance. How you wash it out of your sock I just don't know. Sealed plastic bags of it made to navy specs are available at most surplus stores.

Horseshoe Buoy

As mentioned, these are hard to beat for value. They are made of dense closed-cell (waterproof) foam core with a vinyl plastic cover,

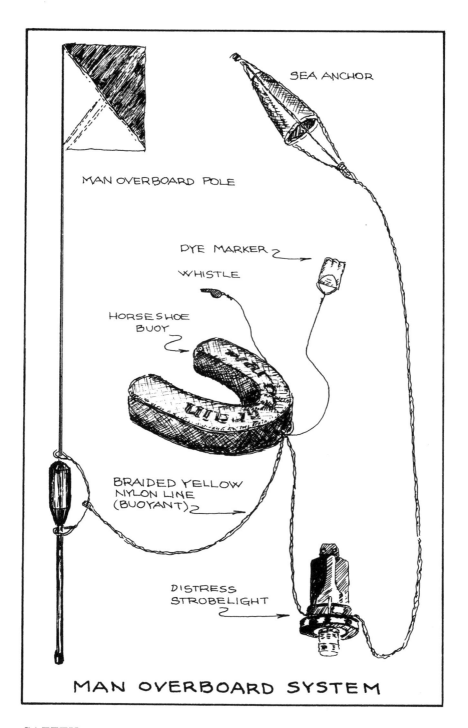

SEA ANCHOR

MAN OVERBOARD POLE

DYE MARKER

WHISTLE

HORSESHOE BUOY

BRAIDED YELLOW NYLON LINE (BUOYANT)

DISTRESS STROBELIGHT

MAN OVERBOARD SYSTEM

zippers, etc. They are U.S. Coast Guard approved and should be aboard.

Plastic Whistles

If the strobe fails and the fog is too dense to see the flag or dye, a plastic whistle might just be enough to attract attention. Since sound travels extremely well over water even in fog, this little 90¢ item might be one of the most important pieces of the whole rig.

Drogue

Once the fallen crew member is out of sight of the boat, he can easily become permanently lost because even though the crew marked course and time perfectly, by the time they return, the wind could have blown the entire rig of buoy and pole completely out of reach of the man. A small drogue of about 12″ diameter, made from scrap nylon (spinnaker material) and attached to the rest of the system, will prevent such costly drift.

Quick Launcher

Speed is of utmost importance in ocean rescue, as aptly demonstrated by an experience Candace had on a voyage from Hawaii to Newport Beach. As they sat forlornly with sails slapping and sun beating down in the Pacific High, Candace decided it was time for a swim. The boat seemed to be almost at a standstill, so over Candace went, big splash and all, and by the time she surfaced, the line trailing from stern was way out of reach, and after a bit of thrashing and a few shouts, the boat disappeared silently behind the huge Pacific swells, and there was ol' Candace, all alone, treading water, with four miles of ocean beneath her. Only some very quick action by the crew and a man in the spreaders brought dear Candace back aboard. Even the finest and most complete man-overboard system is completely useless if it's perched pertly on the yacht's stern, while the fallen crew bobs helplessly in the sunset.

To contain most of the gear aboard and then launch it quickly with the pull of a single lanyard, a canvas (or acrilan) case made to match your sail covers, etc. should be sewn (see Canvas section). And finally, to keep all the goodies from drifting all over the sea, a length of buoyant nylon line (discussions rage on whether this should be short, 30', or long, 75') should tie them all into a single chain so if the man overboard manages to grab anything at all, he'll have access to the whole thing.

BOWSPRIT PLATFORM

One hears endless tirades attacking old-fashioned ideas like bowsprits, terming them unnecessary, dangerous, and an extra expense when paying dock fees. Perhaps all that is true,but bowsprits do make room for large headsails on small boats, and they also evoke something akin to romantic thoughts, and the only real hindrance I find they have is that unless accompanied by a platform and pulpit, their presence will inhibit the use of sails. Off the coast of British Columbia, where islands dot the sea for 300 miles and beautiful anchorages abound, short 10-15 mile daily adventures are most desirable. But I have too often seen sailboats motoring along in a fine breeze, because the crew felt it too much of a task to unfurl their sails. This reasoning comes too frequently from yachtsmen with unprotected bowsprits. Doing a balancing act on a $5''$ radius beam is no one's idea of relaxation, but I advocate not removal of bowsprits, but addition of platforms and pulpits.

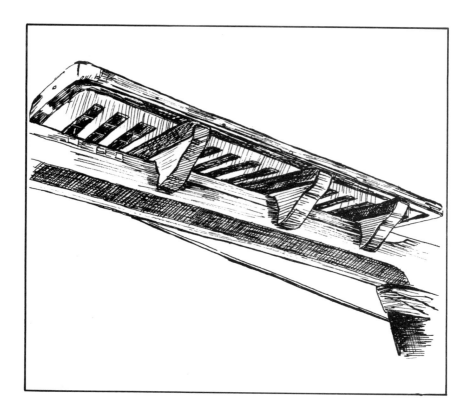

Two basic design theorems should be followed: make the platform strong, and make the platform light. The weight and solid surface should be as little as possible, for some platforms, once buried in a wave, never do come out alive. A grate-like solution seems to be the best. Simpler than grates are parallel teak slats 1½ " X 2" on edge, with spacers between (see photo). They should be resorcinol glued and screwed to each other. Space the screws four to six inches apart. Just gluing and clamping are enough, if that's what you prefer, since the whole platform will be through-bolted onto the bowsprit. These through-bolts will provide more than the necessary strength to hold the pieces together.

The overall width need be no more than 6" on either side for adequate foot support. The platforms will have to be wider if you plan to have them house anchor rollers, but even then one additional 2" piece on the outside will do nicely. The ideal method of attachment is using 1/2" or 3/8" all-thread every 24". This, of course, is run through from side to side, right through the bowsprit, and, hence, requires some very exact long distance drilling. Countersink spaces for lock nuts on either end. Bullnose all edges and round corners.

Beats tight-sprit walking all to hell, doesn't it?

Full grate platform.

Twin stemmed platform (A-frame) eliminates whisker stays.

Warm Rain's platform built from slats.

SAFETY HARNESS

For any offshore or serious coastal cruising, safety harnesses are mandatory, unless your fondest wish has always been to undertake a serious career as shark bait.

An attempt should be made to fabricate your own safety harness, for then, not only will you know how it is assembled, but you can also design it to your own measurements and needs. For the hardware, have a look at the best safety harness money can buy, and buy fittings at least as good.

The belt is the most important part of the harness. It has to be strong, for the line keeping you aboard will be attached to it, and it has to be wide, so the pressure will be well distributed over your back, instead of cutting viciously into vertebrae. Use heavy 2″ seatbelt material and, for extra stiffness, wrap it with two layers of heavy, but soft, dacron to make up a width of 3″. Cut the dacron so its ends come within 4″ of each other in the front (measure this while you're wearing a shirt and sweater to get a medium fit, somewhere between all out foul weather gear and bare skin). Have the seatbelt overlap itself by at least 16″, hanging past the dacron 8″ at one end and 12″ on the other.

Run a couple rows of stitching over the dacron ends to avoid fraying. Next, sew your buckle onto the 8″ free belt, folding the belt back over itself to house the buckle, as in the diagram. Of course, various buckles can be substituted; just be sure they're all brass or stainless, and not plated steel.

Now, using 1″ dacron tape, make up the shoulder pieces. Sew the long piece to the back and sew a short piece (with an adjusting buckle) to the front, just inside the dacron end, as shown. Try to determine what length of shoulder straps you'll be using so you won't have to have yards of tape trailing about. Cross the shoulder pieces in the back and sew them together to keep them from slipping off your shoulders.

Lastly, splice a 5′ length of braid to the triangular fitting, as in the diagram, and fit the line's other end to the best damn stainless snap hook you can buy — one that has at least 1,500 pounds breaking strength.

Two small points to make life easier: a) use different colour dacron wrapping for the belt for every member of the crew, so he can readily grab his own harness, made and adjusted to his own needs, and b) splice two braids with snap hooks to your fitting instead of one. This way, if you're clipped into, say, the lifelines, and you have to move about on deck, when you come to something like a stanchion, where you have to unclip to make progress, you can clip the spare snap hook to the next part of the lifeline past the stanchion, before you unclip the first one. Too many people with single snap hooks have fallen overboard just as they were making this transition.

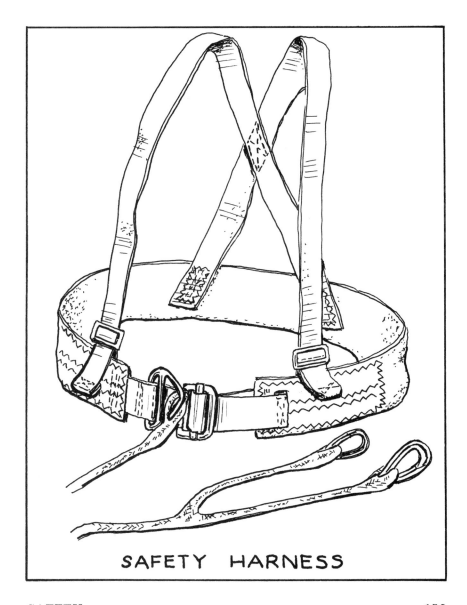

SAFETY HARNESS

ground
tackle

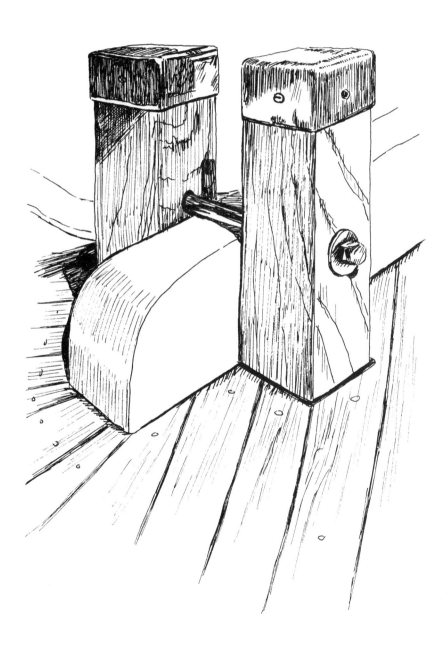

CHAIN PIPES

In many yachts, the mistake is made of leading chain directly through the deck pipe and stowing it immediately below in the bow. This is all fine if one's ground tackle consists of a 20 pound danforth and some line, but when one begins to use 200' or so of 5/16" chain, the weight quickly nears 220 pounds. If this can be lead aft even only two feet, 440' pounds of bow plunging, nose burying energy will have been moved, and that is well worth the effort on any yacht.

The way to achieve this is to lead the chain out of the chain locker aft beneath the V-berth in the fore peak. Most vessels have good space here for both line and chain.

The materials needed here, available from any plumber, consist of 4"diameter PVC pipe and some fittings. The 4" pipe is advisable because large eyes and shackles are often used and often these tangle and wedge themselves in small spaces. A PVC flange, one that can facilitate screws, will secure the pipe to the underdeck while a 45° elbow will take care of the bend and feeding through the bulkhead. The length of pipe should be such that the pipe outlet will come through the bulkhead as high beneath the V-berth and as far aft as possible. This measure is necessary to maximize the amount of space available for the chain beneath the pipe, for it can then drop merrily and stow itself without need for a guiding hand in the form of a crew in the forepeak.

Attach the deck fitting to the vertical pipe and then screw the fitting to underdeck. A 6" × 6" × 1¾" mahogany block should be fitted, screwed and glued onto the bulkhead where the pipe will come through. Drill the pilot hole from fore to aft at the desired angle in the bulkhead and block, and follow that with a 4½" hole saw. Insert pipe into the hole and cut it to the correct length and angle. Glue the elbow to both pieces of pipe. Screw the lower portion of the pipe to the block. If you wish to lead the chain farther aft, use another coupling and add on the desired length of pipe. Try to have the pipe outlet in the middle of the stowage area. If all chain is to be used, that is, no coil of rope will exist to provide bedding for the chain, thought should be given to lining wood or glass hulls with a webbed nylon padding to avoid direct chafe from cascading chain.

THE FINELY FITTED YACHT

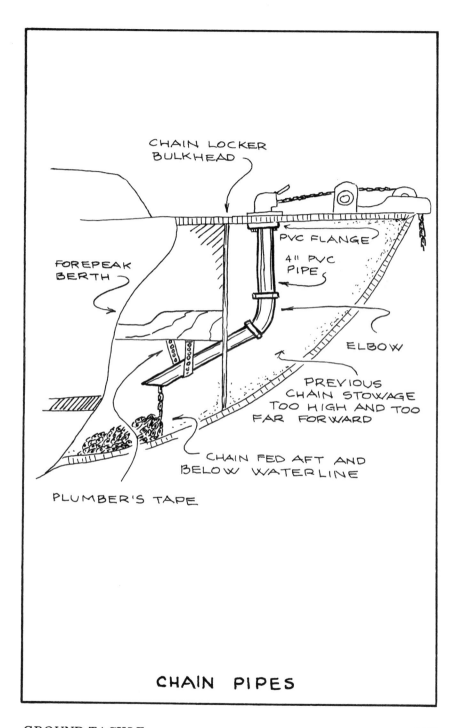

CHAIN LOCKER
BULKHEAD

PVC FLANGE

4" PVC
PIPE

FOREPEAK
BERTH

ELBOW

PREVIOUS
CHAIN STOWAGE
TOO HIGH AND TOO
FAR FORWARD

CHAIN FED AFT AND
BELOW WATERLINE

PLUMBER'S TAPE

CHAIN PIPES

DOCK LINES

I never cease to be amazed by the lack of reverence most people exhibit toward their dock lines. They are, after all, the yacht's only contact with dry land, and if well handled, they can assure most of us that our vessel will be found in roughly the same place some days hence, instead of having drifted off into or under something heavy. Although dock lines seem to be undemanding bits of rope, they do require at least minimal courtesies like proper handling and stowage.

No dock lines should be used without chafe guards. These can be made with a simple piece of leather of very substantial weight and sewn on wherever the line is in constant contact with hawse pipes or fair leads. They should be stitched on tightly and affixed to the line with two through stitches at either end. Make the chafe guards at least 8″ long to allow for variation of onboard attachment. Dock lines, as any lines on a proper yacht, should be whipped. Whipping is an extremely pleasant pastime, resulting in beautiful bits of craftsmanship in exchange for little effort.

The longest lasting and one of the most decorative whippings is the Palm and Needle Whip:

Cut a length of yarn and, using a regular sailing needle, anchor one end to the boat with two stitches. Lay on a number of turns snugly, then "thrust the needle through the middle of a strand and then worm the whipping back to the left side and thrust the needle through the next strand beyond. Now pull the twine up tightly and worm it back to the right side of the whipping, thrust the needle to the next strand and pull tight. Finally worm back to the left side again and again stitch through the strand and tighten." So says Hervey Garrett Smith, and he ought to know.

The stowage of dock lines on many vessels is a disgrace. They are heaved into dinghies, lashed onto dogs, or thrown into the lazarette among oily cans and dripping diesel containers, then hurriedly jerked and yanked out as the boat roars up to the dock. Sacrilege. Dock lines are the simplest things to stow. On the foredeck, they can be left on a samson post and coiled beautifully out of the way, while on the aft, they can remain on the mooring cleat and be coiled as well and used as a sitting pad, if one is lacking. In either case, they will be ready, obviating the need for stuffing the dog into the ice box while his leash is being used to lash the boat to the wharf.

THE FINELY FITTED YACHT

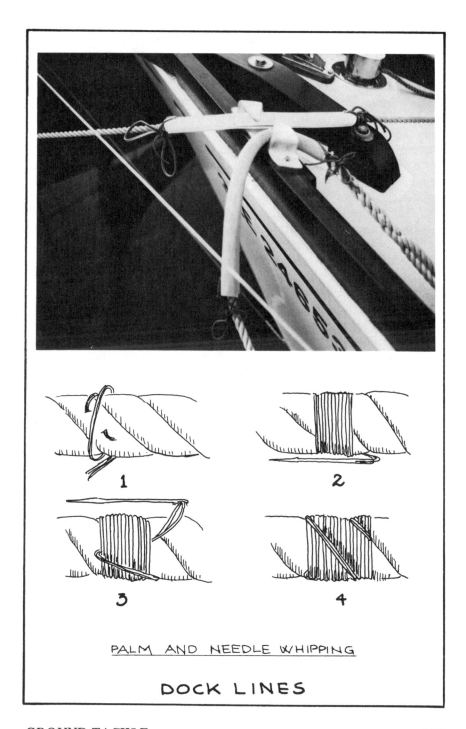

PALM AND NEEDLE WHIPPING

DOCK LINES

GROUND TACKLE   159

STERN ANCHOR CHAIN STOWAGE

Almost everyone accepts the need for stern anchor gear, but few people actually make a serious attempt to design and build proper stowage for it. Having chain and rope heaved into the bottom of the lazarette, with an avalanche of old paint cans and Hibachis and teddy bears atop it, is lunacy, when with very little forethought and minimal effort, accessible and safe stowage can be constructed.

Warm Rain, as most yachts, had a bottomless pit of a lazarette, holding everything and yielding nothing. As a first step, a shelf was built at about half depth and attached with the help of cleat stock to the lazarette bulkhead, and bonded with fiberglass mat and cloth tape to the hull. A tapered opening was cut into the bulkhead below the shelf, leaving 4″ of the bulkhead intact on the sides and 15″ on the bottom. We felt the hole necessary to inspect the chain or untangle it, if it was somehow caught below. A simple door was fabricated to fit over the hole to keep the chain from attacking the engine in rough seas. It was installed with a piano hinge at its bottom, and kept closed with the two brass tension snaps you see in the photo. The hull was lined with a piece of plastic cushioning, the kind people put over their rugs to save them from wear. This was installed because I didn't fancy the thought of the chain cascading down and grinding away the fiberglass. Next, a length of 3″ plastic sewer pipe (the erudite call it PVC) was purchased, its length just sufficient to reach from the top of the lazarette hatch coaming to the bottom of the lazarette shelf. A hole was cut in the shelf, with a hole saw, to accommodate the pipe. It was placed into a corner of the lazarette coaming and secured to it by means of two 1″ pan-head sheet metal screws. The coaming around was lined with very thin brass sheeting. All this is much easier than installing a deck pipe, especially if there is no room to accommodate one.

On the caprail, a bronze fairlead was installed, after the caprail surrounding it was also lined with the brass sheeting. A small Danforth stern anchor was stowed in the lazarette, made fast to the chain, and we lived happily ever after.

CHAIN STOWAGE

ANCHOR ROLLERS

I am endlessly amazed by people who come into anchorages, lift their anchor off the deck and dangle it over the side, scratching glossy paint or chipping gelcoat, all for want of a proper anchor roller. On any vessel with a bowsprit, the lack of an anchor roller is inexcusable, because installing one can be accomplished by the drilling of a single bolt. On other vessels where caprails and stem fittings must be designed around, the undertaking takes on larger, though not insurmountable, proportions.

Generally speaking, the ideal roller will be as large as conveniently possible. Large link chain simply snaps over small rollers, resulting in difficult chain hauling and a lot of noise. Care must be taken that the roller's jaws not be too narrow, or constant chain and rode jamming will occur. In recent years, the synthetic delrin rollers have endeared themselves to yachtsmen. They need no lubrication as their brass or stainless counterparts frequently do, but more importantly, they are almost noise free which the most considerate feel an important factor, especially if frequent late evening anchoring is the norm.

Attention should be paid to the height of the roller's shoulder, for too low a shoulder will often let the chain or line ride off and jam mercilessly in the most undesirable places.

On vessels without bowsprits, the problem is magnified by the fact that it's impossible to fit a large diameter wheel anywhere for lack of available support. Here, the major function of the roller must be to protect the topsides while the chain is being paid out, after which one must transfer the anchor rode into a substantial fairlead in which the rode can spend the night.

The location of such rollers should be close to the stem, otherwise, the shifting vessel will frequently override the rode and cause considerable chafe across the bow. I see no reason why the roller cannot be just off the centreline, giving only adequate clearance past the headstay fittings. A better idea is to have a roller on either side of the fitting, each being a specialist for either rope or chain. If you're lacking a windlass, the installation of a pawl will greatly facilitate hauling the anchor by holding, or more correctly, trapping the chain as it comes aboard.

If you steadfastly refuse to install a roller, would you at least please consent to a skookum fairlead so the next time you come into an anchorage, I won't have to turn away in horror while your caprail is viciously mulched by your chain.

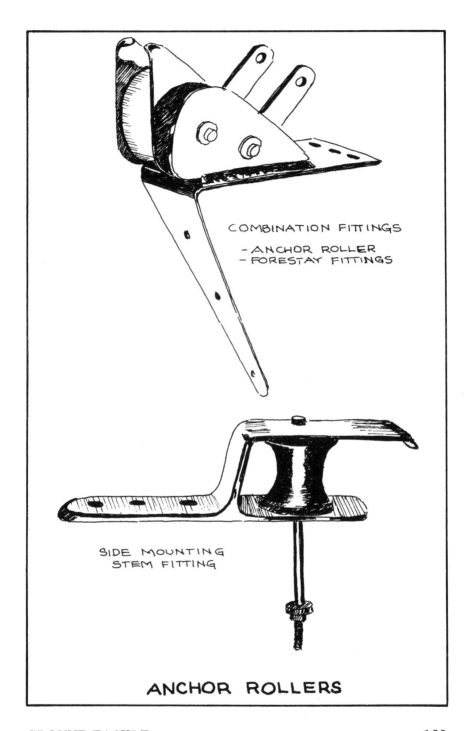

COMBINATION FITTINGS

- ANCHOR ROLLER
- FORESTAY FITTINGS

SIDE MOUNTING
STEM FITTING

ANCHOR ROLLERS

SAMSON POST

Far too often, one hears about a magnanimous gesture by a fellow sailor turning into a most embarrassing disaster that could have been avoided by the installation of a proper samson post for towing. Vessels under tow have had, for lack of a proper fitting, head stay stems, mooring cleats, and stanchions torn out when these were used as towing gear. The following bitt can be safely used on yachts up to seven tons if fabricated as shown and installed as suggested.

The heart of the bitt is a 1/4″ steel plate about 12″ square or tapered, if need be, to fit into the bow. Welded to this should be a 1/2″ plate about 4″ wide and 7″ high forming an upright, with arms protruding about 3″ on either side. A 3/4″ stainless rod can be used here welded to the top of the upright. The ends should be well rounded to minimize torn Achilles tendons.

Oak cheeks milled from 1½″ stock and cut with dimples, as shown, to accommodate heavy lines, should be fixed to either side of the upright. An oak cap from 13/16″ stock should be fitted over the cheeks to minimize weathering of exposed endgrain.

The base plate should be drilled with four 3/8″ holes in the corners for mounting. A 16″-square 1/8″ plate should be fitted below decks for support. If there is any doubt regarding the integrity of the foredeck, the entire foredeck surface belowdecks should be faced with 1/2″ plywood sandwiched between the deck and the back-up plate. The base plate must, of course, be bedded before being seated. Use polysulphide, and use it in the bolt holes as well, to prevent any possibility of moisture seeping into the deck bringing about dry-rot.

Of course, you should hope and pray that your rudder will never break, steering will never fail, and you won't have to be towed, but if doom does come, you won't have to get your boat torn apart while being rescued.

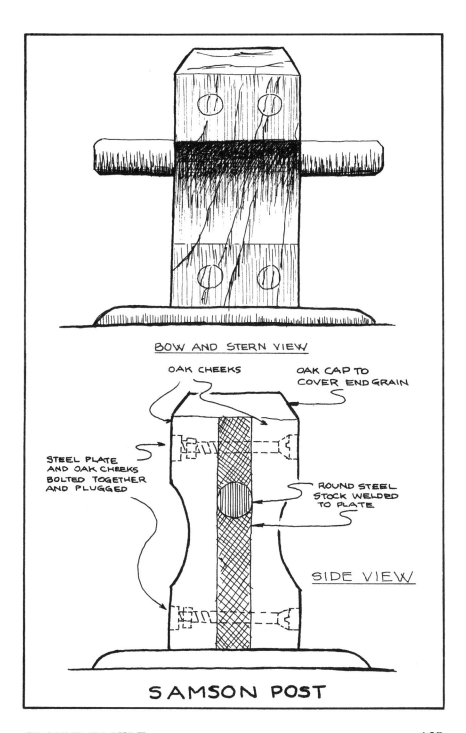

BOW AND STERN VIEW

OAK CHEEKS

OAK CAP TO COVER END GRAIN

STEEL PLATE AND OAK CHEEKS BOLTED TOGETHER AND PLUGGED

ROUND STEEL STOCK WELDED TO PLATE

SIDE VIEW

SAMSON POST

ALL-WOOD TOW BITT

If you have no aversion to cutting a hole in your foredeck, a single piece, all-wood, mooring bitt may be a nicer fitting to use than the metal/wood combination. For boats under five tons, a 3″ × 3″ piece of white oak is sufficient; for boats five to ten tons, 4″ × 4″ is fine; up to 15 tons use 6″ × 6″; over 15 tons get a stump. The above deck height can vary from 6″ to 12″ while below decks you'll go right to the hull.

First fabricate your partner as shown. The thickness of the partner will be determined by: a) the strength of your deck, and b) the displacement of your vessel. With an average deck strength, the best rule is to start with 1/2″ thickness of plywood for up to three tons, and add 1/4″ for each additional three tons. Whatever your thickness, the location of the bitt must be aft of the 2′ beam mark to provide for a partner of sufficient surface. Bond and screw it into place.

Next, form your bitt as shown, then measure for the deck hole to be cut, and cut it with the drilled hole and saber saw method. Do this very exactly. The snugger the fit, the better the hold. Next, rout a 1/4″ × 1/4″ groove around the hole for sealant. Slip the bitt into the hole, go below and establish its exact vertical location and mark the exact position of the base of the bitt accordingly. You will now have to fabricate two low bulkheads — 8″ to 12″ high is plenty — one directly forward and one directly aft of the bitt. Don't scrimp. Use 1″ plywood. Scribe these and fit them, then bond them into place. Double bond each bulkhead forward and aft with two layers of 6″ mat tape and one layer of 8″ cloth. To be sure you won't need any wedges you would do well to screw the bulkheads to the bitt temporarily. For wood boats the task is of course easier, for an existing floor can be reinforced by a step (see diagram) eliminating complicated bulkhead construction. Whether bulkhead or floor is used the bitt must be bolted to it for strength. Use 3/8″ to 1/2″ bolts with the largest washers you can find. Drill the bitt head for a Norman pin of 1/2″ diameter and round off the pin's ends with a file.

To protect the bitt, fit a fine gauge sheet of brass over its top and 1″ down the sides. Caulk beneath it and tack it in place.

If you've followed the above steps your bitt will never tear out; your boat might tear in half but the bitt will be okay.

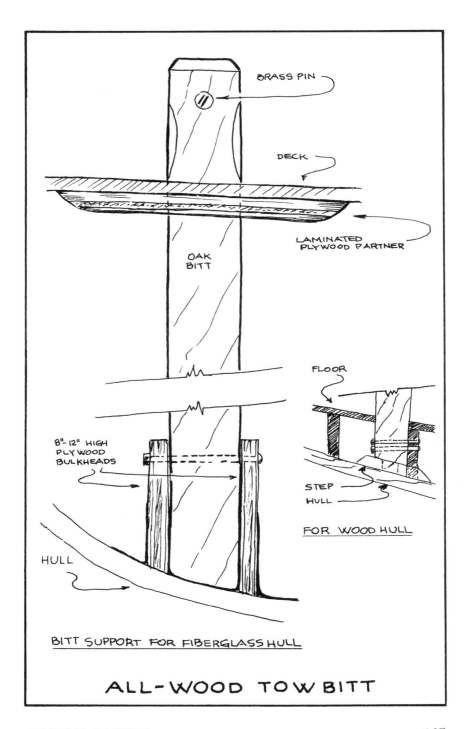

BRASS PIN

DECK

LAMINATED PLYWOOD PARTNER

OAK BITT

FLOOR

8"-12" HIGH PLYWOOD BULKHEADS

STEP HULL

FOR WOOD HULL

HULL

BITT SUPPORT FOR FIBERGLASS HULL

ALL-WOOD TOW BITT

FOREDECK WELL

The best place to stow all ground tackle related gear is in a well in the foredeck. With the lid securely in place, the foredeck is cleared of all lines, chains and windlass, making sail changes an absolute dream. The molded well in the photo is in an *Ontario 30* but a fairly similar job can be done on any yacht if you don't mind taking a saw to your foredeck and doing some uncomfortably tight work in some very small spaces.

Because of the amount of reinforcing needed for an anchor windlass, I would not suggest incorporating it into the well. Rather, I see the well as a good place to stow anchors, chain and especially rope which otherwise has to be fed below decks or coiled and hidden away.

This simplified version will not have a flush fitting lid for one is just too demanding to install. Rather, it will have a very low profile hatch cover, with coamings to keep out the water.

The dimensions of the opening can vary with the individual yacht although I would strongly discourage cutting any opening with longer than 20'' sides or wider than 24'' aft side. The width of the front should of course narrow to allow the sides to follow the lines of the deck. Furthermore, a deck space of at least 8'' should be left all around the opening so as not to endanger the hull to deck joint, and also to enable your hands plus some tools between the well wall and the hull.

Location of the well should be thoroughly considered keeping in mind that you will be taking about 14'' of space directly below the deck in the forepeak. It would be most advantageous structurally to locate the well over the chain locker bulkhead, cutting a piece of the bulkhead out to make room, for then direct support can be returned to the deck by using this bulkhead as part of the foundation. If the yacht is not equipped with such a bulkhead, one would be well advised to make the aft wall of the well into a partial (upper) bulkhead by running it clear from hull to hull and attaching it there either to the frames of a wooden yacht, or bending it directly to the hull of a fiberglass yacht (see diagram).

Other than these precautions, roar on ahead. Measure out your opening and cut the deck most carefully with a saber saw. Reinforce the deck immediately with the 2'' × 1¼'' mahogany cleats (Diagram A). The cleats should be glued, clamped, and screwed to the underdecks after all old paint, etc. has been completely stripped

THE FINELY FITTED YACHT

away. Use epoxy glue and take particular care that neither your countersink drilling nor your screws come out topsides.

Next, determine the depth you will want your well to be. For rope and chain stowage, 10″ is deep enough; if you plan to keep a particular anchor in there, adjust the depth accordingly. Cut your sides from 1/2″ plywood to such a shape that the well sole will have a definite slope to it to facilitate drainage. Install all cleat stock onto your well sides as shown in diagrams, remembering to rip your vertical ones to angles that will make a perfect fit with both adjoining pieces. Now using 1″ #10 S.S. P.H.S.M. screws and epoxy glue, assemble the well in place. The order of assembly will depend on your belowdeck's limitations; do not, however, leave the well sole until the very last for you'll encounter an impossible situation if you do.

Once the well is together screwed and glued, lay strips of cleat stock cut to 45° along the bottom of the well (Diagram A) so the forthcoming fiberglass mat and roving will not have to make so drastic a turn. If they do, the chances of their cracking or delaminating will greatly increase. Glue the strips into place and, using 6″ fiberglass mat tape and 8″ fiberglass cloth tape (in that order), thoroughly seal off all joints of the well. (For directions on fiberglassing, see *From A Bare Hull*, pp. 265-70.) Be sure to work away all loose strands while the resin is still wet so they won't have a chance to become vicious porcupine quills when they harden. Next, clean out and primer the entire well, then cover with at least two coats of very durable enamel.

Now construct the coamings. Cut them from 13/16″ teak to a width that will allow the coaming to stick 1″ above the deck and 3/4″ below the heavy mahogany deck cleat. This lower overhang will form a drip lip, preventing water from seeping into the upper joints. To help the drip lip, cut a saw blade width groove to a depth of 1/8″ along the bottoms of all the coaming pieces. Bullnose all long edges. Now comes the tricky part. You will want to glue and screw the coaming to the heavy mahogany cleat, but *not* into the edge of the deck or you'll delaminate it. To add to the anxiety, you must lay a bead of caulking over the deck's edge where it will butt against the coaming. So, brush resorcinol glue onto your big cleat. Then, lay a thin bead of caulking on the deck edge above it (with caution), then screw the coamings in place. Remove excess caulking and glue.

Next, install your well drain. With a cup of water find the low spot in the well, and proceed to drill a hole for a 1/2″ plastic through-hull. Bed it thoroughly in white polysulfide and fit it with a

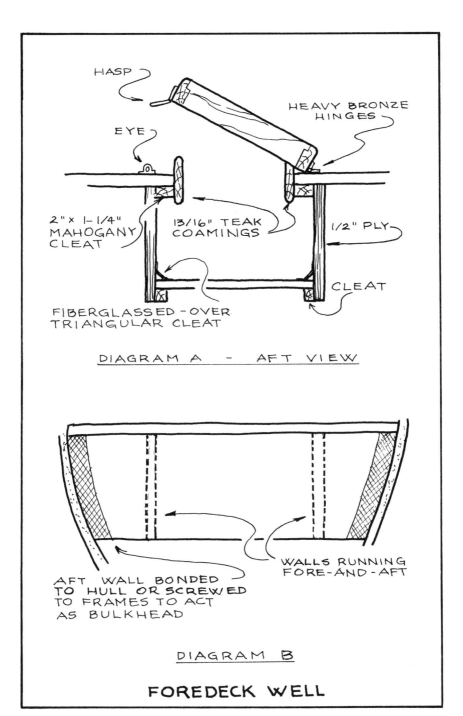

HASP

HEAVY BRONZE
HINGES

EYE

2" x 1-1/4"
MAHOGANY
CLEAT

13/16" TEAK
COAMINGS

1/2" PLY

CLEAT

FIBERGLASSED-OVER
TRIANGULAR CLEAT

DIAGRAM A   -   AFT VIEW

WALLS RUNNING
FORE-AND-AFT

AFT WALL BONDED
TO HULL OR SCREWED
TO FRAMES TO ACT
AS BULKHEAD

DIAGRAM B

FOREDECK WELL

1/2″ nylon hose. At a level just barely below the floor of the well, find a convenient spot on the hull for a 1/2″ brass vent. Drill the hole for it and install it with the opening facing aft and down, that is, about 7:30 o'clock as you face that side of the yacht. Again, bed both inside and outside with polysulfide and tighten well.

The hatch will now have to be fabricated. Cut 1¾″ stock to 2″ width and mill a rabbet in one side 7/8″ wide and 7/8″ deep (see "Skylight") Carry the rabbet end to end on the two side frames, but terminate it at 7/8″ from the ends of the aft and foreward pieces. All four frames must be cut to the hatch's over-all measurements because you'll be using lap joints, i.e. if your hatch is to measure 18″ × 24″, then your pieces will have to be 18″ and 24″ respectively.

For further hatch construction information see "Turtle Hatch" in this volume.

The hatch should be hinged on one side (the foreward end would be safest but then difficulties will be encountered paying out chain and line) with two very heavy bronze hinges. The opposite side of the hatch should be fitted with two hasps and twist-locks of a heavy duty kind. Always keep these securely locked.

Remember, you may just go to the well once too often.

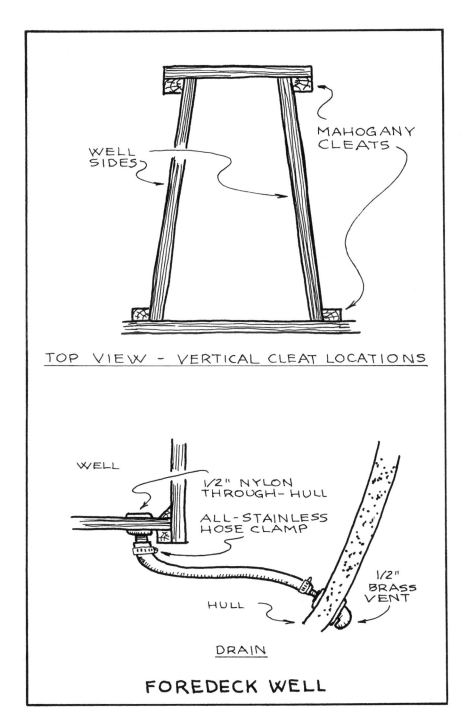

TOP VIEW - VERTICAL CLEAT LOCATIONS

WELL SIDES

MAHOGANY CLEATS

WELL

1/2" NYLON THROUGH-HULL

ALL-STAINLESS HOSE CLAMP

HULL

1/2" BRASS VENT

DRAIN

FOREDECK WELL

GROUND TACKLE

173

ANCHOR CHOCKS

To pretend for even a moment that a single best solution exists to stowing any anchor aboard, would demonstrate unforgivable shortsightedness. Too many different anchors and too many different boats exist for that. Basically, I feel that every attempt should be made to keep the anchor off the deck proper. If a bowsprit exists, the job will be simple, for then plow anchors can be left stowed on the anchor roller affixed to the side of the bowsprit with the stem of the fluke in tight against the roller, and the shank slung along the bowsprit and made fast to it with a short lanyard to keep the shank from banging about.

On a yacht without a bowsprit, accommodation for a CQR is still easily found on a self-stowing bow roller (see diagram).

If an off-centre roller is chosen, you can still atone by fabricating teak chocks that attach to the hull and keep the point of the fluke from gnawing away at the finish.

If you don't have any of the above facilities, you'll just have to bring the damned thing on deck and do what Captain Voss did aboard *Tilikum*, an Indian dugout canoe he sailed around the world in 1904-04, and just fabricate some chocks on deck and trip over them every chance you get.

With a CQR, the best solution is to get that monstrous fluke out of the way against the bulwark and run the shank fore and aft along same. You'll then need to hack out four small pads: two for the fluke, and one for each end of the shank.

Stowing Danforth–type anchors is a somewhat easier task, because they're lighter and have nice long stocks and a tripping palm, both of which are excellent things to hook into brackets of some sort. A most uncomplicated set is available at chandleries. It consists of two strips of stainless steel that clamp to the crosspiece of any stern or bow pulpit, and have notches into which the stock can snuggle. The shank is led down to the bow and made fast to avoid inadvertent anchorings.

Another bracket is available for Danforths, this for yachts without pulpits. It's a single piece design that clamps to a stanchion and holds the anchor securely in an upright position. Both of the above brackets facilitate quick releasing.

If you have neither pulpits nor stanchions, then you don't have to worry about having the anchor stowed and at the ready, because you'll probably fall overboard before you reach the harbour anyway.

THE FINELY FITTED YACHT

CQR ANCHOR

SELF - STOWING ANCHOR ROLLER

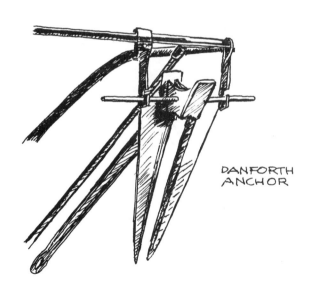

DANFORTH ANCHOR

PULPIT MOUNTED ANCHOR HOLDER

ANCHOR CHOCKS

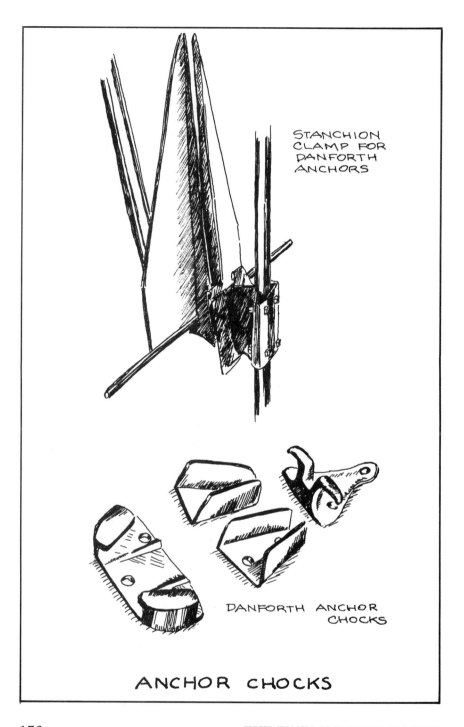

STANCHION
CLAMP FOR
DANFORTH
ANCHORS

DANFORTH ANCHOR
CHOCKS

ANCHOR CHOCKS

THE FINELY FITTED YACHT

ANCHOR CHOCKS

Captain Voss' dugout canoe.

THE FINELY FITTED YACHT

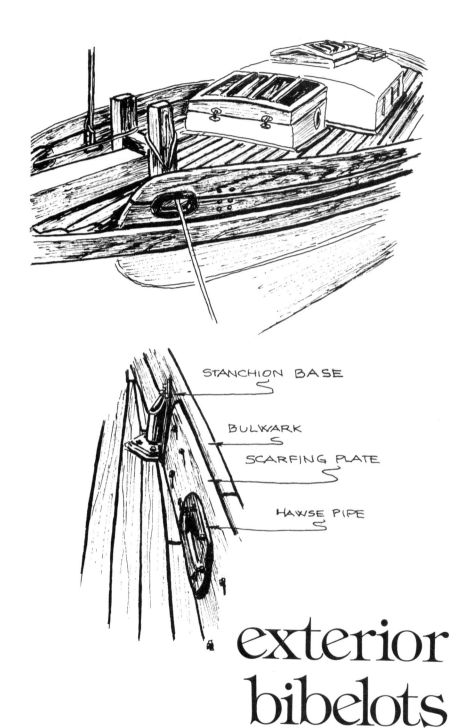

STANCHION BASE

BULWARK

SCARFING PLATE

HAWSE PIPE

exterior
bibelots

SOLAR BATTERY CHARGERS

After a few thousand years of civilization, we are finally giving thought to utilizing the power of the sun for something other than getting brown and growing turnips. We have discovered the phenomenon known as "photovoltaic effect" which allows the conversion of light into electrical energy without moving parts, with the use of silicon crystal based solar cells.

When exposed to sunlight, incoming units of light energy (photons) are absorbed by the electrons within the unit. This creates negative and positive charges which are attracted to their respective chemically treated type silicon of the cell. Consequently a photocurrent flows, voltage and electricity is produced. Thus a power source is created — a photovoltaic generator or a solar cell. It can keep the batteries charged while the boat is not in use, or it can trickle charge and help keep the battery level up during regular usage.

A typical 21" X 21" X 1" unit can produce about 55 amp hours per week in an average U.S. location. In practice that means if you need to run your engine with a common 25 amp alternator (found on most two cylinder diesels) two hours a week to keep up your batteries for your radios and lights, then you can completely replace the engine use with a solar cell. Because silicon crystals are not yet mass produced, the cost of such a unit (about $500) would take about five years of constant boat use to pay for itself in gas or diesel at current oil prices (80¢/gal) but it sure wouldn't take long to pay off in silence.

The construction is of fiberglass and stabilized silicone rubber. Some makes, like the Solar Seamaster, are made especially for marine use and are completely submergible, hermetically sealed, and non-corrosive, without any exposed metal parts or external connections. The cells are protected by a removable 1/4" thick plexiglass cover sturdy enough to walk on if needed.

Installation consists of gluing or screwing the panel to a cabin top or hatch cover, wherever it will get the most exposure (lazarette areas are ideal. See photo.) A single hole well caulked or a rubberized deck connector, will be needed to run the wires down to each battery terminal.

Since there are no moving parts the unit should last until the plexiglass breaks down, but even that can be simply replaced.

The whole thing seems like a very perfect idea; it's just a pity that Henry Ford hasn't gone into solar cell production.

SOLAR PANEL

SOLAR WARM WATER TANKS

A very dear friend living aboard the cutter *Aepomene* in Puerto Vallarta had among his very clever inventions, a most ingenious one, that of solar warm water tanks. He had two fabricated and fitted far forward on the deckhouse, where they were out of the way. They contained enough warm water on most sunny days to provide two fine showers of nearly three quarts each. The tanks measured $2'' \times 20'' \times 10''$, were made of sturdy gauge aluminum (cheaper than stainless, easier to weld and drill, and a better conductor of heat), and painted a very flat black to help heat absorption. They had regular flush-fitting fills on the top and a small vent to allow water flow. At one point, he decided to increase the rate of flow from the tanks for a more dousing shower, so he had two bicycle tire nipples welded to the tanks and would daily pressurize each with a bicycle pump to have, in effect, pressurized water. Outlets were on the bottom and led through the coachroof into the cabin with $1/2''$ copper tubing.

Mounting on deck was achieved by two brackets at either end, tooled out of $1\frac{1}{2}''$ teak stock. These were routed to a $3/4''$ depth in the bottom half to snugly house the tanks, while the upper half was radiused on the corners and bullnosed. The brackets were screwed onto the cabin top after being bedded in Dolfinite. This is a completely serviceable, not unattractive invention that can solve the hygiene problem in any climate providing the sun is out. In the north, you may not be scalded, but you won't get icicles in the under-arms either.

An improved version, that is, one producing warm water at a faster rate, would involve substitution of the tanks with a reconditioned auto air conditioning radiator. The numerous baffles of these vastly increase the exposed surface and can measurably decrease time required to heat the water within. The 1967 Cadillacs have had the smallest and most reliable ones. A plexiglass housing should be made to enclose the whole thing and create a nice greenhouse effect, that is, let in the sun and keep in the heat, as well as keep out cooling winds.

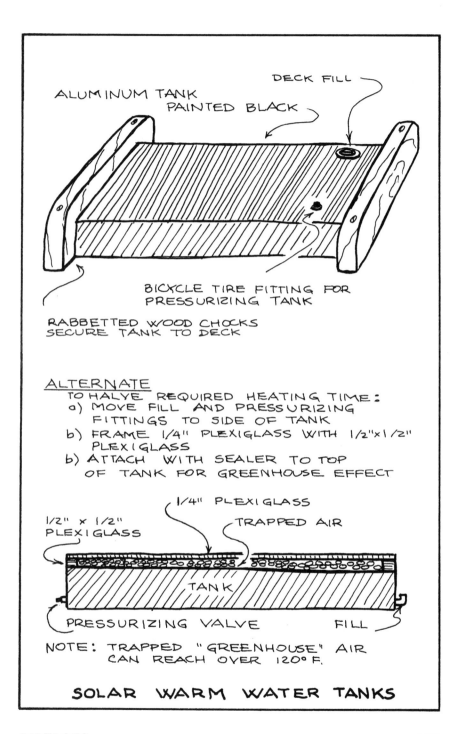

DECK FILL

ALUMINUM TANK
PAINTED BLACK

BICYCLE TIRE FITTING FOR
PRESSURIZING TANK

RABBETTED WOOD CHOCKS
SECURE TANK TO DECK

ALTERNATE
TO HALVE REQUIRED HEATING TIME:
a) MOVE FILL AND PRESSURIZING
   FITTINGS TO SIDE OF TANK
b) FRAME 1/4" PLEXIGLASS WITH 1/2"x1/2"
   PLEXIGLASS
b) ATTACH WITH SEALER TO TOP
   OF TANK FOR GREENHOUSE EFFECT

1/4" PLEXIGLASS

TRAPPED AIR

1/2" x 1/2"
PLEXIGLASS

TANK

PRESSURIZING VALVE   FILL

NOTE: TRAPPED "GREENHOUSE" AIR
      CAN REACH OVER 120° F.

SOLAR WARM WATER TANKS

BOARDING LADDER

I shall not attempt to proselytise everyone to the use of a single type of boarding ladder, for I take immense pleasure in rowing around anchorages studying some of the most stupifying creations since the invention of gargoyles.

Apart from this selfish laissez faire, most boarding ladders should be left alone, for they do work. The simplest can be nothing more than a single piece of line with a couple of wood rungs, drilled and knot-held in place. From watching the owners utilize them, I have concluded that the two dollar and fifteen minute ladders work as well as the store bought $130 jewels.

The ladder to be discussed here is a homemade version of said jewel. First, purchase the hardware shown in the diagram, for you'll have to use measurements from these to cut out some of the wood parts. The whole set is available from H & L Marine.

For a four rung ladder that opens to 40″ and folds to 25″, with rung lengths of 14″ (clear) you will require seven lineal feet of 8″ wide and 1″ thick teak or mahogany. Cut the two 25″ lengths for the sides, and rip what's left (into 3″ wide pieces) for the rungs. Next, on 4½″ and 13½″ centres from the bottom, dado (half depth) the shape of your rungs.

Now, to cut the ladder into two pieces, begin by scribing a line 3″ from the edge of one of the sides all the way from one end to within 8″ from the other end. From this point, scribe a curve reverse to the top curve of the piece (the top curve having, of course, been derived from the shape of your mounting hooks). Next, cut very carefully along the line with a jigsaw remembering that both pieces are to be saved. Now, using this piece as a template, scribe in the opposite side of the ladder. Remember to have the dadoed surfaces facing each other when you're scribing, otherwise you'll end up with two left sides or two rights — whatever they'll be, they sure won't make a ladder.

Now scribe in the inboard cutout as shown. A 4″ high pad near the lower rung will act as a bumper against the hull, eliminating pinched toes between the hull and the rungs. The depth of the pad will of course depend on the hull curvature; one would be well advised to plan using the ladder amidships where this curve is the least drastic. Again, use one cut piece as a template to scribe the other.

The hand holds as shown are 1¼″ × 5″. These can be either routed or drilled-and-cut with a jigsaw. For the latter, drill the two

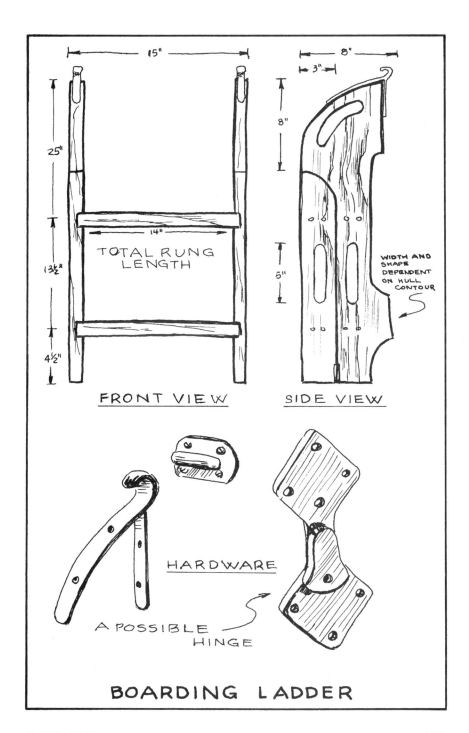

15"

25"

13½"

14"

TOTAL RUNG
LENGTH

4½"

FRONT VIEW

8"

3"

8"

5"

WIDTH AND
SHAPE
DEPENDENT
ON HULL
CONTOUR

SIDE VIEW

HARDWARE

A POSSIBLE
HINGE

BOARDING LADDER

hand hold ends with a 1¼″ butterfly bit, then join the holes with scribed curves and jigsaw out the rest.

Slightly bullnose all edges and sand thoroughly. Install the rungs with resorcinol glue. Glue, screw and plug. The whole unit is under too much strain to rely on glue alone. Wipe all excess glue now.

Install all hardware, then attach the padeyes to the hull with through-bolts or, if that's impossible because of limited interior access, use the most monstrous sheet metal screws that will fit. Bed them well.

Since, even folded, the ladder will occupy a space of almost 16″ X 25″ X 7½″, a good stowage space will have to be found. Hanging it from the underdeck in the forepeak seems to be ideal, with two padeyes housing the mounting hooks on the top, and a set of cabin hook-and-eye (eye on lower inboard rung, hook on underdeck) keeping it in place.

THE FINELY FITTED YACHT

The folding ladder can be used either doubled up (for boarding from a dinghy), or unfolded when required as a swim ladder.

BOARDING LADDER

ROPE BOARDING LADDER

A rope ladder is simple in every way imaginable: simple to make, to use, and to stow. The material should be either teak or mahogany. Some sailors advocate cedar, because it is light and inexpensive, but we're probably discussing three or four rungs maximum, and if you can't lift those with ease, you'd better stop right here in case you herniate flipping the pages.

To determine the number of rungs, measure the free board and divide by 10". Amidships is best, where the hull is most vertical, because it eliminates the need to hang upside down after the ladder has swung under the hull's pinched ends. Add a rung for below the water, unless you're a flying fish.

Mill 13/16" stock to 14" X 4" pieces, cutting out the hull-ward edge of each rung (see diagram) to prevent pinched toes. Two fine grooves, about 1/8", can be cut the length of the surface to act as a non-skid.

Radius all corners, and bullnose all edges. Lay out hole patterns for the rope, 3" in from all edges, and drill 3/8" holes. If you can drill relatively vertically, just mark one step and lay it on top of the others (making sure you align all edges), then drill through as many as you can at once. If your drill bit isn't long enough to drill them all at once, use a rung already drilled as a template for undrilled ones, to save marking time.

The rungs can be held in position along the rope in one of three ways. One way is to tie knots beneath each rung. This is a hit and miss affair, but with a little juggling, it can be done.

The second is to have wood pegs cross-driven through the rope and the rung. Drill 1/4" diameter holes and have them go past the inner edges of the rope holes by about 3/4". Round off the edges of 1/4" dowels, cover them with resorcinol, and drive them home. Trim off the ends.

The third method is to use marlin seizings; that is shown under the headings of "The Proper Mast Step."

Whichever you use, first cut 3/8" line to four times the total length of the ladder. If you are using knots, add about four inches extra per rung (1" per knot). A brass hook fastened onto the bulwark can hold the looped ends of the ladder line.

A word of caution: pull the ladder aboard every evening, or it will bang against the hull through the night.

THE FINELY FITTED YACHT

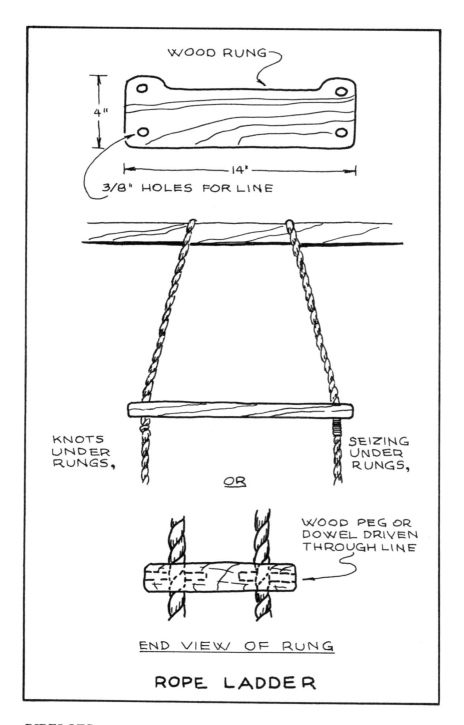

WOOD RUNG

4"

14"

3/8" HOLES FOR LINE

KNOTS UNDER RUNGS,

SEIZING UNDER RUNGS,

OR

WOOD PEG OR DOWEL DRIVEN THROUGH LINE

END VIEW OF RUNG

ROPE LADDER

THE DRAWBRIDGE

Anyone planning to cruise anywhere other than North America should equip his yacht with a drawbridge of sorts. The most common method of tying up from Papeete, to English Harbour, to Monte Carlo is the anchor-out, stern-to-the-seawall system which will usually mean a good healthy leap from ship to shore, unless one is willing to risk the yacht's transom and back down very close to the wall.

The simplest drawbridge consists of a long piece of 2″ × 6″, but these are usually too springy and insufficiently attached to the stern. Constructing a fine drawbridge is straight forward. It should be made of red cedar and mahogany, the first to cut down on the weight, the second to give strength. A plank 12″ in width and 5′ to 7′ in length should suffice on all but the most inebriated occasions.

To start with, construct a ladder from 1″ × 3″ mahogany stock. Let in all the rungs to 1/2″ depth and glue and screw them in place. Space the rungs on no more than 12″ centres. Next, rip some 1″ cedar stock into 2″ widths and glue and screw (or nail) to the rungs and to the frame. Just inside the last rungs on either end of the plank, drill holes and insert brass or stainless bushings with 3/4″ ID's into the sides of the frames, then run a piece of 3/4″ all-thread right through. The all-thread should be of such a length that it protrudes two inches past each side. Lock the all-thread into that position with a washer and locknut. Now, halve a piece of a 20″ length stainless wire, slip a 4″ length of good nylon hose over it, and splice a thimble onto each end. Slip the thimbles over the all-thread and lock them there with large washers on either side and a locknut on the outer end.

The stainless wire harness will be supported by a halyard. Together they hold up the outboard end of the plank. The inboard end will have to be secured by slipping the all-thread into eyebolts or whatever type of fitting can be adapted to the specific yacht. The one in the photo had the plank permanently hinged to the aft pulpit where it could be drawn up vertically to stow. Two stabilizing whisker stays will have to be run from the outboard end of the plank to the beamiest points of the stern (see photo). Any old dacron line will serve nicely; if you want to have it really tight, put it over the sheet winch and haul.

To avoid erosion of the outboard end of the plank by its rubbing against seawalls, fit it with metal skids or a set of plastic wheels (see photo).

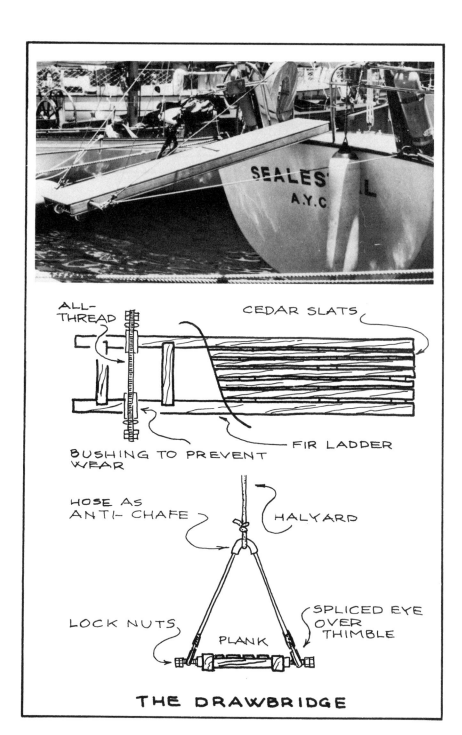

ALL-THREAD

CEDAR SLATS

BUSHING TO PREVENT WEAR

FIR LADDER

HOSE AS ANTI-CHAFE

HALYARD

LOCK NUTS

PLANK

SPLICED EYE OVER THIMBLE

THE DRAWBRIDGE

ADD-ON BULWARKS

Once in a while, a totally new and ingenious concept comes along, a completely multipurpose and visually striking idea, and Naval Architect Lyle Hess's bulwark is one of them. He designed it for his Bristol Channel Cutter, a fiberglass cum teak version of the English pilot cutters, in one of which, *Seraffyn*, the Pardey's have sailed the world.

The bulwark can be fitted onto most modern yachts with very little modification, and aside from giving any vessel a tastefully classic look, it can turn an open side deck into a cozy, safe walkway.

The key to the whole arrangement is the Hess-designed cast-bronze stanchion base. There is only one model, hence only one base-to-stem angle (90°), so different deck angles must be accommodated with shims of either wood or hard plastic. The castings can be purchased from the builder in Vancouver, Canada. On the cutter they've put eight per side, spaced about three feet apart.

The bulwark itself can be cut from 1″ teak, ripped to a width of 2¾″ and bullnosed with a 3/8″ bullnose bit; the top of the top piece only, the bottom of the bottom piece only. Since very few pieces of 25′ long teak exist, two starter pieces can be scarfed amidships where the teak can be doubled up for strength, and a hawse pipe installed for a springline to make the whole thing look more intentional. The foreward and aft ends of the bulwark are rounded and fitted with a sturdy 1½″ thick block, which again houses a set of hawse pipes. Three-eighth-inch carriage bolts have been used to fasten the bulwark to the cast bases.

Installation should begin by laying out the stanchion bases and fabricating the shims. Before bolting in place, apply generous amounts of polysulfide between the deck and shim, then the shim and base. Next, laminate the fore and aft lower pieces together using resorcinol glue and bolts, and tie the plank firmly to the stanchion with the help of lines. Now begin at one end to drill and attach the plant to the castings. Use a half-inch spacer between the deck and plank to attain uniformity. You will need the help of a friend throughout the operation to bend and hold the plank in place while you drill and bolt. Next, with the aid of a quarter-inch spacer, put the upper plank in place, gluing and screwing it to the backup plank amidships. Repeat on the opposite side.

One very nice feature of such a bulwark is that it allows one to make do without a genoa track. An endless strop of good wide tape to distribute the pressure can be made fast to the bulwark at any

THE FINELY FITTED YACHT

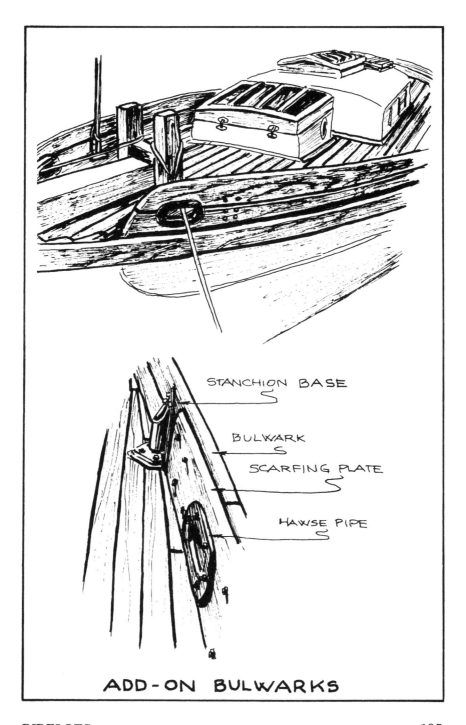

STANCHION BASE

BULWARK

SCARFING PLATE

HAWSE PIPE

ADD-ON BULWARKS

point (see photo) and a block can be shackled to it. Relocating the block requires only a loosening and sliding of the strop.

Whether varnished or oiled, the bulwark will be a feast for the eyes.

Solid block reinforces the end of the bulwark.

Endless strop replaces genoa track.

Bronze base for bulwark and stanchion.

CAPRAIL STEP

I have always been doomed by my own lack of inventiveness, through which *Warm Rain* has had beautifully varnished caprails, but nothing to protect them from people who insist on doing pirouettes on them in golf shoes. All wood rails should have at least one area for feet, an area that is protected as well as non-slippery. Most marine stores offer a chrome beast with rubber inserts, but this looks about as shippy as snow tires. Some marine antique places have cast bronze plates with molded-in non skid, but finding these is difficult at best, impossible at worst.

I found a nice solution aboard a Philbrooks yacht, as shown in the illustration. They used 1/4" teak stock with thoroughly rounded edges, attached to the caprail with wood screws. The idea seems quite good, although I see little need for such long lengths when a step of about 12", intelligently located at the most often used boarding point, near a stanchion or shroud for hand support, would suffice. Thin brass sheeting, treated with a meat mallet (sigh) as described in "Companionway Non-Skid," can provide very nice footing, physically and visually. Generous amounts of caulking should be used under both to eliminate any possibility of water retention, which will quickly destroy and lift varnish, defeating half the purpose for the step.

Other traditional non-skid procedures, like grooving (who wants to hack away at one's caprail) and woven rope mats (the varnish under these will rot away in no time), are not applicable here. The only other feasible solution, useful especially on yachts with bulwarks, is the installation of a cast bronze oval hawse pipe. These are usually wide enough to house a foot, and have the wonderful advantage of providing a perfect fair lead, as well, for a spring line; it is to be located somewhere on the amidships anyway, where stepping aboard will be facilitated by the beaminess of the vessel.

Narrow teak slats protect varnished caprail and make it less slippery.

CAPRAIL STEP

FOLDING WINCH CHAIR

Most sailboats have few places where one can really relax and fish. Granted, feet can be dangled over the caprail, but then lifelines will still be in the way of reeling arms, and when at anchor, the swinging of the boat will necessitate constant repositioning of the body. The winch chair is a perfect remedy, for it fits into a sheet winch, has a nice padded seat that swivels in any direction, and folds up into a 4″ × 14″ × 10″ space. If desired, a back can be fabricated for true comfort.

If you have Barient winches, you can purchase a gleaming naugahyde version for about $80. All others, make your own and pocket about $50 for a fine dinner.

The first step is to secure the most beat-up and/or the cheapest winch handle that fits your winch. Have a machine shop cut the handle off and weld what's left to a 6″ × 8″ plate. From 3/4″ plywood cut a seat with 2″ radius corners. The overall measurements are up to you, but remember, you're building a seat, not a sofa; 14″ × 10″ will accommodate the average derrière. Bullnose the plywood top and bottom to eliminate slivering. Drill eight holes of 1/4″ diameter in your mounting plate, centre it on the plywood, and using the plate as a template, drill your holes. Countersink them slightly and attach the plywood to the plate with 1/4″ bolts and capnuts. Give the wood a good coat of sealer. For padding the top, 1″ closed cell foam should be used. A tidy canvas slip cover can be made with a zipper in one long side. Don't forget to cut a hole in the centre of the bottom for the winch fitting, and reinforce it with double canvas, then hem it.

If you want the luxury of a hinged back, cut a piece of 1/2″ plywood to 6″ × 14″ with radiused corners. Now from 1″ plywood, cut two 14″ × 1″ strips and screw and glue one each to the back and the seat. See drawing. These will act as bases for the piano hinges and enable the thing to fold and stow flat. Install as long a stainless piano hinge as possible. The canvas cover will begin the same as for the backless version, but the back and seat covers should be sewn together at the hinge (inside) and a common zipper installed underneath, running the length of the hinge. Triangular pieces of doubled-up canvas, having leg measurements of 8″ and 6″ will have to be double stitched onto the seat and back part of the cover to act as a restrainer, preventing backward somersaults.

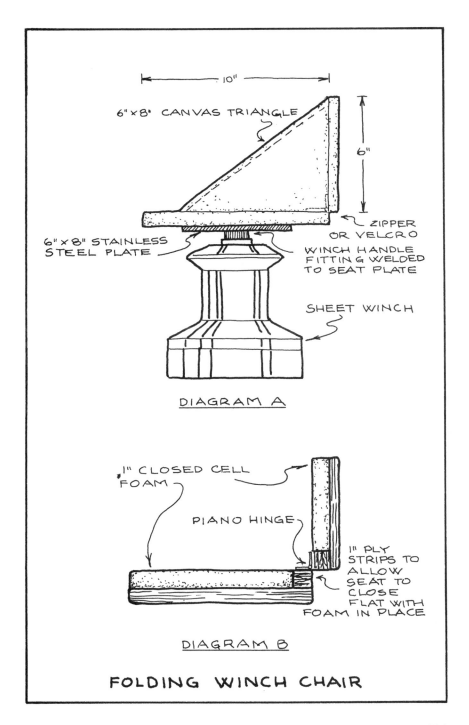

10"

6" × 8' CANVAS TRIANGLE

6"

6" × 8" STAINLESS STEEL PLATE

ZIPPER OR VELCRO

WINCH HANDLE FITTING WELDED TO SEAT PLATE

SHEET WINCH

DIAGRAM A

.1" CLOSED CELL FOAM

PIANO HINGE

1" PLY STRIPS TO ALLOW SEAT TO CLOSE FLAT WITH FOAM IN PLACE

DIAGRAM B

FOLDING WINCH CHAIR

EYEBROWS

No other item that can be produced with as little effort as teak eyebrows, brings about as drastic an improvement to your boat's exterior. Whether the deckhouse is fiberglass or painted wood, a single piece of teak requiring no more than one-half hour of annual upkeep, can visually lower and streamline it.

The piece can be milled from 1/2″ stock. Anything thinner would be difficult to plug and rather chancy to bend and twist without breakage.

The width need not exceed 1″. Length should be measured about 1″ from the foremost and aftmost end of the house, if simple cornerless eyebrows are contemplated. The use of a single length is most desirable. Splicing and scarfing are a pain at the best of times, and man hours are better spent looking for a longer piece. The ends should be well rounded and the whole thing radiused on all outside edges with a 3/8″ bullnose. This is most vital because, from time to time, eyebrows will be stepped on and slid from, and an unradiused corner will, in most instances, crack and splinter. To assure additional prevention of this, the eyebrow should be installed at least 1″ down from the top of the house to be a bit more out of the way of feet.

The next step is to pre-drill and countersink the eyebrow on 10″ centres. A dry run should be made. Remove the countersink from the drill bit and, using a pre-drilled hole as a guide, drill the first hole in the cabin side, then put a screw in it and tighten. Gently. This is no place to build up your muscles. Proceed to drill and screw all holes one by one to make sure everything fits and aligns. Back off all screws, remove the eyebrow, then clean both the cabin side and the eyebrow of dust. Lay a fine bead of Dolfinite on the eyebrow and screw it back in place. Again be gentle or you'll cause the thin narrow piece to explode. Remove excess Dolfinite with a sharp stick. Resorcinol glue and plug.

The more ardent will advocate eyebrows that fully circle the cabin. I know; I used to be one of them until I sat down one morning to fabricate my first compound corner. Later that night, with froth of madness on my lips and a piece of wood resembling a shriveled banana in my hand, I decided on straight eyebrows only.

　　　　　THE FINELY FITTED YACHT

Wanderer IV

Warm Rain

SHORE POWER CORD AND RECEPTACLE

Contrary to what Momma may have told you, running an extension cord into a yacht through a portlight is just not done in better circles. An investment, painful as it is, must be made and the proper shore power cord should be purchased, along with an even more proper shore power receptacle.

Most male receptacles are well made, and waterproof enough when closed, but some I have seen are simple-mindedly fabricated, with the hinges so badly aligned that screwing the lid on can be done only with the help of a sledge hammer. When you are buying the receptable, check it a few times to be sure it functions properly.

Installation should be with the hinge up, so that the natural tendency of the cap will be to fall into a closed position. Even though a rubber gasket is usually supplied with the receptacle, I feel it prudent to run a bead of sealer around the edges after installation. Do not forget to plop a few drops into each bolt hole as well. Do check this seal once every few months, for the receptacle undergoes tremendous forces each time the cord is yanked out.

A note with regard to cord purchase. Be sure you buy complementary hardware. Not all cords fit all receptacles acceptably. Since most are of the twist-lock variety, one should try to buy only those mated perfectly, for poorly fitted ones will require undue force, which, in due time, will cause the prongs to bend and break.

The receptacle should be installed out of the way of feet. I feel a location well aft, as far from normal spray as possible, is preferable to a place in the bow, regardless of the inconvenience this may cause at the home dock.

The female plug should be fitted with a short lanyard that can be run under the hinge pin of the receptacle and tied to hold the plug firmly in place.

When not in use, the cord should be neatly looped and stowed where it won't be bent or nicked by anything heavy or sharp.

THE FINELY FITTED YACHT

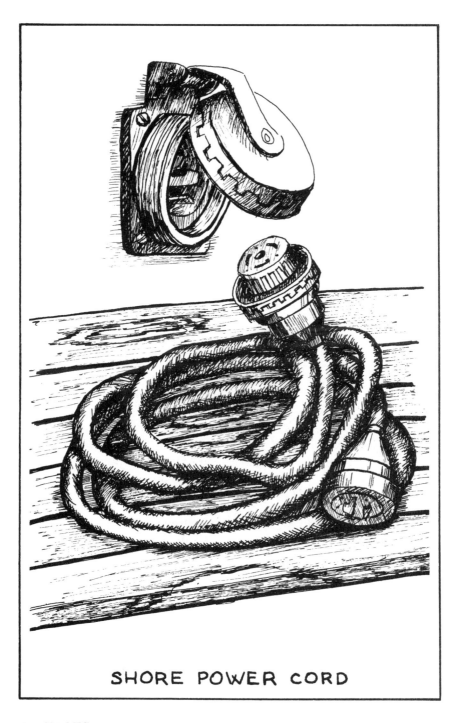

SHORE POWER CORD

SIMPLE SHOWERS

What a wonderfully exhilarating feeling it is to sail into a new anchorage, wash the sea salt and sweat salt from your skin, then sit on deck and just gaze at the sunset. I probably teeter on the brink of insanity as far as cleanliness is concerned, but I just cannot empathize with those people who think that cruising gives them license to stink. Having a shower aboard need not involve hot water tanks and electric pumps and great luxurious shower stalls. Quite the contrary: the simpler the better. The following are but two of the ingenious and extremely inexpensive systems I have found aboard yachts. In almost all cases, preheating water on a stove is step one.

The Cockpit Bucket

The cockpit is of course the most ideal place to hook up a shower. Most have drains, and all are surrounded by materials which will not be hurt or marked by spraying water. Privacy can be gained by lowering the cockpit awning or even more easily by sitting down. If you're a gadget lover, you can rig a nylon curtain (the supple kind like spinnaker cloth are the easiest to stow) by putting a grommet in each of the four upper corners of the curtain and cutting two lengths of plastic battens or poles of bamboo to act as diagonals. Poke their ends through the grommets and suspend them from the boom by means of a lanyard tied at the point of crossover. If you're short of headroom, haul in on the topping lift.

The simplest source of water is of course a bucket; it's very cheap, very easy to fill, and with a slight modification most pleasant to use. The modification involves drilling a hole in the side of a plastic bucket and gluing a threaded flange over it with contact cement. With a male adapter, a plastic valve, the type that's used on a garden hose, can be threaded into the flange. This will enable you to shut the water off while lathering up or looking for the soap. In this way a good shower can be had with as little as two quarts of water. The bucket can be suspended from the boom as well. Installing the spigot on the bottom of the bucket would certainly result in its breaking off after only a few bangings down.

The Spray Tank

Surplus and hardware stores sell portable brass or copper tanks of one or two gallon capacity used commonly to spray insecticides into fruit trees. These are equipped with their own pumps which, with a few strokes, pressurize the tank, and will actually give a very

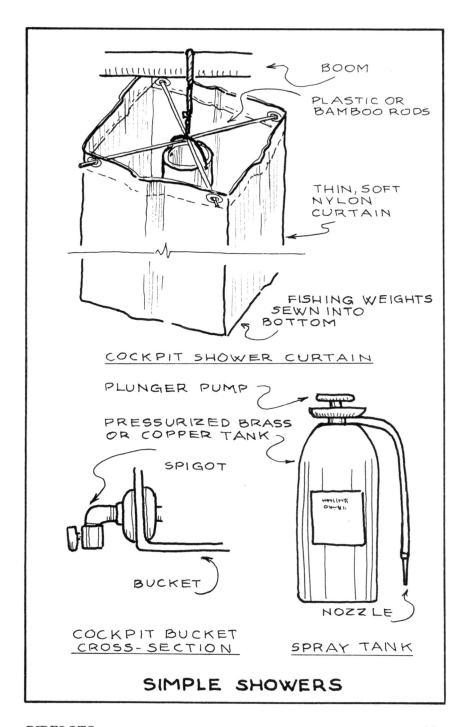

BOOM

PLASTIC OR BAMBOO RODS

THIN, SOFT NYLON CURTAIN

FISHING WEIGHTS SEWN INTO BOTTOM

COCKPIT SHOWER CURTAIN

PLUNGER PUMP

PRESSURIZED BRASS OR COPPER TANK

SPIGOT

BUCKET

NOZZLE

COCKPIT BUCKET CROSS-SECTION

SPRAY TANK

SIMPLE SHOWERS

even and powerful spray. The great advantage of this unit is that it can be filled with water and placed directly on the stove for heating. For greatest water savings, this should be a two person system to free the bather's hands to economize the rinsing.

The Built-In Hand or Electric Pump

If a way can be found to install a shower pan below decks, in or very near to the head, thought may be given to installing a pump (on the head counter if it's a hand pump, and inside a cabinet if it's electric) permanently and equipping it with a flex-hose shower nozzle. The curtain utilized would be similar to the one used in the cockpit, but the grommets could be replaced by snaps which fit into their counterparts on the overhead. The head sink can be filled with warm water from the stove, the free end of the hose from the pump submerged in it, and then the pump can be activated.

Aboard *Warm Rain* we have the most profound shower of them all. The most vital parts are: a tea kettle and Candace. I sit quietly on the cockpit floor while Candace pours warm water over me from the kettle. The spout enables her to refine her aim. The water is guaranteed to be a perfect temperature every time, because she knows full well that when I'm finished, it's her turn.

Oh paradise!

ANTI-CHAFE METALS

Wood is precious stuff. Not only does it drain the pocket initially, but it requires long hours of maintenance; so an attempt should be made to guard and protect it in areas that undergo heavy traffic or wear.

The least demanding and possibly the most visually attractive solution is to use small patches of thin brass sheeting. It can be purchased at most metal salvage or metal fabricator shops, and, since it's mostly sold by weight, a few dollars worth can be made to go a long, long way. It is also a friendly material to use. It can be cut very neatly with tin snips, it can be bent evenly around almost any curve, and it can be held in place by attractive brass tacks.

The most frequent and severe abuse is doled out by ground tackle gear. Both anchor and chain grind and chip away wood mercilessly, so a careful survey should be made around the bow, and all involved areas should be covered with the protective brass. On yachts with bowsprits, the entire area between, and just fore and aft of, the anchor rollers should be so protected. Not only does this part suffer from stray anchor chain, but the swiveled flukes of plow anchors bang and gnaw away at it as well.

As mentioned under other headings, the protective plating is most useful on companionway steps and often stepped-on parts of the caprails. Frequent caprail wear also occurs where fender lines are recklessly hung over the rail. A few small plates and a few harsh words to the crew on the topic of hanging fenders in their designated spots in future, should overcome this problem.

Fairly nasty damage is often caused by dinghies. As they are hauled aboard, the keel strip (brass or aluminum) is often allowed to ride right over the caprail. Since dinghy hauling is more often then not done in the exact same area, a short run (about $8''$) of brass sheeting here could add a lot of protection.

Below decks, the weaponry used against wood is much less formidable, usually taking the shape of boating shoes, so only in the few spots where nervous foot tapping occurs (like under chart tables) should protective measures be taken. Two spots that have suffered on *Warm Rain* are the searails on the counters directly outboard of the companionway ladder. It seems that on an excessive heel, anyone going below takes the most vertical route possible by stepping from the companionway on to the counter. Bring on the brass sheeting.

canvas/
sails

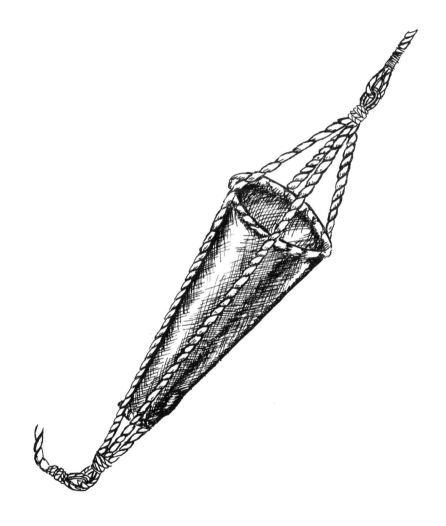

SEWING CANVAS

The equipment you need for sewing with canvas are: tape measure, tailor's chalk, large compass or string and thumbtack, scissors (preferably a bent handled type such as Fiskar's light weight stainless steel, made in Finland, never need sharpening), straight pins, iron, sewing machine with zigzag attachment, size 16 or 18 needle, mercerized heavy duty thread — size 30-40-50, grommets and grommet setter, pencil and string, polyester thread, and a hot knife (a sharpened soldering iron). Following are the basic sewing terms and procedures:

Wrong and Right Side of Material

Simply put, the right side of the fabric is the side you wish exposed, and the wrong side is the one that will not be seen. On most fabrics, this is easily discernible, but on canvas, it doesn't make much difference, unless you are using the very heavy acrylic painted type, as is used for lawn chairs (or beach chairs) and awnings.

Seam

The seam is the point at which you stitch to arrive at the finished size of your product. This is done by placing two pieces of material together, *right* sides together, and stitching on the *wrong* side of the material.

Seam Allowance

This is usually 5/8" (1/2" is used in this book's projects) more than the desired finished size of your product. This allows enough material to finish the raw seams in a number of ways, to prevent ravelling.

Hem

This is the finished edge of any fabric that is not enclosed in a finished seam, such as edges of curtains, tablecloths, and in clothing; skirt hems, shirt sleeves, etc. With a hem allowance of any given width, from 1" to 3", press the raw edge 1/4" to 1/2" to the wrong side of the fabric, then fold to the desired hem length, pin or baste, and stitch.

Seam Finishes

To prevent undue ravelling, there are several finishes for inside seams: a) stitch 1/4" from the raw edge and pink (with pinking

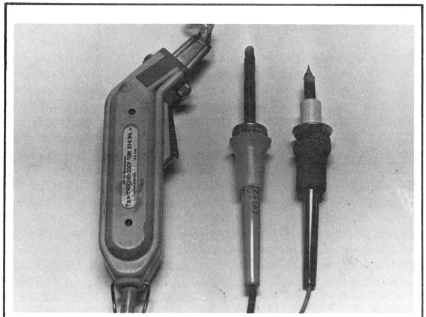

Various hot knives, all cut rapidly and seal edges (as they cut) in synthetic fabrics like acrylic and dacron.

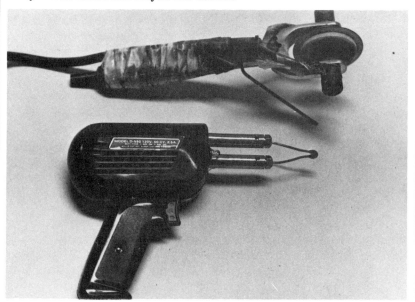

Hot knives. Lower one is soldering gun with sharpened tip.

shears) the raw edge, b) using your zigzag attachment, zigzag your raw edges, being sure the needle enters just inside the raw edge. This can be done to each individual seam edge, or the two seam edges can be held together and zigzag stitched as one, and c) on the wrong side of the material, press the seam open, then stitch through seam allowance and material 1/4" away from the seam on either side. This, of course, will show on the right side of the material, but it looks very nice, especially if another colour thread is used for contrast.

Fastening a Seam — or Back Stitching

If your sewing machine is equipped with a reverse stitch, lower the needle into the fabric about 1/2" from the beginning of the seam. Depress the reverse lever and stitch in reverse until the needle reaches the beginning of the seam. Release the lever and stitch forward. At the end of the stitching line, stitch backward for about 1/2". This secures the thread ends. If your machine does not stitch backward, place the needle 1/2" in from the starting point and stitch forward for 1/2". Leaving the needle in the fabric, lift the presser foot and turn the fabric around on the needle. Lower the presser foot and stitch over the first stitching, continuing to the end. At the end, again pivot the work on the needle and stitch back for 1/2".

Dart

This is a stitched tapering fold in a garment, or any other sewn item, to bring in fullness where not needed. With tailor's chalk, mark on the wrong side of fabric the size and position of your dart. Remember, if you want only 1" darts, fold the material 1/2" (right sides together). Start stitching at the outer edge of the fabric, tapering to a point, then backstitch. If the dart is very large, it can be cut close to the stitching and pressed flat; otherwise, press the dart to one side of the fabric.

Stress Points (Reinforcing)

If you are to be using grommets or heavy duty snaps, the points where these are affixed should be reinforced. To accomplish this, simply cut a square of material 2" larger than your snap or grommet. Place it on the wrong side of the material where the snap or grommet is to be affixed. It can be held there by a basting stitch (either hand or machine). When attaching the snap or grommet, do so through both thicknesses. This will strengthen the stress point. This method can also be used anywhere ties are to be attached at any point in the fabric, such as the edges, corners, etc.

Grommets

This is an eyelet made of metal (preferably brass) used to strength or protect an opening, or to insulate or protect something passed through it. These come in various sizes and must be attached with a grommet setter. They both are available from any fabric shop.

Pin Basting

This is simply placing your two raw edges together (right sides) and pinning every 4" or 5" to prevent the material from slipping when stitching. Place your pins perpendicular to your line of stitching. This way you can stitch right over the pins and remove them after the stitching is completed.

More experienced persons will machine baste (temporary stitching), which means placing your two pieces of material under the presser foot and stitching, while holding the raw edges together with your fingers. When doing this, you should use the largest stitch your machine will make (usually six stitches to the inch). This will enable you to pull out the basting threads when the finished seam has been completed. Do not backstitch machine basting. Before removing, clip threads every few inches.

Grommet set left to right: mallet, grommets, setting block, hole cutter and setter; sitting on plastic cutting pad.

Tension

This is probably the most important control on your sewing machine. The best tension for one fabric may not be correct for another. The required tension depends upon the stiffness of the fabric, thickness of the fabric, numbers of layers of fabric being sewn, as well as the type of stitch you are making. It is best to test the stitching on a scrap of fabric you are using, before starting to sew. The location of the top tension adjustment varies on different machines, while the bottom tension is almost always in the bobbin. A perfect straight stitch will have threads locked between the two layers of fabric with no loops on top or bottom (see Diagram A). If the upper thread is too tight, decrease the tension (see Diagram B). If the upper thread is too loose, increase the tension (see Diagram C). Bobbin tension requires adjusting less frequently than the upper thread tension. When adjusting the tension on the bottom case, make *slight* adjustments with a small screwdriver. To decrease the tension, turn the screw counterclockwise; to increase the tension, turn clockwise. But remember, only a quarter of a turn, or $45°$, is sufficient.

Here is a good way to check your tension balance: be sure to use polyester thread of the same size on the top and on the bobbin, and a sharp, correctly sized needle for the fabric you are sewing. Begin with a full bobbin. Set the stitch length for about 12 stitches per inch.

Fold a 6″ square of fabric in half diagonally, forming a triangle. Make a line of stitching 1/2″ in from the fold.

1) If seam is puckered — both tensions are too tight.
2) If the bottom thread lays on the fabric — tighten the upper thread tension, and repeat test.
3) If the top thread lays on the fabric — loosen the upper thread tension, and repeat test.

Grasp the stitching and pull with a snap to make the threads break.

1) If both threads break — tensions are balanced.
2) If neither thread breaks — both tensions are too loose.
3) If upper thread breaks — loosen top tension.
4) If lower thread breaks — tighten top tension.

Both threads do not have to break at the same place, but they should break on the same snap.

Needle, Thread, and Fabric

The size of the needle should conform with the size of the thread, and both should be suitable to the fabric. Here is a good rule

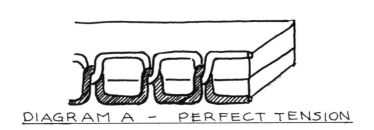

DIAGRAM A - PERFECT TENSION

UPPER THREAD TOO TIGHT

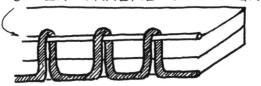

DIAGRAM B - DECREASE TENSION

UPPER THREAD TOO LOOSE

DIAGRAM C - INCREASE TENSION

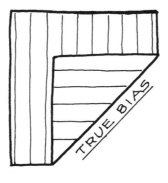

TRUE BIAS

SEWING CANVAS

to remember: the heavier the fabric (e.g. denims and canvas) the larger the needle size (18) and the lower the thread size (30-50, heavy duty); while the sheerer the fabric (silk, tricot) the smaller the needle size (9) and the higher the thread size (80-100). The average sewer rarely uses anything but the medium (thread size 60 and needle size 14) which will sew cotton and cotton blends, shantung, pique, seersucker, velveteen, light weight wool, linen, leather and vinyls.

Casing

A casing is a tunnel to hold either a cord or elastic. If it is to be placed within a circular piece of material, the raw edges of the material should be folded $1/2''$ toward the wrong side of the material and basted in place. This basting will allow you to pull up and gather any excess fullness when turning your casting hem. When you have turned the hem and adjusted the gathers evenly (remember, your casing hem must be at least $1/4''$ to $1/2''$ larger than the material it is to encase), begin stitching, leaving an opening of $2''$ or $3''$ to insert your casing material. If you are inserting elastic, fasten a large safety pin on one end of the elastic and use it as a guide to feed the elastic through the casing. Fasten a large safety pin to the other end of the elastic so you will not lose sight of it, and pull it through the entire casing. When the two ends meet, simply sew, and then close your opening by stitching.

A casing on a flat piece of material is very simple. Determine what you want to encase (cording, rope, etc.), the length of the casing area, and the width of the material to be encased. Cut a strip of material the length of the area you are casing, and an inch to two inches wider than the material to be encased. Lay this strip of material on the area where you want your casing, pin baste, and stitch along each side — leaving each end open. Be sure to fasten or back stitch your stitching. You now have a long hollow tunnel into which you can thread your cord, using the large safety pin; or in the case of rope, if it is stiff enough, tape the end with scotch tape and push through by hand.

Casing for Piping

If you are making cushions and wish to put piping around the boxed edges, you will need to make casing out of bias strips. The bias is a line diagonal to the grain of a fabric, i.e. a line at a $45°$ angle to the selvage. This will enable the fabric to stretch and will make a much smoother tube when sewn over cord. Strips cut out of the lengthwise (warp) or cross grain (woof) of any material, will not stretch and will look bulky when used around corners. (Some of the newer materials will stretch on the cross grain.) See diagram for bias. Bias tape can be bought ready-cut at fabric shops in almost any colour, thus eliminating the need for cutting your own, and if used in a contrasting colour, is very attractive.

Turning Corners

When turning a straight corner, be sure to leave the needle in the fabric, lift the presser foot, and turn the material 90°. Lower the presser foot and continue sewing. Turning round corners is a little more difficult, but can be accomplished by sewing very slowly and easing your fabric around the corner without raising the presser foot.

String and Thumbtack Compass

If you wish to cut out a perfectly round piece of material, a simple compass can be made out of a piece of string, a pencil, and a thumbtack. To make a string compass, cut a piece of string about 5″ longer than the radius of the circle you wish to draw. Tie one end of the string to a pencil near the point. Stretch the string taut and tie a knot at the other end so the section between the pencil and knot is the distance of the radius. Place the canvas on a large flat surface and thumbtack the knot at the centre point of the circle you wish to draw. Holding the pencil perpendicular to the canvas, swing the pencil around lightly to make a circle. Then cut your perfect circle.

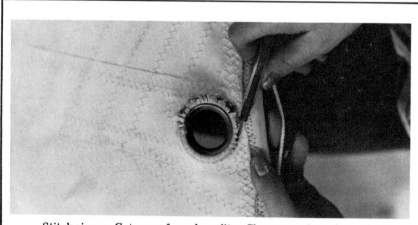

Stitch ripper. Get one of good quality. Cheap ones lose their edges.

CANVAS AND SAILS

COCKPIT CUSHIONS

I'm often accused of having terribly ascetic and Spartan concepts; if this is true, it takes on embodiment in my idea of the proper cockpit cushion. I confess that cushions are mandatory, for no minimally fleshed person can take sitting on a hard teak or fiberglass seat for longer than an hour, all fakirs excluded, but I do not believe in ungodly slabs of foam coated with horrendous naugahyde upon which you sweat in the sun and slither in the rain. Their mammoth size makes them awful to stow and, on deck, they have so much windage that once the wind wedges beneath them, they're overboard in a flash. We have, for some years, used small closed cell pads whose 1" thickness provides as much cushioning as 4" of the cheaper stuff.

We made our foam slabs small; 16" X 12", but have compensated by making the canvas covers for them in unifying sections. This way, as many as three individual pads can be sewn into one long compartment-like sleeve, providing economical usage under varying requirements. If three people require cushions (usually on the same side), the whole thing can be opened up and each person receives one 1" thick foam pad. If two need cushions, one flap can be folded under avoiding the last piece flapping in the wind. One person will, of course, receive double thickness, but then that's life. If only a single crew needs a cushion, the thing can be folded into a triple layer and that, let me tell you, is comfort. A very pedestrian ribbon can be sewn on either end, so the cushions can be tied firmly if used as a single seat.

Acrylic or treated canvas for the cover, I feel, is infinitely superior to naugahyde. It has much greater friction, giving security on a heel and it does not become a sweat pad in the sun nor an ice rink in the rain. It will, of course, get soaked, but it dries as fast as any foul weather gear, so that's no argument. The fact that it lets water through is undeniable, but then, closed cell foam doesn't absorb water, so the cover will dry quickly indeed.

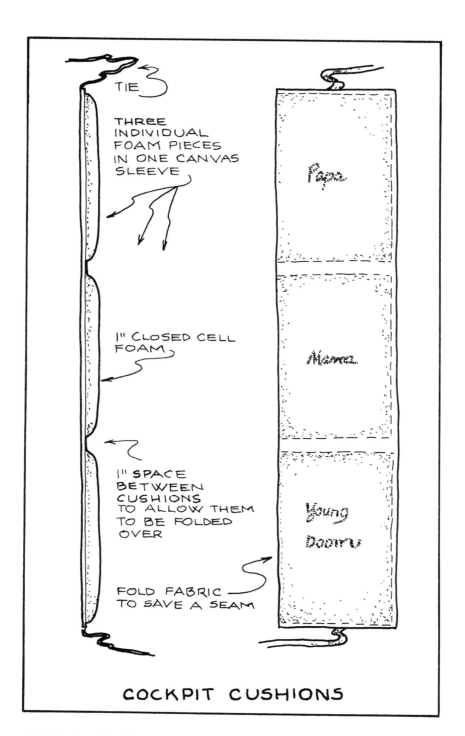

TIE

THREE
INDIVIDUAL
FOAM PIECES
IN ONE CANVAS
SLEEVE

1" CLOSED CELL
FOAM

1" SPACE
BETWEEN
CUSHIONS
TO ALLOW THEM
TO BE FOLDED
OVER

FOLD FABRIC
TO SAVE A SEAM

COCKPIT CUSHIONS

CANVAS AND SAILS

COCKPIT CHART STOWAGE

Charts in the cockpit can be disastrous. When most needed, they fly overboard or end up under hurrying crew's feet, triggering graceless somersaults. But charts abovedecks are often compulsory, and at all times great fun to use, and even the tiniest of cockpits (ours measures 30″ × 42″) will have space for the following clever item.

It is a large canvas pocket that can be snapped or *Velcroed* onto the aft wall of the cockpit. The size of the chart pocket should be 11″ high by 18″ wide. You have to fold a chart in half again to get it in but this can easily be done without permanent creasing. An additional pocket of 2¾″ × 11″ should be added to the outside for stowage of parallel rules, and another 2½″ × 7″ pocket should be sewn for one-handed dividers. If desired, the back portion can be extended to create a flap. Sew three small bits of Velcro onto it (one in, each corner and one in the middle) to help keep your flap shut. The hemming and sewing is identical to previous projects. A piece of Velcro in each top corner, or a snap in the same, should be enough to provide adequate fastening to the cockpit wall.

None of the above is meant to suggest use of this cockpit stowage as an uninterrupted daily procedure, but it would be handy from time to time.

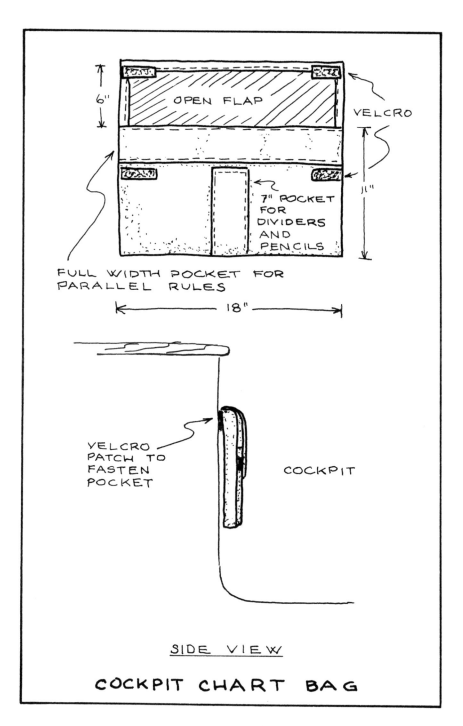

6"

OPEN FLAP

VELCRO

11"

7" POCKET
FOR
DIVIDERS
AND
PENCILS

FULL WIDTH POCKET FOR
PARALLEL RULES

18"

VELCRO
PATCH TO
FASTEN
POCKET

COCKPIT

SIDE VIEW

COCKPIT CHART BAG

WINDLASS COVER

Windlasses are very expensive items that should be rinsed of salt water often and protected by a canvas cover whenever possible. Their gears should be kept well-oiled and salt free.

Since most windlasses are a rather ambiguous combination of curves and points and cylinders, two choices are left to the yachtsman. The first is to fabricate a simple drawstring bag which can be pulled over the windlass and tightened. This is a rather pathetic example of ingenuity, but it works.

Those more civilized can undertake designing and fabricating a canvas Chinese puzzle.

For the typical windlass, with a wildcat for chain and a drum for line, two cylinders, with one end of each closed (much like a winch cover), can be made to cover those parts.

If the windlass has no other eccentricities, each side can then be covered with the addition of two more pieces of canvas. These will have to be fitted with a goodly number of darts to allow for the curve of windlass housing, and a hole in each to allow for the wildcat and the drum. First, cut the holes as tight as possible, then continue darting around until you have a proper fit. Cut a slit below the wildcat to allow the cover to be put in place over the chain, as it goes through the deck fitting. Hem the slit as well as the rest of the cover, then sew the two cylinders in place.

Lastly, sew a piece of dacron tape to the bottom of each side of the slit. These will be ties to keep the cover from sailing off into the sunset.

Any windlass will require a cover made up of a rather ambiguous combination of curves and points and cylinders.

WHEEL COVERS

All sorts of these exist with zippers and snaps and flaps and hinges, when all you need are two pieces of canvas and a drawstring in a casing (heavy elastic will do as well).

Cut a circular piece equal in diameter to your wheel plus $1''$ seam allowance ($1''$ instead of $1/2''$ because this will be double stitched). Next, cut a piece equal *in length* to the wheel's circumference ($2\pi r = C$) plus $1/2''$ seam allowances at each end. Make the width equal to one-third of your wheel's diameter, plus $1''$ for the double-stitched seam allowance, plus $2''$ for a casing. Fold one long edge under $1/2''$, then another $3/4''$ for the casing and run two rows of stitching close together. Hem the ends of the casing and the rest of the ends as well. Now, stitch the other side of the straight piece to the edge of the circular piece, with the wrong sides of both pieces out. Use double stitching. Using the safety pin with line or elastic, run same through the casing. Sew the elastic ends together after you've turned the cover right side out, slipped it over the wheel, and established how tight the elastic will have to be to: a) allow the cover to slip over the wheel, and b) pull the cover tight once it's in place.

If you're using a drawstring, cut the line so it's equal to the wheel's circumference plus $10''$, and after feeding it through the casing, splice the ends together to prevent them from hiding in the tunnel.

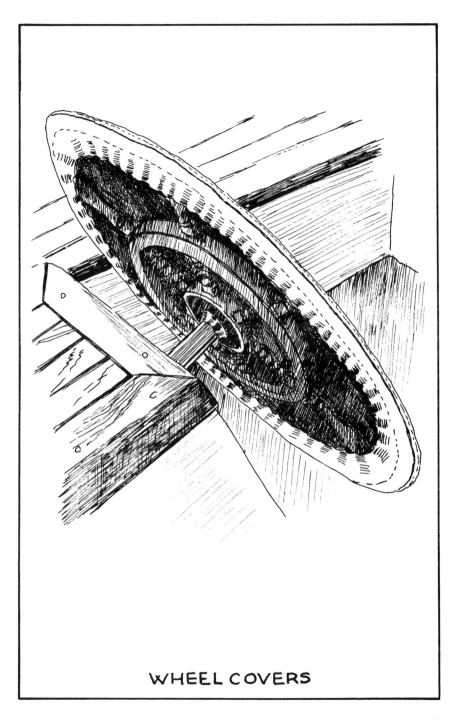

WHEEL COVERS

SEA ANCHORS

Since their highly publicized use by Captain Voss in his circumnavigating dugout canoe, sea anchors have become standard equipment on all yachts engaged in offshore cruising. They are indeed recommended for those venturing even only 15 to 20 miles from the coast, for if forced to run shoreward in a gale, the sea anchor may be the only thing that will save the yacht. Eric Hiscock in *Voyaging Under Sail* recounts when, near the Tonga Islands, a sea anchor, trailed from the stern, slowed them from 5½ to 1½ knots, and enabled them to steer safely a little across the wind, and thus avoid an island and a reef which lay to their lee.

A good sea anchor should be built at least as heavily as the yacht it's trying to slow. The size has been discussed and disagreed upon freely, and although some people carry and use sea anchors with 20" diameter mouths on seven ton yachts, one has to accept the fact that with resistance of such caliber, tremendous forces will be put upon the yacht's fittings. A 10" or 12" opening would seem more reasonable; then, if additional drag is required, warps can be trailed as well. This gives much more flexibility in the amount of drag produced, than the all-or-nothing monster sea anchor.

The most important point of design is the rope framework which must be sewn to the anchor along its entirety. Some sea anchors, whose short bridle extends to the hoop only, are likely to have short life spans as well. The rope hoop can be replaced by a metal one to ensure against collapsing. Use only cotton canvas for the anchor itself, for it has infinitely better chafe resistance than acrylic. The rope should be at least 5/8" braid. Metal thimbles must be spliced into eyes, uniting bridle and towing line. A streamlined lead weight of at least eight ounces should be sewn into a pocket to keep the anchor from riding along the surface. The tripping line is optional and, indeed, often a hindrance, for it fouls around the sea anchor, rendering it useless.

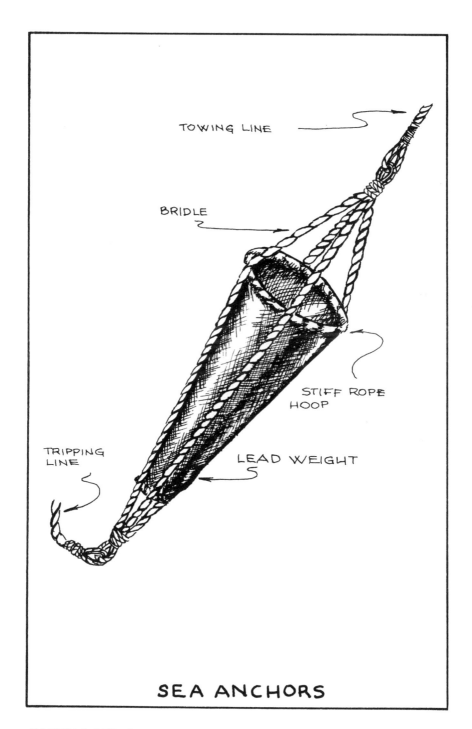

TOWING LINE

BRIDLE

STIFF ROPE
HOOP

TRIPPING
LINE

LEAD WEIGHT

SEA ANCHORS

YE OLD CANVAS BUCKET

An absolute necessity on all yachts is the old canvas bucket. No substitutes exist. A tin bucket is a weapon that turns on its master at every step, or steps on its master at every turn, whichever is easiest for it. The jet age plastic buckets are a joke. One needs only to fasten a line on them and heave them overboard while underway at even a pathetic speed of two knots to witness the separation of the stupid wire handle from the stupid plastic pail just in time to wave goodbye to three stupidly spent dollars. A varnished wooden bucket would be charming, but it has even more ferocity than its tin uncle. Hence, the canvas bucket.

It folds yieldingly into the size of a respectable hankie and even on the rampage, it can do little more harm than a wet noodle.

It should be of 10″ diameter and 12″ height. It should be made of heavy duck canvas so it will stand up when full of water and it must have a stiffening hoop around the rim to keep it from collapsing when being pulled aboard. A piece of canvas 32″ × 15″ will be required for the sides, and a 12″ diameter piece for the bottom. A wooden mast hoop was used in the old days of sailing ships to provide the rim, but those being rather scarce nowadays, one has the option of steaming a piece of 1/4″ × 3/4″ elm, white oak or ash and monel stapling it into a hoop, or resort to a piece of soft plastic of about the same dimensions that can easily be bent and either glued or through-bolted using a cap nut to eliminate any sharp points. The hoop should then be sewn into the canvas and two grommets installed opposite each other below them.

Half-inch line, carefully halved with a thimble seized onto it will do nicely as a bale. Again half-inch line of at least an 8′ length should be used to splice in as a bucket rope. Fit a large knot into the end to protect your handiwork from disappearing into the sea. Some people suggest using a loop around the wrist, but that to me seems a bit drastic, for it can lead to severely bruised limbs or worse — a man overboard. Not even a bucket of your own handiwork is worth that.

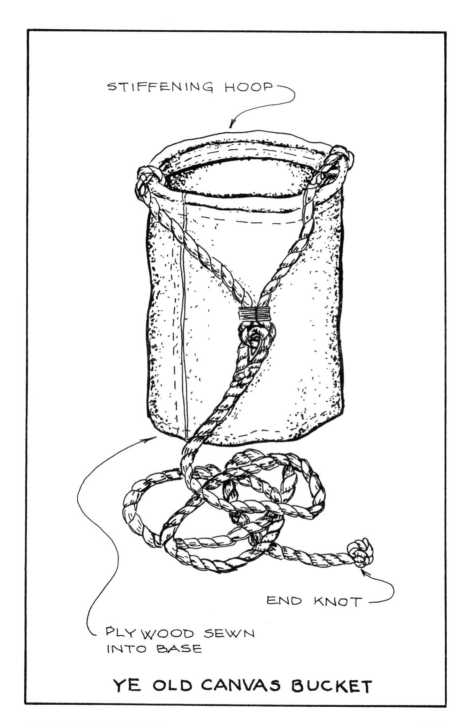

STIFFENING HOOP

END KNOT

PLYWOOD SEWN
INTO BASE

YE OLD CANVAS BUCKET

COMPASS CAP

Compass cards are delicate things, easily damaged by strong sunlight therefore, they should never be exposed unless they are being used. When not in use, a compass cap should be kept over them. Those fortunate enough to have magnificent binnacled, brass shrouds, please flip the page now. The mortals, get out your scissors and sewing kit.

Cut a circular piece of canvas whose diameter is 4″ greater (plus 1/2″ allowance for each seam) than that of your entire compass. At the four points of the compass rose, pinch in your canvas (the sewers call this darting) until you have formed a little dome or cap. Pin and sew these darts. Now, cut two identical rings of canvas whose outside diameter is 1½″ greater than that of your compass ring, and its inside diameter is 1/2″ greater than that of your newly fabricated cap (plus seam allowances). Sew the two rings together. Turn the rings right side out and fit the little cap inside the little ring and sew them together. Cute little beanie, n'est-ce pas? You'll need either Velcro or snaps to attach the cap to the cabin side or compass mount. If your compass is of the vertically mounted variety, three snaps will do, one on top and one on each of the sides. If it's mounted horizontally, use four. Spray with Scotchguard for waterproofing.

Well done, girls. Tomorrow we'll be making tiny underwear for the tiny seacocks.

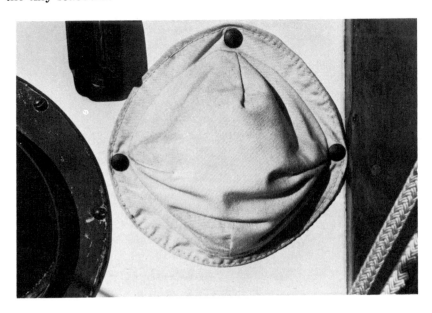

THE FINELY FITTED YACHT

LEE CLOTHS

Any yacht contemplating offshore cruising will have to have its berths fitted with lee cloths, or you might as well just make your bed on the cabin sole (because that's where you're going to spend most of the night anyway); at least then you won't wake up the rest of the crew with your body going thud, thud.

Cotton canvas of moderate weight will work very nicely, although if much voyaging is to be done in the tropics, netting can be substituted to facilitate air circulation.

The cloths should have a finished height of between 14″ and 18″, and an overall length of 20″-25″, with the sides tapering toward the top, again, to facilitate air flow.

Sew the cloth with 1/4″ turned under a 1″ hem, and fit the two top corners with grommets. Install the cloth onto the berth top with screws and finishing washers fitted every 8″ along the bottom edge. Fit the grommets with light lanyards. Lash them to a snap shackle or 1″ piston hank which will, in turn, be snapped into open padeyes screwed to the underdecks.

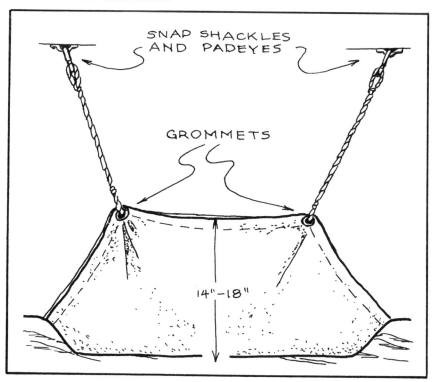

WINCH COVERS

It is recommended that winches be disassembled and greased once a year, and it is suggested that they always be covered when not in use.

The traditional winch covers have a hidden elasticized sleeve inside them, which hold these otherwise leisurely looking little bags in place.

Cut the top circle to the circumference of your winch plus the seam allowance. Cut the side out of a single piece. Make its width the height of your winch (plus seam allowance, plus 1″ for hem), and its length, the circumference of your winch plus two seam allowances of about 1/2″ each. For the little sleeve that lives inside, cut a piece the length of your winch's circumference, plus twice 1/2″ seam allowance, and a width of 3″, plus 1/2″ seam allowance, plus 1½″ for a casing for the elastic.

Begin sewing by stitching the casing. Next, sew the seams of the small sleeve together, then, using the ancient method of the safety pin in the elastic, push the pin in one end of the casing and out the other. Don't cut your elastic to length until you've finished this operation, otherwise — since your elastic will have to be about 6″ shorter than the length of your casing tunnel to function properly — you will forever lose the end of the elastic and end up like a dog chasing its tail. When you've done the threading, gather the casing until its circumference equals that of the narrowest part of your winch, *then* cut the elastic and sew its two ends together, then sew the mouths of the tunnels shut.

Next, sew the seams of the outside full-length sleeve, and hem it. Turn both sleeves wrong side out, set the short one *outside* the long one, then sew them simultaneously to the circular top piece. Now, turn it right side out, slip it over your fist, and give it a little cuddle.

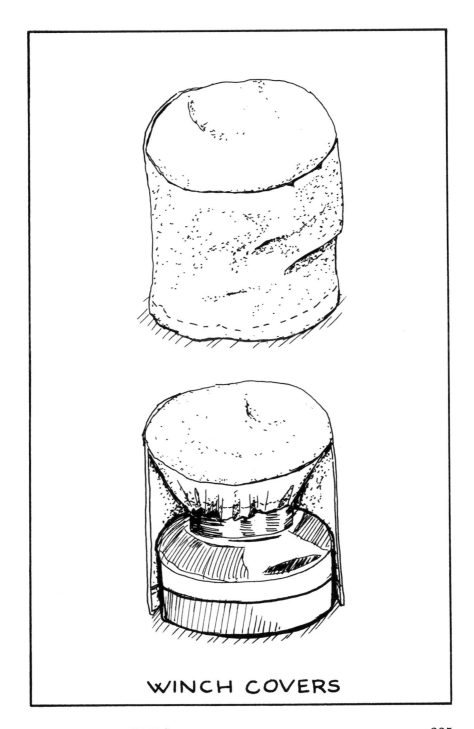

WINCH COVERS

HATCH AND SKYLIGHT COVERS

These are so boringly simple to make that anyone refusing to make them deserves to sand and scrape his woodwork twice a year. They come in very handy over skylights or transparent hatches, both as curtains for privacy, and as screens from the hot sun.

For a hatch with even height sides all around, you will require only one piece for a top, and one long piece to make up all sides. Cut the top to fit snugly, leaving 1/2″ seam allowance all around, then cut the sides so they cover the woodwork completely down to the deck, allowing for seams (1/2″) plus for an elasticized tunnel along the bottom (2½″). Sew the pieces together, leaving an opening for the elastic (or drawstring if you feel you want more secure control), then insert same, and fit in place.

For a gabled skylight, you will have to make the sides out of four separate pieces: two rectangular ones, and two the same shape as the skylight's ends. Ho hum.

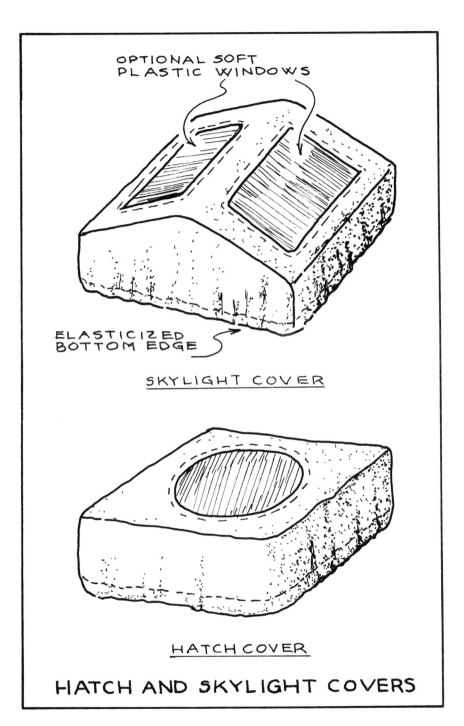

OPTIONAL SOFT PLASTIC WINDOWS

ELASTICIZED BOTTOM EDGE

SKYLIGHT COVER

HATCH COVER

HATCH AND SKYLIGHT COVERS

LIFE BELT STOWAGE

Since most man overboard units are comprised of a number of items like strobe lights and sea anchors, a proper quick release stowage place must be made for them. Hooking all the assorted items over life lines and gallows, like so much laundry, is woefully inadequate.

The bag in the illustration contains stowage for all required pieces, and since its front flap can be released by simply pulling on a lanyard, all gear can be plopped quickly overboard.

First, gather up all your items and try fitting them into the open central part of the horseshoe ring. This can probably house the strobe light, dye markers, whistle, sea anchor, and the needed line as well. If this is indeed the case, then a bag can be made from two pieces of canvas.

Cut a piece of canvas as shown, leaving 1/2" for seam allowances, and 2" for hems. Hem all edges. Sew the bottoms of the sides to the sides of the bottom, but leave the front flap unattached. It should be hemmed. Now cut a piece to form the restraining belt. This should have a finished width of 3", and a length that will let it hang over the front flap by about 2". The other end of the belt will be sewn to the edge of the back.

Sew a small brass padeye into the center of the top of the flap 1" from the edge, and sew two similar padeyes, one on each square flap, 1" from its edge. Place grommets to accommodate the eyes, in corresponding spots of the belt, and the front flap.

Lastly, fit a single piece of light lanyard with three pull pins, which you can bend from good stainless wire; put all your gear into the bag, and close the flap and the belt by running the pins through the padeyes. Sew one end of the lanyard to the bag; the other end will be tied to the last pin. Sew and lash the bag (top and bottom) to the lifelines or gallows, close to the helmsman.

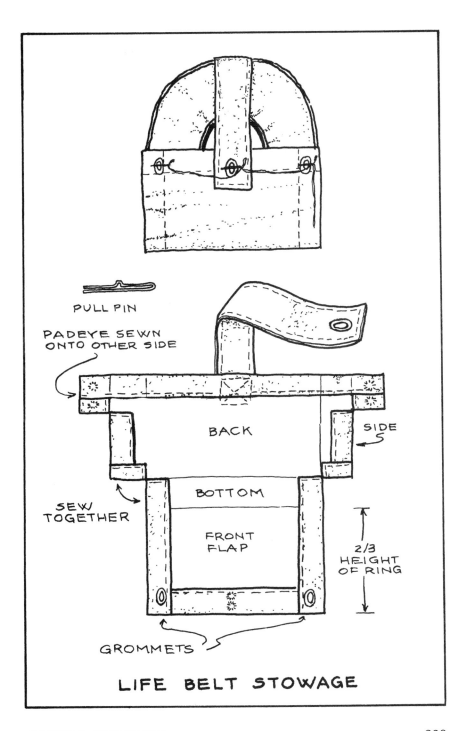

PULL PIN

PADEYE SEWN
ONTO OTHER SIDE

BACK

SIDE

SEW
TOGETHER

BOTTOM

FRONT
FLAP

2/3
HEIGHT
OF RING

GROMMETS

LIFE BELT STOWAGE

WEATHER CLOTHS

These are slabs of canvas strung between the top lifeline and the caprail in the area of the cockpit, traditionally, to keep the crew out of wind and spray, and, more recently, to write the yacht's name upon in horrendously large letters.

They should be so designed, that they run from the stanchion just forward of the cockpit to a stanchion just aft of it. Anything more would just impair visibility, and give precious little in return.

The cloth should be cut to a final size that allows for a $1/2''$ to $1''$ space between it and the lifelines, stanchions, and caprail. This way it can be pulled taut, otherwise, it will chatter horribly in any sort of blow.

Put a generous hem of $1\frac{1}{2}''$ all around, into which grommets for lacing can be set. Cut and sew your major grommets only to begin with, that is, one grommet for the top and bottom of each stanchion, then lash the weather cloth in place, to see how it sets. Now, mark in location for additional grommets (if any), along the bottom, making sure you don't put one in unless you have a place to fasten it to. If no other guiding factors are present, place a grommet every $8''$ along the top and sides.

At this stage, mark out a $6'' \times 10''$ area over which a pocket of the same size can be sewn. This will be a perfect spot for odds and ends, like sailing gloves and caps and sunglasses. If you plan to stow things there on a semi-permanent basis, sew a flap over it, and secure it with a piece of Velcro.

Lastly, set all your grommets, and lace the weather cloth smartly into place.

For yachts with stern pulpits, a more complex cloth can be made to surround the entire pulpit (see photo).

THE FINELY FITTED YACHT

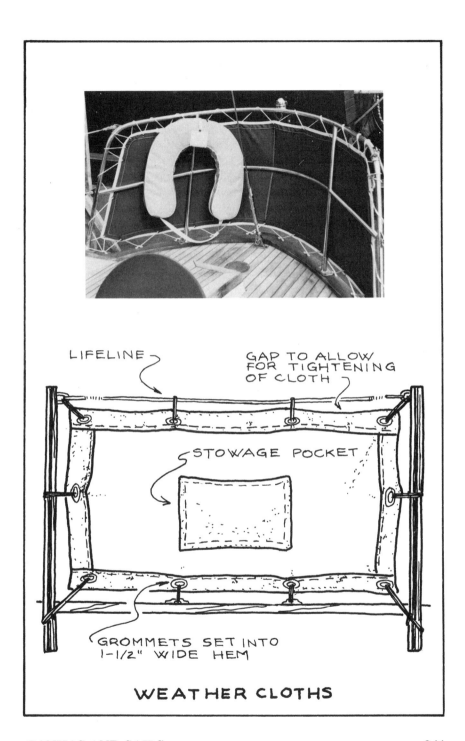

LIFELINE

GAP TO ALLOW
FOR TIGHTENING
OF CLOTH

STOWAGE POCKET

GROMMETS SET INTO
1-1/2" WIDE HEM

WEATHER CLOTHS

DINGHY STRAPS

For dinghys stored upside down, a set of cross straps should be fabricated, as mentioned in the section on dinghy chocks.

The least expensive and most functional material to use is the surplus seatbelt. If you can get it without the buckles, so much the better, for you'll just have to cut them off anyway.

A set of dinghy straps will be made up of two long pieces and two short ones, as shown in diagram. If properly measured and fitted, only a single knot holding the two short pieces together will need to be untied to loosen all the straps to the point where they can be slipped off the dinghy. To be able to accomplish this, the lines (a) and (b) which are fed through the padeyes to connect the long strap to the short one, will have to be of adequate length (between the padeye and the short strap) to allow the long strap to slip back and over the aft corner of the dinghy. This is not nearly as complicated as it sounds, so just go to it and think it out.

At each end of each strap, allow four inches of extra length to be folded back and stitched, leaving a loop for the lines, as in diagram.

Be sure that your two short straps are short enough so that the lanyard, which makes up the single knot atop the dinghy, can be pulled to tighten all the straps firmly. If the straps are so long that they meet — or worse yet, overlap — no matter how ferociously you tug at your lanyard, your straps will still just dangle like soggy spaghetti.

LINE (a)

LINE (b)

STITCHED
LOOP FOR
TIE-DOWN

DINGHY STRAPS

WINDSAILS

In the tropics, some sort of wind funnel system must be installed over a hatch if the belowdecks are to remain habitable. The complicacy of the design depends on one's philosophy of cruising, that is, whether he spends most of his stationary time at anchor or at the dock. If the yacht will be primarily at anchor, a very simple funnel can be made facing permanently toward the bow, since the anchored yacht points predominantly into the wind.

If you prefer being lashed to the land, you'll have to pay in hours invested in fabrication, since you will have to be prepared for the wind coming from any, and all, directions.

Simple

The more aesthetically inclined can attempt to fabricate a six-foot high cowl vent out of canvas, or better yet, spinnaker cloth. The latter is much easier to stow. Those less ambitious can make a square funnel, as in the diagram.

Cut three identical sides (if your hatch is square), with the bottom edges equal to the opening of your hatch, plus $1/2''$ seam allowances, and $1\frac{1}{2}''$ hem allowances. Cut the fourth side to only half height, leaving the top half open for the funnel's mouth. Cut a perfectly boring square piece for the top, with seam allowances on three sides and hem allowance facing the bow. Sew a couple of batten pockets diagonally to the underside of the top (look at any of your sails for proper construction), and cut a couple of discarded battens to fit. Radius the corners very well to keep them from coming through the canvas. Stitch a loop onto the centre of the top to allow for attachment of a halyard, which will be holding the windsail aloft.

Now, stitch all pieces together, attach two snaps in the bottom hem of each side, and screw the reciprocal part onto the outside of your hatch coaming, as close to the deck as possible. The installation of the snaps at such a low point is mandatory, to allow your elasticized mosquito screen (see that section) to be slipped over the top of the coaming. If this is made impossible by your specific coaming arrangement, a permanent screen will have to be sewn into the bottom part of your windsail.

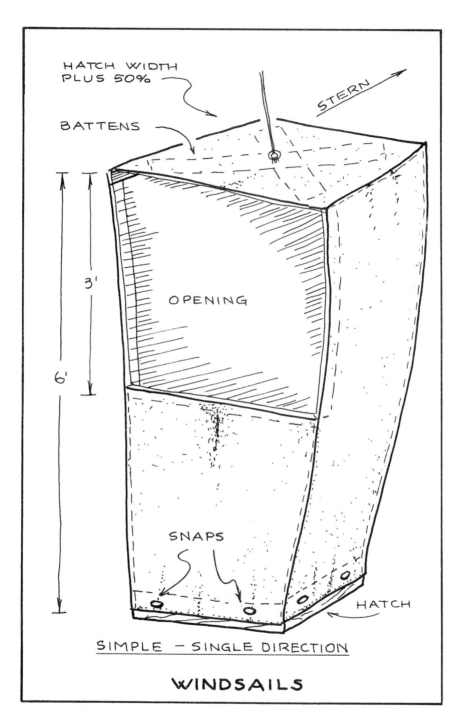

HATCH WIDTH PLUS 50%

BATTENS

STERN

3'

6'

OPENING

SNAPS

HATCH

SIMPLE — SINGLE DIRECTION

WINDSAILS

The More Complex One

Cut four pieces to the shape and size of the half piece in the simple windsail. Stitch these together as above and fit with snaps.

Cut and stitch the square piece for the top with batten pockets, as above, but do not stitch the pockets into place just yet.

Now, measure the diagonal at the tops of the bottom pieces, then measure the diagonal of the square top. Using these measurements, cut two diagonal baffles as in diagram. Add 1″ extra width in one of them for a seam allowance, because this piece will be cut in half and stitched to the centre of each side of the one piece baffle, to form a cross. Hem and stitch these pieces now. Next, stitch the newly sewn cross to the top, then stitch on your batten pockets. Now, let the cross about 10″ into the sides and stitch along the four corners. Use double stitching, for much strain will be experienced by the windsail.

With the bottom of the windsail snapped to the hatch coaming, and its top held aloft by a halyard, it is now ready to funnel air belowdecks, regardless of the wind direction. Oh, the good life!

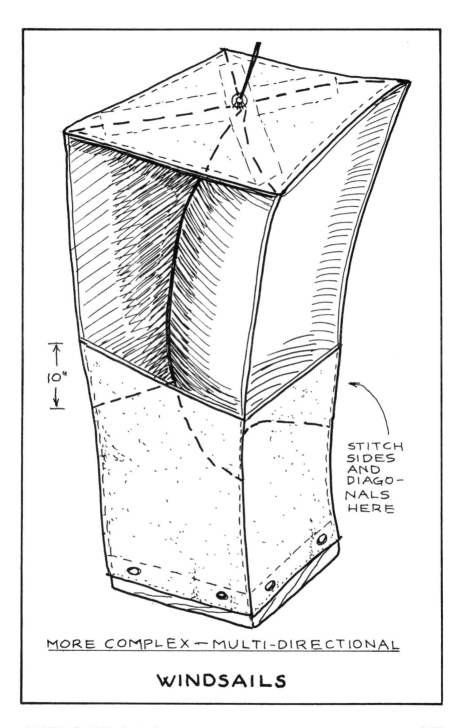

10"

STITCH
SIDES
AND
DIAGO-
NALS
HERE

MORE COMPLEX — MULTI-DIRECTIONAL

WINDSAILS

THE BEST BOSUN'S CHAIR

Dangling 45' high in the air can decidedly be fun, provided the dangling is done from an intelligently designed and conscientiously constructed bosun's chair, and not a pathetic contraption that some deprived individual pilfered from the swing of a neighborhood's playground.

A bosun's chair is called that for a purpose, so one should not settle for a bosun's bench, or bosun's stool, or even a bosun's swing. To be perfectly accurate, it should be called a bosun's *high* chair (about 45'), and as its namesake, it should be fabricated with a back, and sides, and a front, and a part that goes between the legs, so you won't slip out in a careless moment and totally destroy your freshly varnished skylight.

Construction

The chair is basically a double walled canvas sling (not acrylic, because it will chafe through in no time), with a 3/4" piece of plywood in the seat to act as a stiffener. Cut a piece of 3/4" plywood to 10" X 16", radius all corners, and round all edges like you've never done before. Sand to remove all slivers.

Next, cut two identical canvas pieces to a length of 50" and a width of 12". Now, leave the middle 16" at the cut width, and trim the end flaps so they'll form triangles with ends shaped, as in the diagram. Leave 1" all around for double seam allowance. Next, get some heavy dacron scraps from your sailmaker and cut them to two identical pieces, as shown. Now, lay the four pieces together into a four layer sandwich — with the dacron as the bread and the canvas as the baloney — then stitch them all together with two rows of stitches, one 1/4" from the edge, the other 1/2" inside that. Leave one 16" edge of the seat unsewn so you can turn the whole sling rightside out and slip the plywood into place. Now, fold the seam allowances under on these last 16", and double stitch the seam closed.

An additional bit of reinforcement can be had by running a 2" nylon belt (like a seatbelt of a car) between the dacron pieces, from one tip through to the other.

Next, cut and sew two, or four, canvas piggyback pockets onto each side flap, being sure to leave each pocket a goodly belly of 3" extra, so getting hands in and out when aloft will be made possible. A number of small pockets is infinitely superior to one large one, for then standard rigger's tools can have their own special compartments,

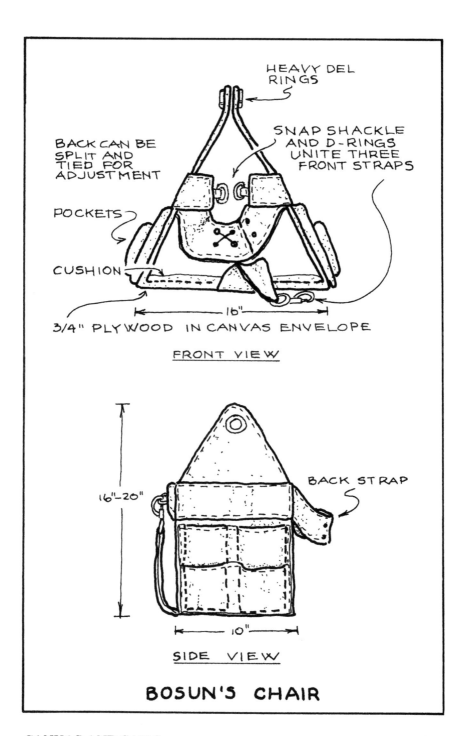

HEAVY DEL
RINGS

BACK CAN BE
SPLIT AND
TIED FOR
ADJUSTMENT

SNAP SHACKLE
AND D-RINGS
UNITE THREE
FRONT STRAPS

POCKETS

CUSHION

16"

3/4" PLYWOOD IN CANVAS ENVELOPE

FRONT VIEW

16"-20"

BACK STRAP

10"

SIDE VIEW

BOSUN'S CHAIR

eliminating lengthy nerve-racking searches. Sew the pockets on most carefully, for you'll be going through six layers of fabric.

Now, cut a strip of canvas to a 6" width and a 50" length and fold and sew it into a 3" × 50" piece, most of which will run clear around the sitter much like a belt. It will be sewn to the outside of both sides of the chair just above the pockets, and will meet in the front, along with a short piece coming up vertically from the bottom of the seat. The vertical piece will consume about 10" of the belt, while the rest can make up as large a horizontal belt as your corpulence dictates. Make it a comfortable fit, remembering that you'll be getting in and out of it, as well as just sitting in it.

Where the three ends of the belt meet in the front, you can either sew them permanently (and securely) together, or install a "D"-ring in the end of the horizontal belts and a snap shackle in the end of the vertical belt.

Lastly, and most importantly, take the chair to a sailmaker and get him to install a good size Del ring (1" hole is minimum) into the tip of each side, for the hauling-halyard to run through. This is done on a machine that exerts 2000 lbs. of pressure, so don't try to do it yourself with pliers. May you dangle happily ever after.

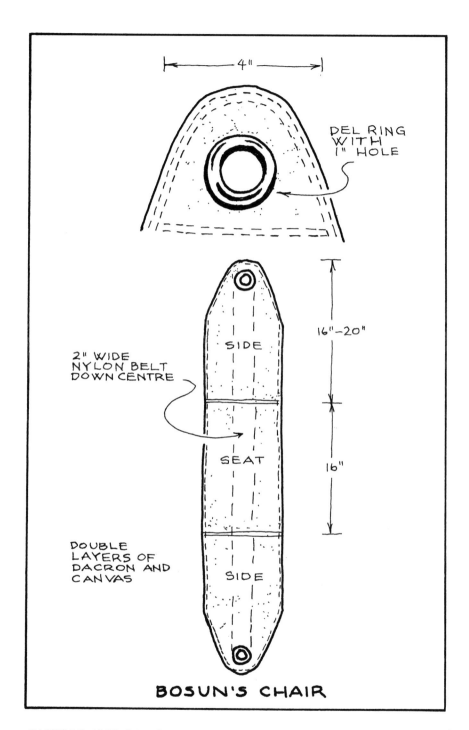

4"

DEL RING
WITH
1" HOLE

16"–20"

SIDE

2" WIDE
NYLON BELT
DOWN CENTRE

SEAT

16"

DOUBLE
LAYERS OF
DACRON AND
CANVAS

SIDE

BOSUN'S CHAIR

WINTER AWNING

Unless one lives in the absolutely perfect climate, that's not too hot and not too cold, not too dry and not too wet, and not too dusty nor too smoggy, one best get the proverbial lead out, along with some needle and thread, and begin sewing an awning. The owner of a yacht with even minimal teakwork — say hatches and caprails — and a painted wood or fiberglass coachhouse, will save himself annual maintenance time of at least one week, by having the yacht covered during the months that it is seldom used. Aside from reducing cosmetic demands, the awning will lengthen the life of the yacht considerably, by keeping rain out of joints and seams. It will also reduce the number of times teak needs to be sanded or cleaned with caustic chemicals, as well as hide paint, gelcoat and metals, from the elements.

Support

To be effective and have a lengthy life, an awning must be kept tight, that is, well supported, and well tied down. The boom is an obvious base for the aft section of the awning. The forward section can be held up by the reaching pole, or even the boat hook. Either can be run from a mast fitting and have its forward end held up by a halyard. This should not be done literally, for then a cutout, collar, etc., will have to be made; instead, the halyard can be tied to a loop sewn into the awning, while the reaching pole can be tied to the bottom of the same line *below* the awning. See diagram. This will, in effect, remove any pull from the awning itself, because the weight of the pole is being borne by the loop.

The outboard edges of the awning will be held up by lifelines, while the front can be supported by the bow pulpit.

Fastenings

As mentioned, the awning must be kept tight, or it will flutter and beat itself to death in a single windstorm. *Warm Rain's* awning did just that, after being left untied in two places. The fluttering acrylic was chaffed through in three spots after a day and a half long storm. Just attaching sandbags to the perimeter of the flaps of the awning is woefully inadequate, for the wind will *lift* the awning's great surface and chafing will begin. The best solution is to have a generous number of tiedowns sewn to the underside of the awning. These can be located anywhere a firm base can be found, e.g. stanchions, boom, pulpits, and rigging. Each tiedown should be sewn

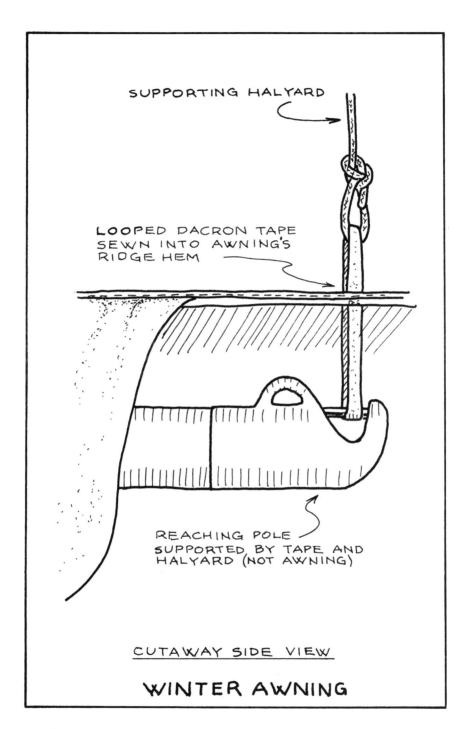

SUPPORTING HALYARD

LOOPED DACRON TAPE
SEWN INTO AWNING'S
RIDGE HEM

REACHING POLE
SUPPORTED BY TAPE AND
HALYARD (NOT AWNING)

CUTAWAY SIDE VIEW

WINTER AWNING

to a sizeable patch to distribute the forces somewhat on the fabric. Don't scrimp. Make the patches as large as possible; you'll have lots of scrap pieces around, so use them. If you're a patch connoisseur, you may consider using heavy dacron instead of canvas or acrylic, for dacron is measurably more chafe resistant than the other two. Any sailmaker will happily inundate you with his scraps.

Chafe Spots

Wherever the awning makes contact with a hard point, a sacrificial chafe patch should be used similar to those used with tiedowns. Again, make the patches large. An awning is usually of a monstrous size, and seldom will it be secured in the same place twice, so a patch should be large enough to allow for any wandering. *Warm Rain's* chafe patches measure 14″ X 14″ over a stanchion top of 1″ diameter. Why not? You can never be sure. Use dacron.

Sectioning

The more utilitarian minded will design his awning in three sections. One section will cover the yacht from the mast to the bow, the next will cover aft from the mast to the rear of the cockpit, and the last piece will cover what's left. In this way, the central piece can double as a sun or rain awning by itself, if so required.

Awning tiedown with large dacron chafe patch.

THE FINELY FITTED YACHT

Joints

Where the three pieces of awning join, an extremely secure, yet quite quickly releasable, attachment should be made. Snaps have no place in a large awning, for they continually corrode and eat away the fabric around themselves. Besides, they usually come apart when you least want them to, and more often than not, they will snap together only after you've dislocated your finger joints three or four times while pressing desperately.

Twist locks in canvas covers are an hilarity. My friend, Gary Storch the sailmaker, told me a story of a two-piece awning held together in such a fashion. From underneath, twist locks look much like snap locks, or at least they did to one fervent crew member, so he grabbed one wing of the awning in each hand, and proceeded to undo the "snaps" with one quick yank; and by God, he did!

Heavy Delrin zippers reinforced with ties, make the most positive joints for, apart from providing an even, noncorrosive attachment, they limit all possibility of spotty joints with large open

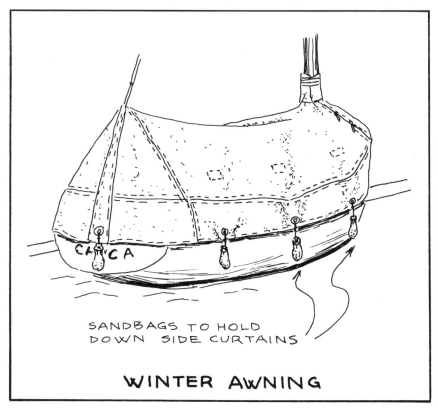

SANDBAGS TO HOLD
DOWN SIDE CURTAINS

WINTER AWNING

spaces between, where water and dirt can enter. The ties should be placed on either side of the zipper (one pair every two feet or so), and the bulk of the fore and aft strain should be taken up by them; the zipper should just more or less keep out the wind. It should be fitted with double pulls, to facilitate closing and opening in both directions.

Since zippers are not waterproof, one should consider having a Velcro-fitted flap hinged from one section of the awning to the other.

Openings

One would appear somewhat tragic standing outside one's beautiful new awning with no way to get in. A short flap about 20″ wide, running 20″ above the lifelines, zippered on its foreward and aft edges, and hinged along the keel line, would show prudence. To gain entrance, the flap could be rolled up and tied in the open position with a tiedown sewn to the awning just above it.

The location of the opening is, of course, important. One's immediate reaction is to place it so it can be used in conjunction with the lifeline gate, and that's all well and good, unless, of course, the gate is misplaced to begin with — or even worse — nonexistent.

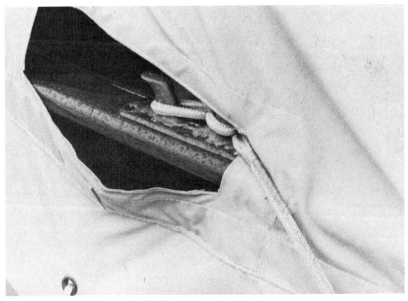

Well reinforced cutout.

In that case, most people would tend to place the opening amidships, especially if the yacht had severely pinched ends, and this would be a mistake. Granted, it is most comfortable to board where the yacht is snuggled to the dock, but once you're in under the awning, doubled over on the side deck, staring at your feet, what will you do? What *will* you do? Waddle — that's what — and that's no fun, especially if you're lugging something heavy, like groceries or an albatross, so *don't* cut the entrance amidships, unless you have a centre cockpit. Then it's okay, but otherwise, cut it somewhere aft, so you can keep your graceless waddling to a minimum.

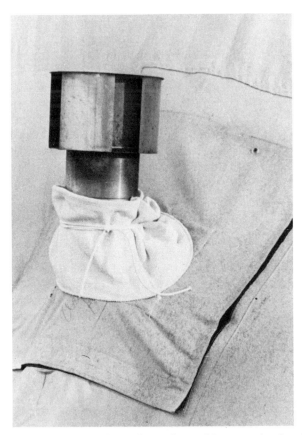

Asbestos collar makes a safe choker to keep chimney-cutout watertight.

If you have a three-hundred-year lease on a dock, and you're not really going anywhere for any length of time, by all means save some money and some labour, and cut an entrance on one side only; if neither of the above, cut two.

Cut Outs

Most well brought up yachts have mooring lines holding them to docks. Areas will have to be cut out of the awning to accommodate them. Like your chafe patches, your cutouts should be big and extremely well reinforced, to allow for chafing. See photo. The finest fitted yacht would probably have its cutout trimmed with a little strip of leather.

Chimney Outlets

In northern climates, awnings do a marvelous job of keeping in heat as well as providing a semiwarm, dry area, to hang umbrellas and galoshes. But to have this warmth in the first place, you need a reliable diesel stove, and diesel stoves have chimneys, which need to stick their noble heads out through the awning. If a standard cutout is made, water will gush in to inundate the deck and house, and the awning will flutter and ripple around the pipe, resulting in pathetic draft. So, a little flap should be fabricated, and held in place with a set of zippers or Velcro, and the centre of the little flap should be fitted (finely) with a little boot made of asbestos. See photo. The diameter of the boot should exceed the diameter of the pipe by 6″, again to allow for slight shifting of the awning.

Flap Hold-Downs

The sides, or flaps, of the awning should be kept from banging around. As mentioned, the awning itself must be secured to the tops of stanchions, etc., with tiedowns, so the securing of the usually short flaps should be no great undertaking. Also, as mentioned, snaps and twist locks should be avoided, as should desperate attempts to elasticise the flap bottoms. Spur-grommets should be set every four feet or so (reinforced with a patch), and made fast with a short line, to either whisker stays or sandbags.

If a bowsprit is present, a single line can be laced through from side to side, below the bowsprit.

The sandbags need not be large, 4″ diameter bags, 8″ high, with a drawstring around the top, should be plenty. A small trick should be used in sewing the bags: instead of cutting out small pieces for say, ten bags, just cut and sew one long tube, 4″ in diameter

THE FINELY FITTED YACHT

Sandbag hold-down.

Collar for shroud outlet.

CANVAS AND SAILS 259

(remember 1/2″ seam allowances on either side of the piece), with a length of ten times 10½″ (8″ for bag, twice 1/2″ for seam allowance, top and bottom, and 1½″ for the tunnel for the drawstring). When sewn, simply cut the long tube into 10½″ sections, sew in the bottom, and finish the top.

General Design Points

Cutouts in the top of the awning should be as few as possible. The topping lift (and the staysail stay as well on cutters), should be disengaged and stowed against the shrouds.

The mast collar should be generously high, with ample length of tape (about 20″ each), to be wrapped tightly around the collar. The ends of the tape (halving a single 48″ piece is preferable) should be stitched to the top corner of the collar, so an inadvertent funnel won't be created.

Shroud-cutouts should be fitted with hinged flaps, and held in place with Velcro. Make the width of your cutouts at least 3″, to allow for some fore and aft play. Fit the bottoms of the flaps, as well as the piece they adjoin, with grommets and ties, or the weight of the sandbags will pull the flap away.

Slopes

Be sure all surfaces are generously sloped or water will settle in areas and, with the pressure of its weight, either tear the awning, or at least drip through.

Laying-Out and Assembly

Fabricating an awning of this nature takes more time to design than to sew. Remember, you can't just fold bits of cloth every which way and hope they'll fit. They won't. You will have to create a great number of panels, each of them accurately measured and laid out on a diagram. Don't be frightened by all the odd shaped pieces you come up with, just measure and label all sides accurately. Run your fabric fore and aft, to lessen the number of small pieces required. Allow 2″ or more per hem; 3″ if grommets are to be set in them. It would show prudence to cut out and machine bast only the centre section of the awning first, then take it down to the boat, fit it, and mark in all needed adjustments. The centre section is the easiest to make, having the fewest triangles, so it's the best one to practice on.

Some people recommend sewing all the bits and pieces (ties, reinforcements, etc.) onto each small part before incorporating it into a section. This is folly. Indeed, none of the above should be even

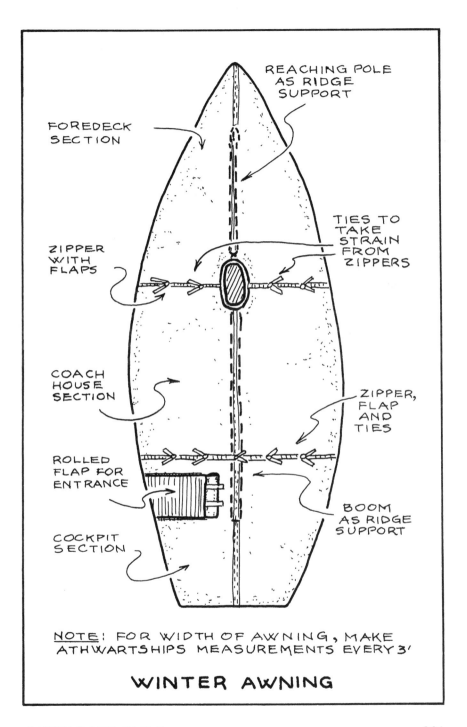

REACHING POLE AS RIDGE SUPPORT

FOREDECK SECTION

TIES TO TAKE STRAIN FROM ZIPPERS

ZIPPER WITH FLAPS

COACH HOUSE SECTION

ZIPPER, FLAP AND TIES

ROLLED FLAP FOR ENTRANCE

BOOM AS RIDGE SUPPORT

COCKPIT SECTION

NOTE: FOR WIDTH OF AWNING, MAKE ATHWARTSHIPS MEASUREMENTS EVERY 3'

WINTER AWNING

thought about until *all* sections have been adequately fitted together, for, although I'm first to admit that small pieces are easier to handle and sew onto than large ones, I just cannot conceive what good an easily sewn on chimney collar is going to do three feet aft of the chimney.

The ridge of the awning should be reinforced its full length, for great tension will be put upon it. This can be done by running an 8″ wide piece of fabric over (or under) the ridge seam. *Over*, will help waterproof the seam, *under* will act as a chafe patch. Up to you.

Seams should be sewn so the high piece will overlap the low piece, otherwise, you'll be sewing handy little troughs for water and dirt to be caught in.

Flaps (sides) can be sewn on last, since their fit is not nearly as vital as that of the top pieces. This will cut down on the amount of bulk you'll have to handle during fitting.

Dacron tape — not grommets and line — sewn per diagram should be used for all ties.

Good luck.

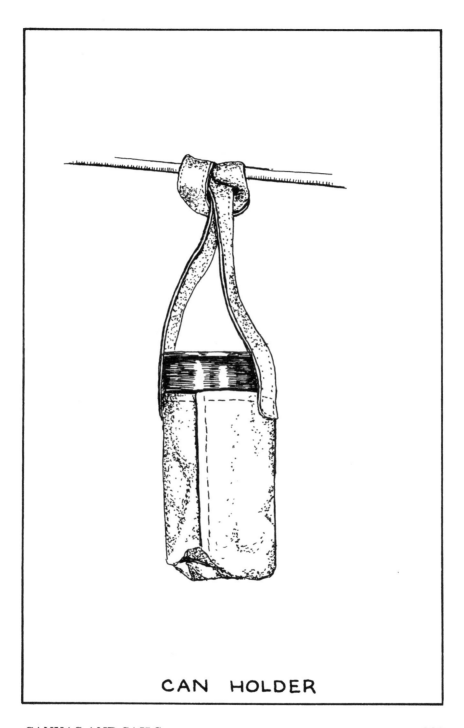

CAN HOLDER

SUN AWNING

The varieties of these have such a great range that I'm almost afraid to begin; but here goes.

Cockpit Only

In temperate climates, where the avoidance of the sun is mandatory only on uncustomarily hot summer days, a small awning fitted just over the cockpit, will be quite adequate. In its simplest form, it could be made up of the dinghy sail slung over the boom and lashed to the lifelines.

A more advanced awning would be a rectangular piece of treated canvas (Vivatex), supported in a similar fashion, except that the boathook could be slung athwartships over the boom, to act as a spreader to give a bit more head room.

Coach House Awning

If the sun is severe enough over a long period to overheat the deck and coach house, an awning, stretching as far forward as the mast, should be fabricated. Side curtains could be bypassed in favour of uninterrupted ventilation.

Full Cover

If you're in such vicious heat that the coach house awning is not enough, you should give thought to either moving to another climate, or constructing an awning that covers the yacht from stem to stern. In such a case, the construction would be very similar to the winter awning, except that the precautions against water leakage could be bypassed.

With all three awnings, rapid rigging and stowing are most important, for if the thing is a monster to use, then sewing it will be a waste of time, because no one will ever bother putting it up anyway.

Construction

Cut your pieces of canvas with allowances for seams (1/2″), and hems (2″), making sure that the edges always fall short of their intended anchoring spot, so they can be pulled taut. Since much windage and strain will be encountered by most of these awnings, the corners should be reinforced with a patch of canvas or dacron before the spur grommets are set in, or dacron tape tiedowns sewn on.

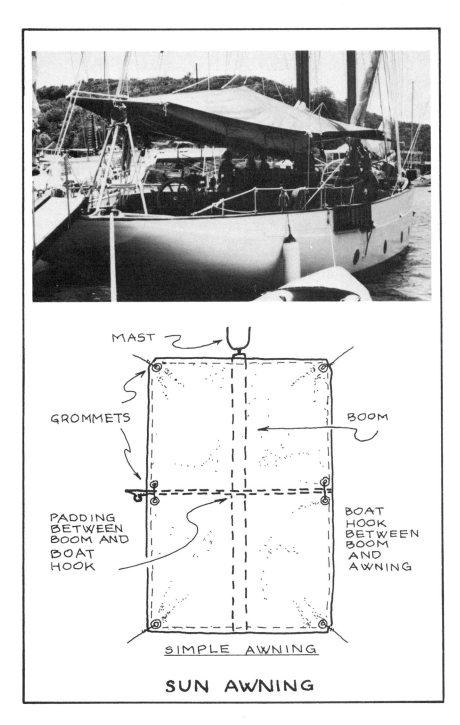

MAST

GROMMETS

BOOM

PADDING
BETWEEN
BOOM AND
BOAT
HOOK

BOAT
HOOK
BETWEEN
BOOM
AND
AWNING

SIMPLE AWNING

SUN AWNING

For added stiffness, a ridge rope can be installed in much the same fashion as the piping in cushions. See "Cushions" section.

If side curtains are required for early morning and late afternoon sun, the best solution may be a single portable flap, about 3' × 6', which could be moved from one spot to another depending on the yacht's position.

A most commendable secondary function of sun awnings would be to trap rain water. This can be simply done by reverse rigging most canopies, that is, having a trough down its spine instead of a ridge. To do this, hang the foreward end of the awning from the shrouds (slung *below* the boom), and the aft end, spread by the boat hook, from a lanyard on the backstay. Tilt the awning foreward or aft, as you prefer, then simply place a bucket at the mouth of the trough and call in the bucket brigade. In the tropics (where sun is the longsuit and good drinking water the short), I have seen a 40 gallon water tank filled in 45 minutes during one of their average drizzles.

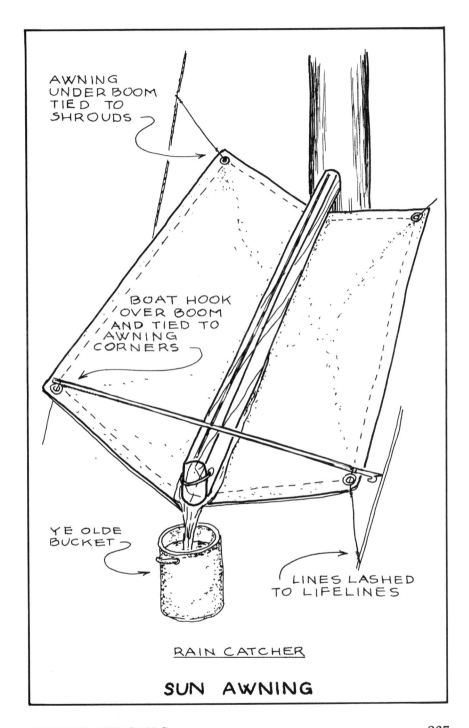

AWNING
UNDER BOOM
TIED TO
SHROUDS

BOAT HOOK
OVER BOOM
AND TIED TO
AWNING
CORNERS

YE OLDE
BUCKET

LINES LASHED
TO LIFELINES

RAIN CATCHER

SUN AWNING

SAIL CARE

Intricate adjustments are made to the amount and type of resins. Coating and impregnation procedures are complex. Weave constructions become more specialized. And the cost of sails continually goes up, making it easy to understand why, whether you race or cruise, keeping your sails in top shape is all-important.

Racing Sails

For all of you lunatic fringe sailboat racers (and I'd include myself in that category), your main interest is to keep your sails fast, recognizing that the "racing life" of the sail is probably substantially shorter than the sail's structural life. That fundamental axiom applies to all racing sails — unresinated, resinated, soft or firm. Here's what you do to keep them in shape.

Don't use your best racing sails when you don't have to. Any sail has a limit to its racing life, and since sails aren't cheap, daysailing or practicing boat handling with your newest, hottest rags is a fast way to make them slow. You might even want to use one suit of sails for major regattas and another for less important events or club racing.

Store your sails dry. Racers can dry their working sails on a lawn or on their boat if there isn't too much wind. It is especially important for resin-coated fabrics to be dried thoroughly, as they tend to soften up a bit and can develop reduced stretch resistance if they remain wet. If you sail in salt water, it's especially important to keep sails dry. Salt draws the moisture out of the air and tends to keep sails damp.

The amount of sunlight a sail receives when drying can be more detrimental for big boats than small boats. This is because the ultra-violet degradation that can break a sail down, though the process takes quite a while, is more critical on big boats that must sustain higher wind loads.

However, sunlight *can* affect nylon spinnakers, which are very sensitive to ultra-violet light due to their light-weight construction. A three-quarter-ounce spinnaker fabric can lose 50 percent of its strength after just two weeks of direct exposure to sunlight.

Always fold or roll your sails. This will keep them smooth and flat and *much* faster especially in light air. Some people prefer to fold their sails on the same crease time after time. Others don't care. I'm in the "don't care" school. It seems to me that if you have many small creases over the sail that will eventually disappear you're better off than having five or six large, semi-permanent creases that can cause resistance to air flow, just as a rough bottom can slow a boat's progress through the water.

Rolling sails has been in vogue for the past four or five years, although rolling very stiff, resin-coated fabrics finished with Condition Yarn Temper or Duroperm has been around for even longer. There is no doubt that rolling keeps sails smooth. I have never felt any particular need to roll mainsails, but I'm convinced it helps keep jibs fast. The best way to roll a jib is to start from the head and roll to the foot. That will keep the head of the sail in the center of the rolled tube when you're finished and the luff wire — if you have one — will stay in the tube better as well. The luff wire can actually act as a coil inside the tube which makes the rolled sail stiffer and easier to transport. If you have a jib with hanks, roll from the head straight down the luff. When you're ready to hoist, all the hanks will be at the front of the tube, ready to snap to the headstay.

If your spinnaker has a fairly stiff finish, keep it folded as well. Many wrinkles can eventually break down some of the newer spinnaker fabrics. To roll a stiff-finished chute material, join the clew and then the rest of the sail laterally, rolling it from the head down to finish the package. That way, the luff tapes won't crinkle as badly either, which at times can cause the luff itself to shrink.

Don't worry about dirt or blood on sails unless the stain can easily be rinsed off with water or truly bothers your aesthetic sensitivity. Dirt doesn't slow sails down, but washing highly-resinated sails can make them softer and cause them to lose their shape.

Never let your sail luff unnecessarily. Sheet them in just enough to keep them quiet, reducing the vibration and shaking that strains cloth and also loosens shackles, tangles sheets and pushes battens out of mainsails. Obviously, it's important to take sails down at the dock, but you can also lower your mainsail between races and sail around on the jib.

Cruising Sails

It isn't crucial to have wrinkle-free cruising sails, so it's okay to leave them stuffed in their bags for a week or so. It's also okay to leave them wet for short periods of time, although if you're planning on storing your sails for long periods, it's important they be dried thoroughly to prevent mildew. Mildew won't grow on synthetic fibres and will not affect their strength, but it can grow on the dirt that gets on sails and it can develop into an unsightly mess.

Unlike racing sails, washing cruising sails will not damage them. In fact, while removing salt and dirt, washing your sails will make them softer and easier to handle. Use warm water and a mild detergent. Probably the easiest technique is to lay the sail flat on an asphalt driveway or lawn and scrub it with a long-handled brush. Be sure to rinse the sail thoroughly and dry it in the shade if possible.

A good cover is essential for the cruising sail. Ultra-violet radiation over a prolonged period can seriously weaken your sail fabric and a sail that is left in the sun, especially in the tropics, can lose a serious amount of strength after less than a year. Acrylic fabrics, although expensive, make the best covers because they are absolutely insensitive to ultra-violet rays and because they won't fade.

Make sure your sails are furled securely before leaving your boat for any length of time. Sails can become completely destroyed in a squall or a storm because a portion of the sail was left loose and started flapping. That goes for roller-furling headsails as well. Make sure the sails are furled smoothly and the furling lines are secure.

It's extremely worthwhile to have your sails checked periodically by your sailmaker. He'll be able to repair small rips or weak seams before they become a problem and he'll wash and fold them properly.

Basically, a small amount of time spent caring for your sails can, in the end, make you race fast or cruise efficiently. Fortunately, there are no mysteries in sail care — only a little common sense.

Stain Removal

Any of the suggestions below will help you on new stains. If you're serious about cleaning a stain, do it soon. Waiting will probably make the job impossible.

Blood Stains

Scrub the stain with a concentrated mixture of dry detergent and warm water. Make the mixture as thick and pasty as possible and apply it to the stained area with a brush. Let the mixture stand on the stain for about 15 to 30 minutes to let the detergent work, and then rinse with warm water. If the stain is still there (and at least some of it probably will be) you can bleach the stained area with something like Clorox and warm water and then re-rinse. Bleach nylon only at room temperature and then rinse thoroughly.

Oil, Tar and Wax

Oily, black stains are extremely tought to remove from sails, but try the following: first, scrape off the excess gook with a spatula. Do not heat the stain because it will drive the stain deeper into the fabric. Place some drycleaning fluid on a soft, absorbent cloth and then place the sail stain side down on the cloth. Next, pour some more fluid on the sail so it will soak through the cloth and carry the stain out onto the absorbent cloth. Sail cloth is so tight that this method will probably take a while. Squeezing the fluid through the sail with another absorbent pad will help. Also, coated sail cloth (most three-quarter-ounce spinnaker cloth, Duroperm or CYT) won't allow fluids to soak through, so you'll have to blot from one side. After you've done what you can, soak the stain in warm water with a laundry pretreatment product, rinse, scrub with a mild detergent and rinse again.

Mildew

Mildew won't affect the strength of your sail, but it's best to remove any stain soon or you'll have it for a long time. Wash the stain in hot, sudsy water (with some bleach added), then rinse and dry. Moisten the stain with lemon juice and salt and let it dry in the sun. Rinse in warm water.

Rust

Soak the stain in oxalic acid for 15 to 30 minutes and then rinse thoroughly. You can get oxalic acid powder at a drug store. Use manufacturer's recommendations about the amount of water to cut it with.

Things To Avoid

Dacron polyester is essentially unharmed by any normal chemical commonly used around boats — including battery acid, acetone, gasoline, etc. Some solvents will tend to soften the resins (especially resins used in coating rather than impregnation), but the resin will reharden after the solvent evaporates.

Nylon, on the other hand, is sensitive to some acids and bleaches, especially in warm solutions. Since spinnakers (which are almost universally made from nylon) tend to get very tight and relatively weak, you should keep them away from acids and bleaches. When removing stains (such as mildew stains) on spinnakers, make sure you are using a room temperature bleach solution, and make sure you rinse the sail thoroughly after cleaning.

SAIL CLOTH

A key ingredient of sail design is in the cloth, where myriad combinations of weaves and finishes can interact at a microscopic level to create the perfect sail.

Fortunately, your sailmaker has given the problem of sail cloth selection a lot of thought and has probably chosen well from the staggering array of available fabrics which have been developed out of the infinite variety of weaves and finishes.

In most cases, it is wise to rely on his recommendation since his choice is based on a deep understanding of fabrics as well as first hand experience with sails suited for your boat and the conditions you will be sailing in. But sometimes there is a choice among several materials or finishes, each of which might be satisfactory for your sail. Understanding what tradeoffs are involved will help you assist your sailmaker in choosing the right cloth for your sailing aspirations. At the very least, it's important to understand the theories a sailmaker employs in selecting cloth.

One simple tradeoff, for instance, and the one people are most used to dealing with, is whether to opt for "soft" or "firm" material. This is an overly simplified way of classifying cloth since "soft" cloth for one maker may mean "firm" cloth for another, just as a big breeze to a Long Island Sound sailor may seem pretty insignificant to a native of San Francisco Bay.

When it comes to designing your sail, a sailmaker is aided primarily by knowing what boat you sail, where you sail it and what the average wind and sea conditions are. In addition, he has to know or at least be familiar with, how your mast and rig behave. These pieces of information help him to decide how to design the sail's shape and size, and, just as important, they help him choose the right cloth.

Many people underestimate or ignore the importance of sail cloth on sail performance, though more and more people are coming to realize that in addition to affecting the feel or handling properties of a sail, sail cloth can also influence shape, performance and the longevity of a sail just as strongly as the sail design and construction. Sailmakers have realized this as long as sails have been made, and as a result, they spend a lot of time analyzing available fabrics to determine what will work best.

For instance, a 505, Cal-20 and Finn mainsail might all be roughly the same size, but each will have different characteristics which would lead your sailmaker to choose widely different fabrics for each sail. Before looking into the choices your sailmaker might make, let's look at what goes into the various fabrics he would be choosing from.

First, sail cloth is made by interlacing continuous strands of filaments called yarns. Weaving these groups of filaments in various ways allows each interlaced yarn to spread out or compact as it moves in and out in the weave. This also makes the resulting fabric pliant and non-porous. For instance, in spinnaker cloth, the filaments are spread out to minimize porosity in spite of the loose packing of the yarns. The number of yarns per inch in the weave are kept to a minimum to save weight. In mainsail and jib fabrics, the filaments move in such a way as to allow the yarns to deform and brace the weave to provide maximum resistance to stretch.

Yarn for sail cloth is almost exclusively either nylon or polyester. Polyester is sold under many trade names by various fabric producers, but Du Pont's Dacron is by far the most common polyester yarn used in sail cloth. The individual properties of nylon and Dacron determine what fabrics they are used in. Nylon, because it is very strong and light weight for its size and bulk, is best for spinnaker materials.

Nylon's relative stretchiness isn't a factor in spinnakers. Dacron, which is denser and less stretchy, although weaker (stretch resistance and strength have nothing in common) than nylon, is extremely well-suited for working sail fabrics, where stretch resistance rather than ultimate strength is the major factor. In addition, both nylon and Dacron shrink with heat. This shrinkage is extremely important — even crucial — in finishing modern, tightly-packed fabrics. For nylon materials, this shrinkage isn't terribly important. For Dacron materials, however, where maximum tightness is important in reducing bias stretch (stretch along a line diagonal to the warp and fill yarns; warp yarns run parallel to the cloth panel and fill yarns run perpendicular to the panel). Any amount of tight packing produced on a loom would be insufficient to provide the fibre packing density that a combination of tight weaving and shrinking with heat can produce. Even the tightest fabrics produced on the most powerful looms can be tightened anywhere from 10 to 20 percent through heat shrinkage.

Nylon or Dacron yarns used for sail cloth are available in certain specific sizes. Because of this, and because there is an infinite number of spacings that can be chosen for the warp yarns and fill yarns, describing fabric by weight only is sort of like describing a boat by weight only. If someone told you he had a 5,000-pound boat, you

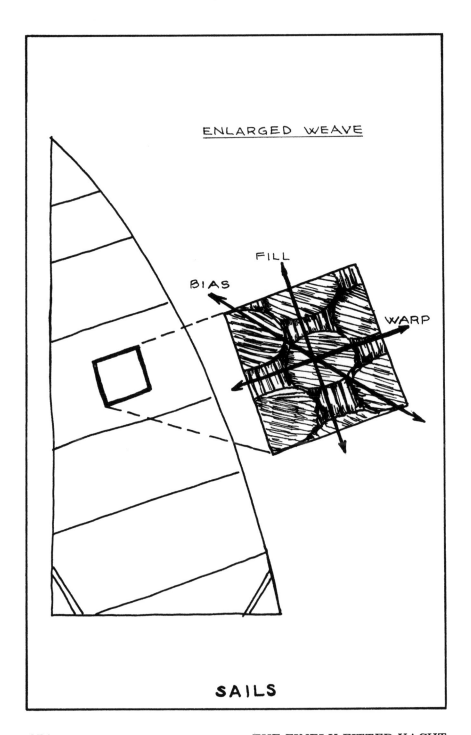

ENLARGED WEAVE

FILL

BIAS

WARP

SAILS

THE FINELY FITTED YACHT

would know as much about his boat as you would about a fabric you were told weighs five ounces. The term "five ounces" refers to the weight of a piece of fabric 36″ X 28½″, a sailmaker's yard — at least in the U.S. Elsewhere, sail cloth weight refers to ounces for a square yard, or in the metric system, to grams per square meter.

For any weight and type of cloth, it is the stretch properties of the particular fabric which determine how a sail made from it will be shaped and how that shape will change with changes in wind velocity, sheet tension, mast bend, stay sag, and other factors. As one example, a sail made out of a material that stretches very little along the leech and quite a bit on a line between the clew and the middle of the sail will tend to develop a deep draft aft with increasing wind loads. If that's the case, the correct balances of stretch and stretch resistance have not been considered and the sail will not perform properly. For instance, another case where balances must be carefully weighed is in high-aspect and low-aspect mainsails. Because there are high leech loads on high-aspect mains, stretch resistance in the fill yarns is extremely important. In low-aspect mainsails, fill stretch resistance is not as important, but controlling the bias stretch, which affects the large center area of the sail, becomes more important. For most genoas, it's important to minimize the bias stretch and to carefully balance the stretch in the warp and fill yarns. Stretch properties, and how they are used effectively, have many variations.

Sailmakers generally measure the stretch properties of sail cloth by pulling on it and recording the stretch in various directions. What is more interesting is how those properties get into the cloth in the first place and why.

Stretch properties depend primarily on two things — weave and finish. The weave builds inherent stretch properties into the cloth by placing certain sized yarns and a certain yarn spacing in both the warp and fill. Two basic categories of weave are mainsail weaves and genoa weaves.

Mainsail weaves tend to have larger fill threads to withstand the higher leech loads they are subjected to. Genoa fabrics are designed for maximum stretch resistance in the bias direction. In these fabrics, fill and warp stretch are balanced to allow the stretch between the leech and the mid-sections of the sail to work together to prevent or delay the sail from becoming too full or the draft from moving aft as wind pressure builds.

After weaving, a sail cloth must be finished so its final properties are precisely tailored to the requirements the particular sail is

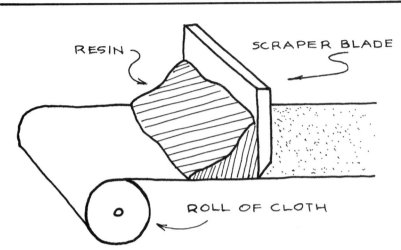

RESIN   SCRAPER BLADE

ROLL OF CLOTH

RESIN LIES <u>ON</u> TOP OF SAIL CLOTH
MAKING IT <u>STIFFER</u> AND MORE STRETCH
RESISTANT.

<u>RESIN COATING</u>

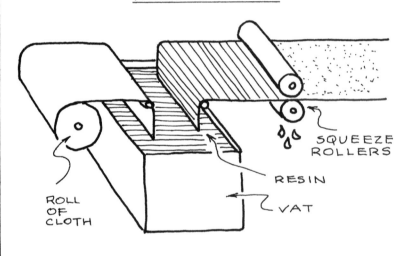

SQUEEZE ROLLERS

RESIN

ROLL OF CLOTH

VAT

RESIN SOAKS <u>INTO</u> SAIL CLOTH
MAKING IT SOFTER AND MORE PLIABLE.
PURPOSE IS TO <u>CONTROL</u> STRETCH.

<u>RESIN IMPREGNATING</u>

SAILS

destined for. Due to the wide range of possible finishes, the end use is vitally important. A one-design boat might need a firm finish to lock in the shape while a cruising sailor might desire a fairly soft finish for ease of handling. A tightly-woven fabric can be made soft (but relatively stretchy), hard and difficult to handle with extremely low stretch, or anywhere in between the two. The process requires taking the fabric as it comes off the loom and cleaning, shrinking, crushing and otherwise treating the cloth.

Beyond simply making the cloth stretchier or softer, the details of the stretch properties can be changed in finishing. For instance, the relative amounts of stretch in various directions can be adjusted to make the fabric work better for a certain application. This is an area that almost borders on alchemy and is very important in producing highly engineered, long-lasting sail cloth.

The two most important areas of finishing are shrinking the fabric with heat and applying resin to it. Dacron shrinks approximately 10 to 20 percent by panel length with heat. Shrinking an already tightly woven fabric causes additional tightening or jamming of the yarn intersections in the fabric and stabilizes the inherently unstable lattice structure of the weave. Shrinkage with heat combined with tight weaving builds power and resiliency into fabrics and gives them the guts to stand up to repeated luff tension, sheet trimming, wind loading and other factors.

Resins can also be used to further stabilize the fabric's structure. Currently, there are two types of resin applications in common use — impregnation, where the resin is put *into* the fabric, and coating, where the resin is applied to the surface of the fabric.

For sail cloth, the most widespread of these two methods is impregnation. In this process, the cloth is first passed through a solution containing a structural bonding resin, then squeezed to give uniform penetration, and finally dried at a closely regulated temperature. This process physically places the bonding agents into the fabric and between the filaments and yarn intersections where it ties the structure together from the inside. Resin curing is then carried out at high temperature and pressure, providing extraordinary internal bonding. A carefully resin-impregnated fabric will show no surface resin at all, even at a microscopic level. The additional resistance to stretch is built *into* the fabric. By playing around with the amount and type of resin that gets put into the fabric, many degrees of stretch resistance can be obtained.

When extremely high degrees of stretch resistance are required, Dacron fabrics are usually coated — one side only — with a very

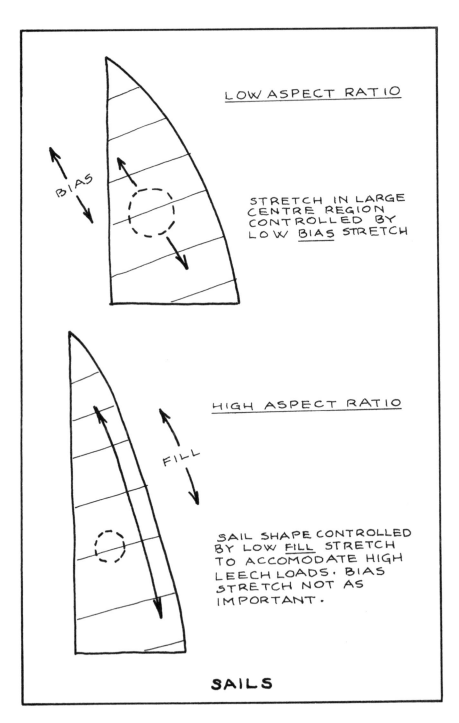

LOW ASPECT RATIO

STRETCH IN LARGE
CENTRE REGION
CONTROLLED BY
LOW BIAS STRETCH

BIAS

HIGH ASPECT RATIO

FILL

SAIL SHAPE CONTROLLED
BY LOW FILL STRETCH
TO ACCOMODATE HIGH
LEECH LOADS. BIAS
STRETCH NOT AS
IMPORTANT.

SAILS

tough, very low stretch, resin. Dacron fabrics of this type are marketed under various names by various manufacturers (Condition Yarn Temper or Duroperm are just two) and are extremely crisp to the touch. They might be tough to get down a hatch, impossible to bag unless folded, and, generally, difficult to handle on a boat. However, they have extraordinary shape-holding capability. Sails built out of these fabrics hold their designed shape over a very large wind range and can eliminate the necessity to have special sails for various wind conditions.

In many cases, proper attention to the choice of fabric stretch properties (that is, the balance between fill, bias and warp stretch inherent in a particular weave) will allow you to avoid crispy, hard-to-handle fabrics with little or no reduction in sail performance. However, there are also many applications where a high degree of stretch resistance (even with increased handling problems) is very important. For instance, in most one-designs, the only way to get a jib to perform efficiently over the widest range of conditions is to use fabric that has been heavily impregnated or coated. On offshore racing boats as well, headsail materials, especially for lighter, full-sized genoas which must hold their shape over huge changes in wind loads, must be resinated to some degree. Remember, however, that resinated fabrics do not have to be ultra crisp. They can be very soft — almost indistinguishable from resin-free fabrics — and still have significantly reduced stretchiness. Your sailmaker knows best what the tradeoffs are for your boat and for your sailing, so if you want a sail that's easy to handle and don't care about ultimate shape holding, or if you don't care about handling as long as you're fast, he can probably make a recommendation on the best fabric to use.

A great deal has been said about the lasting properties of resinated fabrics, and the subject of resin in sail cloth is a controversial one. First of all, it is important to realize that resination is not black and white. The point is that there exists an infinite range of possibilities.

All fabrics, unresinated and resinated alike, become stretchier and softer for use. However, any good, tightly-woven, resinated fabric will never become softer or stretchier than an unresinated fabric of comparable weave that has been used — or abused — equally.

Modern resinated fabrics, even though they will eventually lose some of their resistance to stretch, have extraordinary lasting qualities. This is due largely to the fact that the resin actually prevents the stretching and inter-fiber movement that causes fabrics

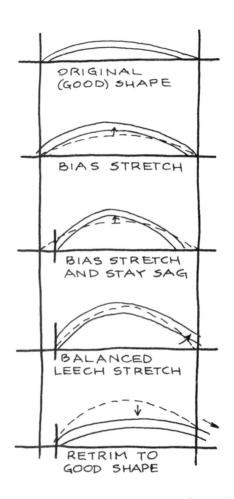

ORIGINAL
(GOOD) SHAPE

BIAS STRETCH

BIAS STRETCH
AND STAY SAG

BALANCED
LEECH STRETCH

RETRIM TO
GOOD SHAPE

BALANCING LEECH STRETCH (FILL) AND
BIAS STRETCH IN GENOA FABRICS
INCREASES THE USEFUL RANGE OF
THE SAIL. SHOWN ABOVE IS A
SEQUENCE OF STRETCH AND ADJUST-
MENT IN A TYPICAL GENOA AS
WIND STRENGTH CHANGES.

SAILS

to break down. In addition, modern fabrics have resin stretch properties and fabric stretch properties arranged so the two complement and reinforce one another. This is tricky to do, but results in maximum ruggedness and shape-holding, combined with an excellent life span. My personal experience has been that, except on the very highest racing level where people tend to be a little superstitious, a sail built out of properly resinated fabric will stay fast for at least one or one-and-a-half seasons of hard racing — as long as the sail isn't severely abused.

The other side of the coin is that really excellent sails can be made out of extremely soft fabrics as long as the greater stretchiness of the fabric is understood and allowances are made by the sailmaker. These sails will be long-lasting, easy to handle, simple to store, and, generally, a joy to have around. If you're cruising, they're a must. If you race, there are lots of applications where soft sails will work fine. If you race seriously, you might have some sails you wish were softer to the touch, but you'll be thankful for their range because you won't have to keep changing them when the wind changes, and your boat will go faster.

Now, let's get back to our choice of fabrics for three boats — Finn, 505 and Cal-20.

The main differences between a Finn main and a 505 main are as follows: the 505 main sits on a mast that is stiffened by spreaders and deck level support and is therefore not very "bendy". Also, with a trapeze, the 505 becomes overpowered only in a very strong breeze. Even then, it can plane to windward by cracking off a bit and by allowing the sails to keep generating full power. A Finn, on the other hand, has no mast bend control at all and extremely limited stability. Therefore, the main must respond to mast bend and depower the boat simultaneously as the main sheet is trimmed in response to increasing wind strength.

The 505 main, then, needs to be able to maintain its shape over a very broad range of wind strength with relatively little mast bending taking place which would tend to flatten the sail. In this application, an extremely stiff fabric would be in order — with enough fill stretch resistance to keep the leech clean and controlled. Generally, a 4.5- to 5-ounce weight fabric with a "square" construction (equal weight yarns in warp and fill) might be necessary, giving good bias and fill stretch resistance, finished with either a super-stiff coating (like Duroperm or Condition Yarn Temper) or a firm impregnated resin. Actually, either fabric finish could be chosen, the final choice depending on how the sailmaker chose to design the sail.

For the Finn, a reasonable fill stretch would be desirable, but too stiff a fill would prevent the leech from opening enough to allow the sail to depower. However, in this case, a great deal of bias stretch and resilience is required to allow the sail to keep up with the mast bend and not over-flatten the sail. Of course, too much bias stretch would cause the sail to become fuller, so in this case, with sharply limited stability and a limited control of mast bend, choosing exactly the right balance of bias and fill stretch is critical if the sail is to allow the boat to be sailed effectively in a broad range of conditions. To obtain the correct amount of bias stretch, a lighter, softer fabric (say 4-ounce) is required, which, in addition, would have heavier fill yarns to resist the leech loads.

For the Cal-20, with its larger, overlapping jib, the main would tend to be trimmed tighter than a 505 main and would probably require stretch resistance on the fill. In addition, the larger jib tends to "pre-bend" the air in front of the main and reduce the pressure differentials which cause the sail to get fuller. That, combined with the desire on the part of many Cal-20 owners to have an easily handled sail, would lead a sailmaker to choose a softer fabric with less bias stretch resistance.

These hypothetical choices are not necessarily gospel however, since different sail designs and different sailing techniques can require different sail fabrics. It is your sailmaker's job to combine your boat's characteristics and your sailing needs to come up with a fabric choice and a sail design that will work best for you.

Jim Linville is the president of Dimension Sail Cloth in Putnam, Conn., a former world Tempest champion and an active one-design and offshore competitor.

tools

ACCESSORIES

The Dovetail Jig

It is difficult to ascertain why a dovetail joint carries such prestige, and why it evokes memories of the great days of fine craftsmanship — perhaps it reminds one of the times when joints such as these were done by hand, one dovetail at a time.

Romantic reminiscences aside, the dovetail is still an extremely functional joint, virtually unequalled in strength and practicality, especially for interior work. On the exterior of a yacht, the somewhat delicate dovetail could become a victim of weathering, especially if the wood is not varnished conscientiously.

The jig in the photo enables one to prepare an average joint (God only knows what that is) in about the same time as most other methods of joining would require. The only tool needed is a 3/8″ chuck electric drill motor. This should be of good quality, as the jig must be used at high revolutions (about 3,000) to perform the cleanest cuts with the fewest tear outs.

The jig comes with grid, bit assembly, guide handle (with depth stop) and, most happily, detailed illustrated instructions. It is obtainable for about $25 from the Princeton Company.

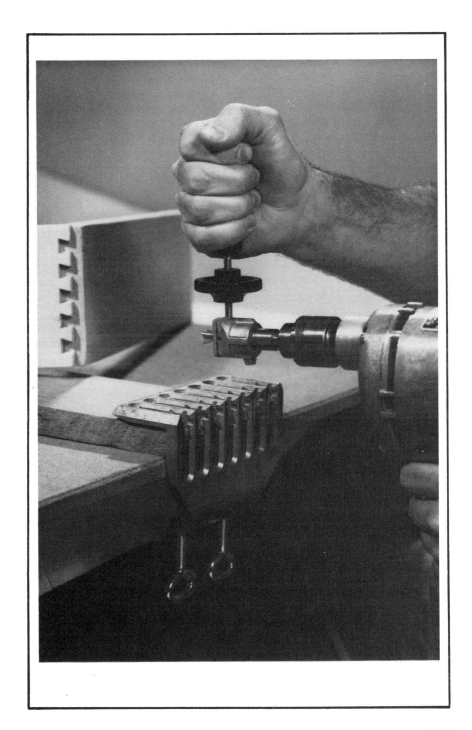

Centre Doweling Jig

Doweling is probably the best way to join boards, edge to edge. Using a tongue and groove joint is acceptable, but when working with expensive hardwoods, one does not want to waste even 1/2″ for a lap joint. Doweling is a rapid operation that leaves the full widths of the boards intact. The only equipment needed is a drill motor and a jig (see photo) which costs about $20.

The jig clamps boards from 7/16″ to 2-1/8″ in thickness, and its automatic self centring yields accurate centre drilling even on round stock. The drill guide is hardened, and the guide holes are drilled and reamed for extreme accuracy. Drill bit sizes accommodated are 1/4″, 5/16″, 3/8″, 7/16″ and 1/2″. If you're contemplating cabinet work of any quantity, you may as well fork over the $20 and get it over with.

Doweling Jig Clamps

Using dowels on right angle joints will save a great amount of time, because it eliminates the plugging of externally drilled holes. The doweling clamps shown make drilling of doweling holes simple and accurate. The clamps position the pieces and align the holes. The guides supplied are for 1/4″, 5/16″ and 3/8″ drill bits, and should be enough for most occasions.

The freestanding clamp (without the holes) remains stationary, while the guide clamp (with the holes) can be slid along as the drilling requires. The jig (as apparently most things nowadays) costs about $20, and again, if major cabinet work is anticipated, the investment can be well justified.

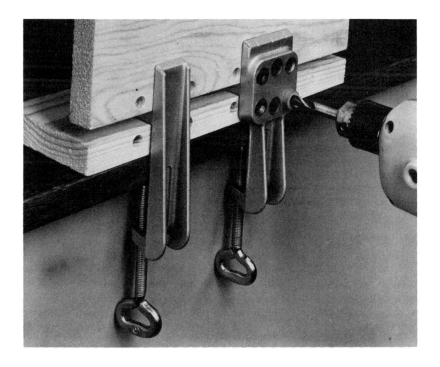

CHISELS AND KNIVES

Chisels

A good chisel should be well balanced, and designed for the work required. Delicate arcs cannot be cut with a 1″ wide blade and, conversely, attempting to chisel away a large mass with a 1/4″ sliver-picker is proof of lunacy.

I do not for a minute suggest that a different chisel be purchased for each line cut; indeed, a handful (small hand) of well thought out ones like 1/4″, 1/2″, 3/4″ and 1″, will do for all projects in this book. There are various things to examine when purchasing chisels and the following section will elaborate on these.

Generally

The bevel edge cabinet maker's chisels and square edge framing chisels are used for all general forming work and are usually struck with a mallet.

Mortise chisels are narrow chisels with thick heavy blades and a very broad bevel angle which serves to break waste when the chisel is employed to cut deep, square holes (mortises). These chisels are also meant to be struck strongly.

Conversely, chisels not designed to be struck are paring chisels. These are usually longer and more delicate and are always kept shaving-sharp, as they are moved solely by hand pressure.

Using any chisel requires a knack, one easily acquired, but nonetheless a knack. Practice makes perfect. However, here are a few hints: first, mark out your work carefully and accurately using a solid square of the right size for easy handling. Second, always begin work inside your marked lines and cut into the waste wood. Third, rough out the whole cut, pare away the waste carefully, and then pare carefully down to the mark for your final finish trimming. Using these basic rules, you'll have a nice clean-sided, flat-bottomed hole when you are finished.

Blade Stems

Basically, two types of blade stems exist, the socket and the hooped.

(a) Socket. The handle fits into a socket that is actually cast as part of the blade. These tools are designed for heavy malleting. This type of handle will retain a firm joint for a long time.

(b) Hooped. Here the end of the blade fits *into* the wood handle which is reinforced and kept from splitting by a metal hoop.

Normally, these are for lighter work, and are sometimes equipped with a leather stock-washer between the handle and the shoulder of the blade, to avoid unnecessarily "shocking" penetrations into the wood.

Handles

The modern composition handles seem to work very well although the connoisseur may prefer wooden ones. The best handles are made from rather rare boxwood. Ash is second best. Any wood handled chisel required to do heavy work should be equipped with a steel hoop at the free end to keep the handle from being mulched. An alternative is leather tipping.

Knives

A retractable bladed razor knife is a must for all workshops. It can cut insulation, sharpen pencils, and make very fine line markings on wood. The retractable blade is beautiful for stowing and eliminating nicks in the searching hand.

A refined cousin of this is a wooden handled European model, with a sheath over the blade. It can be sharpened instead of being replaced. It runs the entire length of the handle and can be gradually pulled out as the edge is ground.

Care

All chisels and knives should be sheathed when stored, to preserve the edge. Very simple inexpensive sheaths can be fabricated from cardboard and duct-tape. Make them and use them.

Lastly. A chisel is not an axe, a prying tool, screwdriver or wire cutter. It should be used with care. Cut to a small depth at a time, clear away rubble, then cut deeper.

Stones

Never use a stone without using ample oil. By carrying away the metal chips and bits of stone which have been ground off, the oil keeps the stone from clogging. If a stone becomes clogged with debris, put some oil on it and rub briskly with a rough cloth.

Washita is the most rapid cutting of the four grades of natural stones (Soft Arkansas, Hard Arkansas and Black-hard Arkansas being the others), and will produce the fastest edge. Soft Arkansas is the best general purpose stone and will produce a very sharp edge. Hard Arkansas is the best all-round stone for the final polishing of an already sharp tool. Black-hard Arkansas is the ultimate finishing stone. It's very slow cutting, but will produce an absolutely razor edge (for perfectionists).

India and Crystolon stones are man-made. India doesn't cut as fast as Crystolon. Fine India is roughly equivalent to Natural Washita, and therefore is a preliminary final honing stone. Crystolon is most useful when an edge is very dull or has been chipped and you need speed more than a sharp edge.

What to Buy

It's a good idea to have at least one very fast cutting stone to remove a lot of metal when you nick a blade or try to salvage a badly worn edge. Coarse Crystolon or Coarse India are best.

Next, you may have never gotten your tools as sharp as you can and should. The very sharpest edge works best, and once you've achieved it, occasional honing on a Hard or Black-hard Arkansas or stropping will maintain the edge; however, if the steel you are using is not the first quality, all the honing in the world won't help as the edge will crumble.

Lastly, you can skip a grade as you move up. In other words, you can move from a Washita to a Hard Arkansas as you are honing. A single stone with two different surfaces back to back is the best basic unit.

Honing Guide

Chisel and plane blades must have accurate bevels to work at their best. This can be hard to ensure when holding a blade by hand. A honing guide guarantees accurate bevels. There are a number of tools available to do this. The bevel you put on the blade is determined by how far back on the guide you hold the blade. The jaws of the guide are screwed tight to hold the blade in position, and then the guide is run along the stone on its roller. The usual angle is 25°.

MARKING TOOLS

Accurate, well made tools which help you lay out your stock are invaluable. These tools are a delight to hold in your hand, to look at and, most important, to use. Excellent marking tools are not a luxury; they will help you avoid mistakes. Remember, measure twice and cut once.

Cutting Gauge

This is especially useful for scoring across the grain. A super sharp blade cuts cleanly without tearing. Solid brass strips inlaid in the rubbing face will make for long wear. It is adjustable with a thumb screw.

Double Slide Marking Gauge

This is a particularly useful tool. Both sides have a hardened steel pin for general marking, and top and bottom adjust independently with two steel thumb screws. The scales are usually fitted into the slide on both sides, allowing easy reading of the distance of the pin from the rubbing block. It can easily be used for mortising layout also.

Folding Rules

Folding rules fold neatly to fit into your pocket. They should be tough and close grained. Most are marked in inches (1/8″ graduations on one side and 1/16″ on the other).

Sliding Bevel

This is essential for marking off odd angles, dovetail work, and framing. It should have brass fittings to protect the ends against damage and a solid brass locking lever to allow adjustment.

Scratch Awl

A scratch awl is particularly good for light marking of layout. A very sharp point will scratch a super fine mark on the wood surface.

Calipers and Dividers

Inside calipers are designed for transferring or measuring interior dimensions, and outside calipers for transferring or measuring outside dimensions very accurately. Dividers are used for scribing arcs and circles, and can also be used to mark off absolutely straight or curved parallel lines. The bow springs and threaded spool mechanism ensures sensitive adjustment and that the settings will not change when transferring dimensions or marking out.

FILES

Filing is one of man's oldest arts. A good file or rasp used properly should cut cleanly and smoothly. The teeth should not "catch" the wood fibres. The right file does the work you want to do better and usually faster.

Files are formed by raising a continuous tooth evenly across the file. There are two basic kinds of files: single cut and double cut. The teeth in single cut files run in one direction only, but run in two directions on the double cut files. (The latter will cut quicker and more coarsely.)

Rasps differ from files in that the teeth are formed individually and are not connected to one another. Files will cut smoother than rasps, but when used on wood, will work much slower and are susceptible to clogging.

In order of ascending smoothness of cut, files are graded: Coarse, Bastard Cut, Second Cut, and Smooth. Rasps are graded in ascending order: Wood Rasp, Cabinet Rasp Bastard, Cabinet Rasp Second Cut, and Cabinet Rasp Smooth. In general, a longer file or rasp will have somewhat coarser teeth than a shorter one.

Your stock should be held firmly in a vise or clamp. For general filing, the stock should be at about elbow height. If the work requires heavier filing, it should be lower, and if that is finer, it should be near eye level.

In general, the file or rasp at the handle end should be held in your hand with your thumb along the top edge. The other end of the file or rasp should be grasped with the thumb and forefinger of your other hand.

PLANES

Until 30 or 40 years ago, a craftsman could literally get hundreds of different types of planes.

In this day of power-driven tools, we are apt to forget how important hand planes are for fine woodworking. Each plane has its own special purpose — work which it can do more easily and accurately than any other. Not only can you usually do more careful (and better) work with a hand plane, but also — often because of power tool set-up time — you can work faster. For example, the scrub plane can rough out stock very rapidly.

Skill at hand planing is one of the most important abilities of any craftsman. Experience with hand planes will help you understand exactly what a power tool is doing when you use it for a particular job (an important and subtle appreciation if one is to achieve consistently good results with power tools). Also, a hand plane is a far more forgiving tool. Careful work sacrificed for speed can ruin more otherwise good work than anything else.

Here are a few hints about using any plane. First, keep the blade as sharp as possible. The Bench Oilstones and the Honing Guide are excellent for this purpose. Second, generally plane *with* the grain. (Look at the side of the stock and you can easily see which way the grain runs.) If you don't work with the grain, you run the danger of "catching the grain," lifting chips of wood and producing a rough surface.

When planing end grain, push the plane one way to the middle of the board only; then repeat this process going in the other direction. This prevents splitting the board at the edge.

Sharpening Plane Irons

There are two steps to putting a proper edge on any plane iron: grinding (i.e. shaping) the edge, and honing. Grinding may be required when the edge has developed a nick, whenever the edge has become "thick" due to frequent honing, or if the bevel has become rounded due to rocking on the oilstone.

When grinding, a good natural grindstone used with water is best. Thus, there is no danger of drawing the temper out of the edge by excessive heat buildup. The shape of the edge for a bench plane when used for rough, course work can be rounded slightly by 1/64" to 1/32". For more general work, a square edge with the sharpness just rounded off the corners is preferred. For jointing, the entire edge must be dead square.

Wooden Body Planes

In Colonial days the standard plane used by cabinet makers and carpenters alike had a wood body. A fully equipped workshop might have as many as 30 or 40 — one for every shape needed. A wood block wedged in the body of the plane was used to hold the steel cutting blade in place. In North America, we gradually have grown accustomed to using the "Stanley-type" steel body plane, as the knurled knob blade adjuster was easier to use than the wood wedge.

However, there is no real substitute for the wood-bodied plane. Although not now best for casual carpenters, a wood plane will produce better results on important pieces. The wood sole will not mar the work surface, and the wood-to-wood contact between the sole and the stock lets the plane slide easier than with a steel-bodied plane. Also, because a wooden plane is lighter than a comparable steel plane (superior planing is accomplished by pushing a sharp blade *through* the wood, *not into it*), it is less fatiguing to use.

The Use of Bench Planes

Of all the bench planes, the Jack is usually the first to be used — for the preliminary cleaning up and squaring of stock and the accurate truing of short edges. For truing long edges, the Jointer (Trying) Plane must be used. The Smooth Plane is used for final smoothing on flat surfaces of any roughness after a Jack Plane has been used and after gluing.

The most common fault when using bench planes is "dipping". For accurate results, it is critical to avoid this. Just pay attention to the following two simple rules:

— At the beginning of each stroke, put slightly more pressure on the front of the plane.

— At the end of the stroke, keep slightly more pressure on the back of the plane.

THE FINELY FITTED YACHT

HAND SAWS

The difference between an adequate saw and the best lies in the balance of the tool, the ruggedness and comfort of the handle, the quality of the steel (plus the accuracy and sharpness of the teeth), and, in general, ease of use.

There are many different types of saws — both as to size and design. As usual, each will perform its own special function best. For example, you can crosscut a board with a Rip Saw, but it will work much slower and will produce a very rough finish. In contrast to a Rip Saw where the teeth are set and filed to cut with their points, Crosscut Saw teeth are filed to cut with their edges and shaped with no hook to prevent snagging on wood fibers. Select the proper saw for each job and you will do better work.

CLAMPING TOOLS

Woodworking is made unnecessarily difficult when you are not able to hold or clamp your work in the proper position — quickly, easily, and accurately — with no movement of the stock.

Every workshop should have a number of clamps with different functions, as each does its job better than any other can.

Usually, when using any portable clamp, place a wood pad between the clamp and the wood surface. Always wipe up excess glue right away and apply pressure gradually. Clamps can exert tremendous force, so apply only enough to get the job done. Check squareness and alignment as you draw up.

Now, a word or two about how to select your clamps. There is an old saying in woodworking that you can never have enough clamps. While certainly not literally true, the saying has a certain ring of truth to it because most woodworkers never think about what clamps they need until the last minute — often just before gluing up. At that point it's really too late, and they find themselves trying as best they can to make do. At the very least, the result is a lot of aggravation. At worst, it means out of square frames, buckled panels, or glue set before final assembly can be completed and aligned.

Don't ignore the needs of your shop for proper clamps. Think about what you really had to have (but didn't) during the past year. You should have on hand at least three of each size or type of the clamps that you do decide to maintain. Also, in general, stock longer or larger clamps than short ones — although the very small ones are terrific for work on smaller pieces where the larger, heavier clamps would simply overwhelm the workpiece.

Miter Clamp

Here is an interesting "one evening" project that will provide you with an uncomplicated clamping jig with many advantages for mitering. It is adjustable to any size frame; it applies uniform pressure to all four joints simultaneously; it leaves joints visible so you can be sure they are *straight and tight*; it is light and easy to handle, minimizing the danger of damage to frames; and it eliminates the necessity of buying a clamp for each joint.

This practical jig overcomes the disadvantages of most other "miter clamps" which hold work of very limited size range, and apply little, if any, pressure to the joint itself.

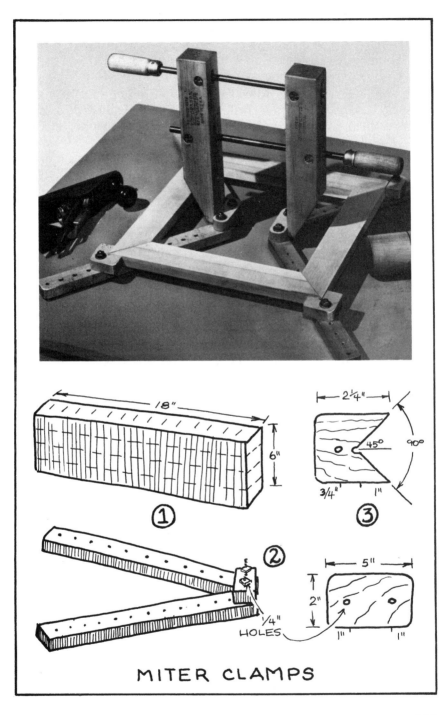

① 18" 6"

② ¼" HOLES

③ 2¼" 90° 45° ¾" 1"

5" 2" 1" 1"

MITER CLAMPS

Legs

(Four required.) Use straight, clear hardwood strips 1″ × 1¾″ × 18″ long, or as much longer as you wish, for the jobs intended. To make the legs, take a piece of 2″ × 6″ (1¾″ × 5½″), stand it on edge, mark its centre line down its spine, then very carefully mark 1″ intervals along the line and drill 1/4″ holes as marked through the entire width. Accuracy is important. Now rip the wood into four 1¾″ × 1″ pieces.

Counterbore all holes on the underside of each leg to accommodate the flat-head machine screw to be used in the assembly of the clamp. This will permit the clamp to lie flat on the bench.

Swivel Bars

(Two required.) Use the same 1″ × 1¾″ hardwood cut 5″ long. Locate centres 1″ in from each end, and drill 1/4″ diameter holes. Round the ends for neat appearance.

Corner Blocks

(Four required.) Make these from the same hardwood stock, cut 2¼″ long. Mark for two 1/4″ diameter holes, with one of them being 1″ in from the end so it will be centred at the bottom of the right-angle "V". This will provide relief for the corners of the frame being clamped so that it will draw up properly, without crushing any sharp corners on the frame. Cut perfect 90° recesses into each block.

Assembly

You will need eight 1/4″ × 2¼″ flat-head machine screws, with nuts or wing-nuts to fit. Assemble the swivel bars onto the legs as illustrated. The corner blocks are assembled into each of the legs at positions determined by the size of the frame to be mitered. Make certain that the corner blocks are assembled at the same relative position in each leg.

Clamping

With both pairs of legs placed on the bench so that the swivel bars are on top, the four corner blocks can be roughly positioned to fit the frame. The swivel bars should be parallel to each other, and separated by some convenient distance. Pressure is applied by drawing the swivel bars together by means of a Handscrew. On very large frames, the swivel bars may be a considerable distance apart, in which case a bar clamp can be used.

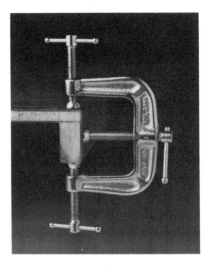

Three-way edging clamp provides "right-angle" pressure to the edge, or side, of work.

CATALOGS

Spyglass
2415 Mariner Square Drive
Alameda, CA 94501

> *The* Spyglass *catalogue is actually a very beautifully produced reference volume, edited by a most gracious gentleman by the name of Dick Moore. The contents depart from standard catalogue fare with many articles and outfitting tips, aside from the few hundred pages of all marine gear imaginable.*

Thomas Foulkes
Landsdown Road, Leytonstone
London, England, E11 3HB

> *This has been the bible of cruising boat outfitters for many years. The catalogues normally run about 200 pages and cost about $10, but are well worth the price.*

Lands' End Catalog
2317 N. Elston
Chicago, IL 60614

Mariners Catalog
National Fisherman and International
Marine Publishing Co.
Camden, ME

James Bliss Co.
Dedham, MA 02026

Manhattan Marine
116 Chambers Street
New York, NY 10007

Jay Stuart Haft
8925 N. Tennyson Dr.
Milwaukee, WI 53217

　　　　　　　　　THE FINELY FITTED YACHT

SPARS

Le Fiel
Mast and rigging, aluminum
13700 Firestone Blvd.
Santa Fe Springs, CA 90670

Shepperd Woodworks
Wood spars
21020 70th West
Edmonds, WA 98020

Super Spar
Masts, aluminum
7231 Rosecrans Ave.
Paramount, CA 90723

Forespar
Spars and fittings
3140 Pullman St.
Costa Mesa, CA 92627

Metal Mast Marine
Aluminum spars and related fittings
P.O. Box 471
Putnam, CT 06260

Sparcraft
Masts and assorted hardware
P.O. Box 925, 770 W. 17th St.
Costa Mesa, CA 92627

Forespar, Inc.
Rigging and spinnaker poles
3140 Pullman St.
Costa Mesa, CA 92626

WOOD

American Forest Products
All hardwoods and marine plywood
14103 Park Place
Cerritos, CA 90701

American Hardwood
1900 E. 15th St.
Los Angeles, CA 90021

Rogers Woodworking
Custom marine woodwork
874 W. 18th St.
Costa Mesa, CA 92627

Albano Marine Woodwork
Custom wood parts
% Wave Traders
1702 Bridgeway
Sausalito, CA 94965

H & L Woodwork
2965 E. Harcourt St.
Compton, CA 90221

The Harbor Sales Co.
Marine plywoods
1401 Russell St.
Baltimore, MD 21230

Penberthy
5800 S. Boyle Ave.
Los Angeles, CA 90058

RIGGING

Forespar
3140 Pullman St.
Costa Mesa, CA 92627

Hood Industries Rigging
951 Newhall St.
Costa Mesa, CA 92627

Ronstan (Alexander Roberts)
Running rigging
1851 Langley Ave.
Irvine, CA 92705

Universal Wire Products, Inc.
Rigging
222 Universal Drive
North Haven, CT 06473

DECK HARDWARE

American Precision Marine
Deck hardware
1260 Montauk Highway E.
Patachoque, NY 11772

Barient
Winches, etc.
936 Bransten Road
San Carlos, CA 94070

Barlow Winches
Alexander Roberts Co.
1851 Langley Ave.
Irvine, CA 92705

Clamcleat
Sneve-Nysether Co.
Box 1201
Everett, WA 98206

Gibb
Winches, turnbuckles, hardware, Hasler vang gear
82 Border St.
Cohasset, MD 02025

Harken
Blocks
1251 E. Wisconsin Ave.
Pewaukee, WI 53072

Hye
Deck gear
1075 Shell Blvd., #12
Foster City, CA 94404

Johnson Yacht Hardware
Lifeline hardware
Main Street
Middle Haddam, CT 06456

Lewmar Marine Yacht Hardware
Winches and rigging hardware
892 W. 18th St.
Costa Mesa, CA 92627

Merriman Holbrook
Complete line of deck hardware including winches
301 River St.
Grand River, OH 44045

Navtec Inc.
Rigging hardware
P.O. Box 277, Maynard Industrial Park
Maynard, MA 01754

Nicro-Fico
Complete line of hardware for running rigging
2065 N. Ave 140th
San Leandro, CA 94577

Ronstan (Alexander Roberts)
1851 Langley Ave.
Irvine, CA 92705

Schaeffer Marine
Complete line of deck and running rigging hardware
Industrial Park
New Bedford, MA 02745

Wilcox-Crittendon
Complete line of marine hardware
Middletown, CT 06457

GENERAL HARDWARE

Harding Machine Marine Parts
Individual custom hardware
1733 Monrovia Ave., Suite N
Costa Mesa, CA 92627

Harris Marine
Individual custom hardware
1281 Logan
Costa Mesa, CA 92626

Vic Berry
Best fuel and water tanks in the whole world
760 Newton Way
Costa Mesa, CA 92627

R.C. Plath Co.
Bronze hardware and anchor windlasses
337 N.E. 10th Ave.
Portland, OR 97232

Caseco
All types stainless steel fasteners
1215 S. State College Blvd.
Fullerton, CA 92631

Moritz Foundry
Windlass and other beautiful bronze cast marine hardware
133 Industrial Way
Costa Mesa, CA 92627

Beckson Manufacturing
Pumps, vents, hatches, etc.
Box 3336
Bridgeport, CT 06605

Danforth
Anchors, compasses, instruments
500 Riverside Industrial Parkway
Portland, ME 04013

Mariner Yacht Hardware
Blocks, deck hardware
1714 Seventeenth
Santa Monica, CA 90404

Nicro-Fico
Complete line of hardware for running rigging
2065 W. Ave 140th
San Leandro, CA 94577

PYHI
ABS plastic portlights and vents
1647 N. Avalon Blvd.
Wilmington, CA 90744

Rostand, Inc.
Ecclesiastical brass and marine hardware
Milford, CT 06460

Seagull Marine
Avon, Whale pumps, CQR anchors and Simpson Lawrence
Windlass and British hardware
1851 McGaw Ave.
Irvine, CA 92705

Wilcox-Crittendon
Complete line of marine hardware
Middleton, CT 06457

Yacht Specialties Co., Inc.
Wheel steering
15 5 E. St. Gertrude Place
Santa Ana, CA 92705

Bomar Company
Hatches
1021 E. State St.
Westport, CT 06880

ELECTRONICS

Dawn Electronics Corp.
Knotmeter and taffrail log
P.O. Box 91736
Los Angeles, CA 90009

Davis Instruments
Navigation supplies
857 Thornton St.
San Leandro, CA 94577

Fisheries Supply
Everything
Pier 55
Seattle, WA 98101

Kenyon Marine
Navigation instruments, hardware
New Whitfield St.
Guilford, CT 06437

Ray Jefferson
Radios, electronics, instruments
Main & Cotton St.
Philadelphia, PA 19127

Signet Scientific Comp.
Yacht instruments
129 E. Tujunga Ave., P.O. Box 6489
Burbank, CA 91510

Telcor Instruments Inc.
Yacht instruments
17785 Sky Park Circle, Box CC
Irvine, CA 92664

VDO Instruments
Knotmeters
116 Victor
Detroit, MI 48203

GENERAL

Ferro Corp.
All fiberglass materials
18811 Fiberglass Road
Huntington Beach, CA 92648

Detco Grove
Two part polysulfide caulking for teak decks
3452 East Foothill Blvd.
Pasadena, CA 91107

Larwyck Development
Windvanes
17330 Raymer St.
Northridge, CA

Dickinson Marine
Diesel stoves and heaters
#103 4241 21st Ave. West
Seattle, WA 98199

Marine Vane Gears
Windvanes
Cowes, Isle of Wight
England

Alco Mining
Lead ballast casting
16908 S. Broadway
Gardena, CA

Norcold Inc.
Refrigerators
11121 Weddington
North Hollywood, CA 91601

Norton Products
Holding plate refrigeration systems
173-M Monrovia Ave.
Costa Mesa, CA 92627

Thalco Uniglas Co.
Fiberglass
1212 McGaw Ave.
Santa Ana, CA 92705

Boat Transit
Boat hauling cross-country
P.O. Box 1403
Newport Beach, CA 92663

Fatsco
Beautiful solid fuel ship's stoves
251 N. Fair Ave.
Benton Harbor, MI

Lavender Fasteners
All stainless steel fasteners
884 W. 18th St.
Costa Mesa, CA 92627

Southwest Instruments
Navigation aids, marine supplies, books and
everything you can dream of
235 W. 7th St.
San Pedro, CA

Aquadron/Acme
First aid kits
1113 Johnston Building
Charlotte, NC 28281

Atlantis
Foul weather gear
Waitsfield, VT 05673

Canor Plarex
Foul weather gear
4200 23rd Ave. W.
Seattle, WA 98199

Aonolite
Reinforced fiberglass foam
425 Maple Ave.
Carpentersville, IL 60110

Doris Hammond
Canvas bags
260 Kearny St.
San Francisco, CA 94108

Edson
Steering equipment
480 E. Industrial Park Road
New Bedford, MA 02745

Guest
Yacht lights
17 Culbro Drive
West Hartford, CT 06110

Interlux Paints
Marine finishes
220 S. Linden Ave.
So. San Francisco, CA 94080

A.B. Optimus
Stoves and lanterns
P.O. Box 907, 1251 Beach Blvd.
La Habra, CA 90631

Paul Luke Inc.
Stoves and cabin heater
East Boothbay, ME 04544

Sailrite Kits
Sail and awning kits
2010 Lincoln Blvd.
Venice, CA 90291

Samson Cordage Works
Dacron and nylon braided line
470 Atlantic Ave.
Boston, MA 02210

Z-Spar Koppers Co. Inc.
Marine finishes
1900 Koppers Building
Pittsburgh, PA 15219

Woolsey Marine Ind.
Marine finishes and winches
201 E. 42nd St.
New York, NY 10017

TOOLS

The following companies have some of the most beautiful tools imaginable. Their catalogues alone are a feast for the craftsman's eyes.

Brookstone
127 Vose Farm Road
Peterborough, NH 03458

Garrett Wade
302 Fifth Avenue
New York, NY 10001

Leichtung
701 Beta Dr. #17
Cleveland, OH 44143

Adjustable Clamp Co.
417 N. Ashland Ave.
Chicago, IL 60622

The Princeton Co.
P.O. Box 276
Princeton, MA

WOODWORKINGS

H&L Marine Woodworking Inc.
2965 E. Harcourt St.
Compton, CA 90221

H&L is the major North American source of prefabricated teak or mahogany wood workings. Their range spans from the simplest flag pole, through items like towel racks, doors, drawers, magazine racks, book racks, etc. They will also custom fabricate hatches, cockpit grates and swimsteps to your specifications. Their work is usually of very good quality and their prices are most reasonable. A number of ideas in this volume were taken from their products.

GLOSSARY OF TERMS

— A —

Acetone — A very combustible, fast evaporating, fluid used for cleaning surfaces. The only thing that will dissolve and clean polyester resin.

Arbour — An attachment used with a drill motor; supports hole saws of different sizes. Usually has a drill bit inserted through its center.

— B —

Back-Up Plates — Reinforcing plates, usually steel or brass, used when bolting through vulnerable material such as wood or fiberglass.

Bedlog — A set of raised tracks upon which the main hatch slides.

Bevel — The act of cutting to a taper.

Bevel Square — An adjustable tool which, with two arms and a wingnut, can be used to duplicate or record angles.

Bolt Rope — Roping around the edge of a sail or awning, needed to distribute the strain on the cloth.

Bull-Nose — (A) to round off a sharp edge; (B) a concave bladed router bit used to round off a sharp edge; (C) the rounded edge itself.

Butt Connector — A metal press fitting that unites two wires end to end without complex splicing.

— C —

Cap Nut — A finishing nut with one side sealed off.

Carriage Bolt — A smooth-headed bolt with squared shoulders to keep it from turning.

Center Punch — A pointed tool for making marks on wood or metal.

Cleat Stock — Square cross-sectioned strips of wood used to join perpendicularly uniting pieces of plywood.

Countersink — To set the head of a screw or bolt below the surface; tool used for this purpose.

— D —

Deck Beams — Athwartship beams that support the deck.

Dolfinite — A very oily bedding compound best used on fiberglass to wood, or wood to wood joints.

Dovetailing — A very positive method of corner joints for wood, using intermeshing wedge shapes for each piece as fasteners.

Dovetail Saw — A very stiff-bladed hand saw with a well reinforced blade for very accurate cutting.

Dowels — Wood turnings used as a common attachment, usually to join boards edge to edge.

— E —

Elbow Catch — A spring loaded catch for cabinet doors, usually hidden and accessible through a finger hole.

Epoxy Glue and Resin — A high strength synthetic adhesive that will stick anything to anything.

Eye — A closed loop, in wire-rope or line.

— F —

Feather — To even two adjoining levels into each other.

Flare — To widen or ream the end of a pipe for coupling purposes.

Flathead — A bevel-shouldered screw.

— G —

Gelcoat — A very hard outer coating (usually color pigmented) of a fiberglass boat.

Grommet — A brass eye sewn or pressed into canvas work.

— H —

Hack Saw — A very fine tooth bladed saw (the blade is removable) made for metal cutting.

Hatch Coaming — Built up buffer around the inside of a hatch opening to keep out water intruding under the hatch.

Hole Saws — Circular, heavy walled saw blades of infinite diameters used in conjunction with a drill motor to cut holes.

Hose Barb — A tapered fitting, with terraced ridges that allow a hose to slip on but not off.

Hose Clamp — An adjustable stainless steel ring used to fasten hoses to fittings.

Hose Ties — Plastic ties with a barbed tongue and eye used to fasten hoses to bulkheads, sole, etc.

— I —

Inboard — Toward the centreline.

— K —

Key Hole Saw — A very narrow bladed hand saw with one end of the blade unsupported, used for hole or curve cutting.

— M —

Machine Screw — A fine threaded, slot headed fastener made to be used with a tapped hole.

Mat — An unwoven fiberglass material made up of randomly layered short fibres.

Miter Box — A wood or metal frame which is used with a hand saw to cut material at a given angle.

Miter Gauge — The sliding fitting on a table or band saw against which the piece of wood is laid to assure a straight cut. The gauge itself is adjustable to any angle required.

Molding — Trimming pieces of wood or plastic that hide joints or mistakes or both.

— O —

Oval Head — A screw with a head of that shape.

— P —

Pad Eye — A through bolted deck fitting to accommodate blocks, lines, etc.

Pet Cock — A small 90° turn off-on valve ideal for fuel switch.

Plastic Resin Glue — A powder base, mixed with water, that forms a very strong, water-resistant glue.

Plug — A tight fitting wood dowel used to fill screw-head holes.

Polysulfide — An unbelievably effective, totally waterproof sealing-bedding compound.

— R —

Rabbet — A groove cut in a plank.

Resorcinol Glue — A two-part, completely waterproof, glue.

— S —

Scribe — To reproduce the curve of a surface onto another surface by using a compass with pencil.

Sheet Metal Screw — Coarse treaded, self-tapping screw.

Shrink Tubes — Plastic tubing slipped over wire splices then shrunk by heat to seal the splice.

Silicone Seal — A quick drying non-hardening sealing compound.

Swedge — Method of attaching, by pressure, fittings onto a wire rope.

— T —

Thimble — A round or heart-shaped metal–eye chafe protector, around which rope can be seized.

— V —

Vented Loop — A bronze fitting with a valve that prevents siphoning of water into appliances below the waterline.